James
and Jude

James
and Jude

JOHN PAINTER
and
DAVID A. deSILVA

Baker Academic
a division of Baker Publishing Group
Grand Rapids, Michigan

James © 2012 by John Painter
Jude © 2012 by David A. deSilva

Published by Baker Academic
a division of Baker Publishing Group
PO Box 6287, Grand Rapids, MI 49516-6287
www.bakeracademic.com

Printed in the United States of America

Library of Congress Cataloging-in-Publication Data
Painter, John.
    James and Jude / John Painter and David A. deSilva.
        pages cm — (Paideia: commentaries on the New Testament)
    Includes bibliographical references and index.
    ISBN 978-0-8010-3634-7 (pbk.)
    1. Bible. N.T. James—Commentaries. 2. Bible. N.T. Jude—Commentaries. I. DeSilva,
David Arthur. II. Title.
    BS2785.53.P35 2012
    227′.9107—dc23   2012022166

12   13   14   15   16   17   18   7   6   5   4   3   2   1

For DWBR in gratitude and with thanks
J. P.

In honor of N. Clayton Croy,
a reliable friend, meticulous scholar,
and faithful Christ-follower
D. A. deS.

Contents

Figures and Tables

Figures

Tables

Foreword

Paideia: Commentaries on the New Testament is a series that sets out to comment on the final form of the New Testament text in a way that pays due attention both to the cultural, literary, and theological settings in which the text took form and to the interests of the contemporary readers to whom the commentaries are addressed. This series is aimed squarely at students—including MA students in religious and theological studies programs, seminarians, and upper-division undergraduates—who have theological interests in the biblical text. Thus, the didactic aim of the series is to enable students to understand each book of the New Testament as a literary whole rooted in a particular ancient setting and related to its context within the New Testament.

The name "Paideia" (Greek for "education") reflects (1) the instructional aim of the series—giving contemporary students a basic grounding in academic New Testament studies by guiding their engagement with New Testament texts; (2) the fact that the New Testament texts as literary unities are shaped by the educational categories and ideas (rhetorical, narratological, etc.) of their ancient writers and readers; and (3) the pedagogical aims of the texts themselves—their central aim being not simply to impart information but to form the theological convictions and moral habits of their readers.

Each commentary deals with the text in terms of larger rhetorical units; these are not verse-by-verse commentaries. This series thus stands within the stream of recent commentaries that attend to the final form of the text. Such reader-centered literary approaches are inherently more accessible to liberal arts students without extensive linguistic and historical-critical preparation than older exegetical approaches, but within the reader-centered world the sanest practitioners have paid careful attention to the extratext of the original readers, including not only these readers' knowledge of the geography, history, and other contextual elements reflected in the text but also their ability to respond correctly to the literary and rhetorical conventions used in the text. Paideia commentaries pay deliberate attention to this extratextual repertoire in order to highlight the ways in which the text is designed to persuade and move its readers. Each rhetorical unit is explored from three angles: (1) introductory matters; (2) tracing the train of thought or narrative or rhetorical flow of the argument; and (3) theological issues raised by the text that are of interest to the contemporary Christian. Thus, the primary focus remains on the text and not its historical context or its interpretation in the secondary literature.

Our authors represent a variety of confessional points of view: Protestant, Catholic, and Orthodox. What they share, beyond being New Testament scholars of national and international repute, is a commitment to reading the biblical text as theological documents within their ancient contexts. Working within the broad parameters described here, each author brings his or her own considerable exegetical talents and deep theological commitments to the task of laying bare the interpretation of Scripture for the faith and practice of God's people everywhere.

Mikeal C. Parsons
Charles H. Talbert

Abbreviations

General

//	indicates textual parallels	i.e.	*id est*, that is
BCE	before the Common Era	Lat.	Latin
ca.	circa, approximately	*m.*	Mishnah
CE	Common Era	MS(S)	manuscript(s)
cf.	compare	n(n)	note(s)
chap(s.)	chapter(s)	no.	number
contra	in opposition to	n.s.	new series
ed.	edition, editor	NT	New Testament
e.g.	*exempli gratia*, for example	OT	Old Testament
Eng.	English	par.	and parallel(s)
esp.	especially	pl.	plural
ET	English translation	p(p.)	page(s)
Gk.	Greek	v(v.)	verse(s)
Heb.	Hebrew		

Bible Texts and Versions

ESV	English Standard Version
LXX	Septuagint
MT	Masoretic Text
NA[26]	*Nestle-Aland: Novum Testamentum Graece*. Edited by Kurt Aland et al. 26th ed. Stuttgart: Deutsche Bibelstiftung, 1979.
NA[27]	*Nestle-Aland: Novum Testamentum Graece*. Edited by Barbara and Kurt Aland et al. 27th rev. ed. Stuttgart: Deutsche Bibelgesellschaft, 1993.
NASB	New American Standard Bible
NEB	New English Bible
NIV	New International Version
NLT	New Living Translation

NRSV	New Revised Standard Version
REB	Revised English Bible
RSV	Revised Standard Version
UBS²	*The Greek New Testament.* Edited by Kurt Aland et al. 2nd ed. London: United Bible Societies, 1968.
UBS³	*The Greek New Testament.* Edited by Kurt Aland et al. 3rd corrected ed. Stuttgart: United Bible Societies, 1983.
UBS⁴	*The Greek New Testament.* Edited by Barbara and Kurt Aland et al. 4th rev. ed. Stuttgart: Deutsche Bibelgesellschaft / United Bible Societies, 1994.

Ancient Corpora

OLD TESTAMENT

Gen.	Genesis
Exod.	Exodus
Lev.	Leviticus
Num.	Numbers
Deut.	Deuteronomy
Josh.	Joshua
Judg.	Judges
Ruth	Ruth
1–2 Sam.	1–2 Samuel
1–2 Kings	1–2 Kings
1–2 Chron.	1–2 Chronicles
Ezra	Ezra
Neh.	Nehemiah
Esther	Esther
Job	Job
Ps(s).	Psalm(s)
Prov.	Proverbs
Eccles.	Ecclesiastes
Song	Song of Songs
Isa.	Isaiah
Jer.	Jeremiah
Lam.	Lamentations
Ezek.	Ezekiel
Dan.	Daniel
Hosea	Hosea
Joel	Joel
Amos	Amos
Obad.	Obadiah
Jon.	Jonah
Mic.	Micah
Nah.	Nahum
Hab.	Habakkuk
Zeph.	Zephaniah
Hag.	Haggai
Zech.	Zechariah
Mal.	Malachi

DEUTEROCANONICAL BOOKS

1–2 Esd.	1–2 Esdras
Jdt.	Judith
1–4 Macc.	1–4 Maccabees
Sir.	Sirach
Wis.	Wisdom of Solomon

NEW TESTAMENT

Matt.	Matthew
Mark	Mark
Luke	Luke
John	John
Acts	Acts
Rom.	Romans
1–2 Cor.	1–2 Corinthians
Gal.	Galatians
Eph.	Ephesians
Phil.	Philippians
Col.	Colossians
1–2 Thess.	1–2 Thessalonians
1–2 Tim.	1–2 Timothy
Titus	Titus
Philem.	Philemon
Heb.	Hebrews
James	James
1–2 Pet.	1–2 Peter
1–3 John	1–3 John
Jude	Jude
Rev.	Revelation

DEAD SEA SCROLLS

CD	*Damascus Document*
1QH	*Hodayot*, or *Thanksgiving Hymns*
1QpHab	*Pesher Habakkuk*
1QS	*Serek Hayaḥad*, or *Rule of the Community*

RABBINIC LITERATURE

'Abot	*'Abot*
Roš Haš.	*Roš Haššanah*

OLD TESTAMENT PSEUDEPIGRAPHA

Apoc. Ab.	*Apocalypse of Abraham*
2 Bar.	*2 Baruch*
1 En.	*1 Enoch*
Jub.	*Jubilees*
Pss. Sol.	*Psalms of Solomon*
T. Ab.	*Testament of Abraham*

T. Ash.	*Testament of Asher*
T. Dan	*Testament of Dan*
T. Iss.	*Testament of Issachar*
T. Levi	*Testament of Levi*
T. Naph.	*Testament of Naphtali*
T. Reu.	*Testament of Reuben*

APOSTOLIC FATHERS

1–2 Clem.	*1–2 Clement*
Did.	*Didache*
Herm. Mand.	*Shepherd of Hermas, Mandate*
Herm. Sim.	*Shepherd of Hermas, Similitude*
Herm. Vis.	*Shepherd of Hermas, Vision*
Ign. Pol.	Ignatius, *To Polycarp*
Ign. Trall.	Ignatius, *To the Trallians*

NAG HAMMADI CODICES

Gos. Thom.	*Gospel of Thomas*

Ancient Authors

ANAXIMENES

Rhet. Alex.	*Rhetorica ad Alexandrum*

ANONYMOUS

Rhet. Her.	*Rhetorica ad Herennium*

ARISTOTLE

Eth. nic.	*Ethica nicomachea*
Rhet.	*Rhetorica*

ATHANASIUS

Ep. fest.	*Epistulae festales*

AUGUSTINE

Civ.	*De civitate Dei*
Doctr. chr.	*De doctrina christiana*

CICERO

De or.	*De oratore*
Fin.	*De finibus*
Nat. d.	*De natura deorum*

CLEMENT OF ALEXANDRIA

Strom.	*Stromata*

DIO CHRYSOSTOM

Or.	*Orationes*

DIOGENES LAERTIUS

Vit.	*Vitae philosophorum*

EPICTETUS

Ench.	*Enchiridion*

EUSEBIUS

Chron.	*Chronicon*
Hist. eccl.	*Historia ecclesiastica*

HESIOD

Theog.	*Theogonia*

IRENAEUS

Haer.	*Adversus haereses*

JEROME

Vir. ill.	*De viris illustribus*

JOHN CHRYSOSTOM

Hom. Act.	*Homiliae in Acta apostolorum*
Hom. Gal.	*Homiliae in epistulam ad Galatas commentarius*
Paenit.	*De paenitentia*

JOSEPHUS		Leg.	*Legum allegoriae*
Ant.	*Jewish Antiquities*	*Mos.*	*De vita Mosis*
J.W.	*Jewish War*	*Opif.*	*De opificio mundi*
Vita	*Vita*	*Post.*	*De posteritate Caini*
		Prob.	*Quod omnis probus liber sit*
LUCRETIUS		*Sobr.*	*De sobrietate*
Rer. nat.	*De rerum natura*	*Spec.*	*De specialibus legibus*
ORIGEN		PLATO	
Cels.	*Contra Celsum*	*Phaed.*	*Phaedo*
Comm. Jo.	*Commentarii in evangelium Joannis*		
		QUINTILIAN	
Comm. Matt.	*Commentarium in evangelium Matthaei*	*Inst.*	*Institutio oratoria*
Comm. Rom.	*Commentarii in Romanos*	SENECA	
Hom. Exod.	*Homiliae in Exodum*	*Ben.*	*De beneficiis*
Hom. Jes. Nav.	*In Jesu Nave homiliae xxvi*		
Hom. Lev.	*Homiliae in Leviticum*	SOPHOCLES	
		Ant.	*Antigone*
PHILO			
Abr.	*De Abrahamo*	TERTULLIAN	
Decal.	*De decalogo*	*Cult. fem.*	*De cultu feminarum*
Det.	*Quod deterius potiori insidari soleat*		

Modern Works, Editions, Series, and Collections

BDAG   W. Bauer, F. W. Danker, W. F. Arndt, and F. W. Gingrich. *A Greek-English Lexicon of the New Testament and Other Early Christian Literature.* 3rd ed. Chicago: University of Chicago Press, 2000.

NPNF   *The Nicene and Post-Nicene Fathers.* Edited by Philip Schaff and Henry Wace. 2nd series. 14 vols. Reprint, Grand Rapids: Eerdmans, 1979.

PG   Patrologiae cursus completus: Series graeca. Edited by J.-P. Migne. 162 vols. Paris: Migne, 1857–86.

PL   Patrologiae cursus completus: Series latina. Edited by J.-P. Migne. 217 vols. Paris: Migne, 1844–64.

James

John Painter

Preface to James

Orientation to Reading James and the Introduction

More than fifty years ago, as a student at Moore Theological College in Sydney, Australia, I heard a sermon on James 1:17 preached by D. W. B. Robinson, then vice-principal of the college and later the archbishop of Sydney. Though I remember little of the sermon, the words of the text have remained indelibly imprinted in my mind, as are the image and the echo of D. W. B.'s distinctive enunciation of that text: "Every good gift and every perfect gift is from above, coming down from the Father of lights. . . ." Since that time, I have had a growing conviction that this text expresses a profound insight into the depths of the mystery of God and resonates with strands of the Jesus tradition found in the Gospels and paradoxically has the power to withstand the trials and temptations that assault believers in the world. Reflection on this text and its place in the epistle as a whole was renewed when, late in 1988, D. Moody Smith invited me to write a book on James the brother of Jesus in a series that he was editing. I was delighted to take this on, although only passing treatment of the epistle was possible. Now, in this commentary, I hope to do more justice to the theme. But this can only be comparatively so, because here we plumb the mystery of God in relation to the enigma of the world and our place in it.

The distinctive language of the epistle signals that James develops this theme in a distinctive way, though not without significant relationship to the Jesus tradition and connections and tensions with Paul. This short epistle uses sixty-three words not found elsewhere in the NT, and ten of these are first known in James. Another nineteen are found only in James and Paul, and one of these is first known in their writings. The distinctive language not found elsewhere in the NT suggests that the epistle emerges from a stream of early Christianity not well represented in the NT. The language used only

3

by James and Paul in the NT attests more common ground between the two than is usually acknowledged but also bears witness to significant tensions even in their use of shared distinctive language.

Already in 1892, J. B. Mayor drew attention to James's use of the Wisdom literature and the sayings of Jesus found in the traditions used by Matthew and Luke. More recent scholars have reiterated his observations. They have added little to the detail but have built much on this basis. Strong support has been given for the recognition of a connection between James and the sayings traditions in oral or written form rather than to the Gospels. The question has been raised as to whether the relationship of James to the wisdom tradition is via the wisdom of Jesus. Though the relationship to the Jesus tradition is evident, the use in James is distinctive. The evidence confirms that James uses the Jesus tradition for his own purposes and does not quote it. The vocabulary and the language of James are closer to the Jesus tradition than to the writings of Paul.

James also has a relationship to Hellenistic literature and the writings of the Greek moralists. Though James and Paul are much closer in thought than is usually recognized, the use of language in James is generally different from Paul's, and when it is the same, it is often used to assert a difference between them. This is the case with the notorious "faith and works" dispute. Though James and Paul are not as distant from each other as James implies, a significant point of difference remains even when allowance is made for their different use of the same language. Why do they use the language of faith and works differently? Why does the one give priority to faith and the other to works?

Authors construct meaning from existing pools of language. Words are like the individual pieces of a jigsaw puzzle; their meaning is discerned through seeing the way they are used in a large sample of puzzles. Not only do different speakers/authors use the same words in different and distinctive ways; the same author/speaker may use the same word in multiple ways. Further, some pieces/words are distinctive to certain puzzles. Thus, recognition of word choice and word use is important for understanding.

Whereas lack of the language of the Jesus tradition in the Letters of Paul has led scholars to question his knowledge of it, James seems to be saturated with echoes of it. Yet James belongs more to the world of Paul than to the world of Jesus. The letter is addressed to the Diaspora, and any sense of Jerusalem with its temple is entirely absent from it. From this perspective, James shares with 1 John the sense of the allure of the "world," though what the world offers is vacuous and a distortion of the reality of the gift-giving God. Yet humans are susceptible to its attraction because of a propensity to self-deception arising from desire. Here there is an overlap with Paul's treatment of desire (Rom. 7:7–8), but James is conceptually closer to 1 John than to Paul on this issue, though there too significant points of contact occur in the midst of overall differences. James does not seem Johannine in vocabulary, style, or dominant themes, but at points overlap is evident: in the portrayal of the confrontation with the same alluring world and in a comparable understanding of God, though expressed in different language.

James emerges from a distinctive strand of early Christianity that, though not unrelated to other strands, stands alone in the NT. It stands alone because what might have been the dominant voice of its time had become an anachronism by the time the NT took canonical shape. By then a distinctive Jewish Christianity had been overwhelmed by the burgeoning church of all nations. Although the collection of Catholic Epistles, in which James was given first place, was probably a Jewish collection, it was received as a collection addressed to the church generally. Both James and 1 Peter retain their Diaspora addressees but were read allegorically as if addressed to Christians as strangers and pilgrims in an alien world. The remaining five Catholic Epistles were also probably of Jewish origin and orientation. Thus, there is a question concerning the original use of "catholic" to describe them. While "catholic" might express the perceived orientation of their address, it could be an assertion of their reception as canonical epistles, rather than remaining disputed or being rejected as heretical.

Although James stands as one of seven Jewish documents in the corpus of General (Catholic) Epistles, it stands apart from the other six despite various points of contact. Even Jude (Judas), who identifies himself as "brother of James," is distant from James and more Pauline in form and expression. Thus James stands out even in this collection. The Johannine Epistles stand more with the Gospel of John than with the other Catholic Epistles, though the conception of the world and the problems to be faced in it is shared with James and to some extent with the other Catholic Epistles. The vision expressed in a fragmentary way in James needs to be discovered from the fragments that make up the epistle, and without too much help from other early Christian writings. Though the parts are fragmentary, the whole is more than the sum of its parts. The collection of thematic units in James can be described as a gallery of diverse images that seem to hang together to produce a unified vision of life in the world in relation to God. In the process of reading, we move from *fragmentary words to a unifying vision*.

For Heidegger (1976, 312; 1979), "language is the house of Being." Because this imagery is evocative, precise implications of meaning remain less than clear. There seems to be some connection with Heidegger's hermeneutic involving preunderstanding and the hermeneutical circle. Words are the building blocks of meaning. Language is not only the way we communicate with others but also the way we come to understanding—whether of ourselves or of ourselves in relation to others and the world. This is true whether language is the foundation of all knowing or is the way unreflected knowing becomes conscious understanding. Words are important; they are the building blocks of meaning, and it is notable that authors have favorite, characteristic, and

5

distinctive word choices. That is why the quest to understand the writing of another person, in this case James, begins with the examination of the widest possible range of meanings and seeks to narrow and make precise the way a particular author uses words. Dictionaries define possibilities that need to be refined in the light of the author's particular usage.

In the case of James, the accumulation of words found exclusively in this letter in the NT, a number of which are known first in James, confronts the reader with difficulties that are masked by translation, especially since these words are used only once or twice. The difficulties are increased because our knowledge of this author is confined to five short chapters of just 1,632 words. The five chapters contain 410, 415, 285, 275, and 247 words respectively. This more or less declining chapter length does not belong to the original text, which was not divided into chapters and verses. These divisions sometimes obscure the flow of meaning in the text. On the whole, this is not a serious problem, because of the way James is composed. It does not develop a progressive argument but rather presents a series of related images or sayings that lead to a coherent vision or understanding. Nevertheless, the division between chapters 3 and 4 unhelpfully breaks up thematically related material, and the thematic break in the middle of chapter 2 is likewise obscured by the modern chapter divisions. Thus, in this commentary James is discussed in eight major divisions, not the five corresponding to the traditional chapter divisions.

My extensive introductory chapter lays out the evidence for reading the Epistle of James as a legacy of James of Jerusalem but issuing from a later time in the Diaspora and directed to the Diaspora. The attention to detail there is necessary because of the widespread failure to grasp the problems that lead to this view and the weight of the evidence on which it is based. Nevertheless, those who are anxious to get to the text of James can proceed directly to the text and interpretation, referring to the introductory discussions when so directed by a cross-reference. This is not the recommended approach, but it will work for those impatient to get to the text.

It remains only to thank Micheal Parsons for the invitation to contribute to the Paideia series and to thank him and Charles Talbert for their patience in waiting for the manuscript. Thanks too to James Ernest, Wells Turner, and his team for their patient help in the editorial process.

John Painter
Charles Sturt University
Canberra, Australia
November 2010

Introduction to James

This introduction is meant to be an aid to reading the epistle and the commentary. Familiarity with the text of James, gained from reading through this short work at a sitting, will enhance the value of the introduction. It gathers together what is relevant from various places in the commentary, where it is referred to when relevant by cross-references such as "see 'James and the Canon' in the introduction." There are advantages in coming to the text and commentary with some knowledge of these matters and turning back to them for deeper reflection in the discussion of specific texts. The name "James" is used by convention, although the author who gave his name to this epistle was named "Jacob," after Israel's third great patriarch. The connection with the patriarch is explicit in James 1:1, and the authority of the relationship is expressed in the dominating use of the imperative (commanding) mood throughout the epistle. In this commentary, "James" refers to either the author or the epistle; the context should make clear which is in view. (On the need to understand "Jacob" when reading "James," see "The Name 'James' or 'Jacob'" and "Jacob as Patriarch" below.)

James and the Canon

The attempt to understand James can profitably begin by tracing its path into the Scriptures known as the New Testament. The origin of this epistle is shrouded in mystery. By starting at a point when James is clearly known but struggling for "canonical" recognition, we can move more confidently as we journey back into the uncertainty of earlier times.

The Canon

The Greek word *kanōn* (canon) denotes a regulatory role, and it has a broader use than defining the Scriptures. It also denotes "the *rule* of faith" and the canons of councils, which sometimes define the canon of Scripture. We have no evidence of the use of this term to denote the authoritative list of authoritative Scriptures until the fourth century (see Metzger 1987, 131, 289–93). Around 320 CE, Eusebius (*Hist. eccl.* 6.25.3) refers to Origen (ca. 185–251 CE) in his commentaries defending the canon of the church (*ton ekklēsiastikon phyllatōn kanona*).

This rare use of *kanōn* describes Origen's defense of the four-Gospel canon. Origen was building on the clear defense of the four Gospels by Irenaeus (*Haer.* 3.11.8) around 180 CE. Eusebius's use of "canon" expresses the authority of the church to define the scope of the Gospels, but there was no settled NT collection. Canonical consciousness is expressed in the use of *kanonikos* in canon 59 of the Council of Laodicea (360 CE), where it means "within the canon of Scripture." In 367 CE, Athanasius uses the verb *kanonizō*, which means "to include in the canon" (*Ep. fest.* 39.2 [PG 26:1177]). Here for the first time we have a canonical list of precisely the twenty-seven books of the NT.

Eusebius (260–339 CE)

Eusebius grew up in Caesarea in Palestine, where the great Origen had spent the latter part of his life. Caesarea had inherited not only the tradition of Origen but also his library. Eusebius made good use of this inheritance, though he was a very different kind of scholar than Origen. Eusebius was not a brilliant theologian, and though he was skilled as a biblical exegete, his great gift was as a historian who set new standards in the gathering of literary evidence as a basis for his own historical narrative and commentary. He knew how to identify, select, collect, and comment on important sources to show the providence of God in history to bring the church through persecution to an ultimate triumph of the faith in and through the person of Constantine, the first Christian Roman emperor. Eusebius's elevation to be bishop of Caesarea (ca. 313–339 CE) was in the train of the triumph of Constantine. Early in Constantine's supreme reign, Eusebius wrote *In Praise of Constantine*, and his *Life of Constantine* was almost finished when Eusebius died in 339 CE. His history of the church (*Ecclesiastical History*), his most famous work, was probably begun by about 300, but it was not completed until around 320, almost certainly before the Council of Nicaea in 325, which he does not mention. The great value of this work is the preservation of fragments of critically important sources from the earliest history of the church to his own time, many of which have not survived independently of his collection. A precursor of this work is his little-known *Chronicles*, in which he sets out the chronology of the events to be described.

To describe the character of Scripture, Eusebius uses another group of terms. He refers to "the sacred Scriptures [*tōn hierōn grammatōn*]" (*Hist. eccl.* 6.15.1; 6.16.1; 6.18.2; 6.25.1); "the divine Scripture [*tēs theias graphēs*]" (*Hist. eccl.* 6.13.4; 6.18.4; 6.19.2); "all holy Scripture [*pasan hagian graphēn*]" (*Hist. eccl.* 5.24.7; cf. 3.14.1); "covenantal" Scripture, which is often misleadingly translated as "canonical." Thus, Eusebius notes that 1 Peter was accepted by "the ancient elders," but 2 Peter "we have not received as covenantal [*endiathēkon*]" (*Hist. eccl.* 3.3.1). He also refers to "all the covenantal Scripture [*pasēs tēs endiathēkou graphēs*]" (*Hist. eccl.* 6.14.1; cf. 5.24.7). In *Hist. eccl.* 6.25.1–3, Eusebius tells of Origen's provision of a catalog of "the sacred Scriptures of the Old Covenant [*tōn hierōn graphōn tēs palaias diathēkēs*]" containing twenty-two "covenantal books [*tas endiathēkous biblous*]." The close proximity of these connected terms (*diathēkēs* and *endiathēkous*) demands the translation of the latter as "covenantal." Following reference to Origen's outline of the twenty-two books, Eusebius turns to Origen's *Commentary on Matthew*, where he treats the books of the distinctively Christian Scriptures. The use of "Old Covenant" to describe the one implies the name "New Covenant/Testament" for the other, though neither Origen nor Eusebius uses those words here. Eusebius does summarize the writings of the NT (*tēs kainēs diathēkēs*) in *Hist. eccl.* 3.25, especially 3.25.1. (The importance of this observation calls for recognition, for which see "Scripture and the Mission to the Jewish People" below.)

Only by the mid-third century is James clearly attested by Origen, who recognizes that its authenticity is questioned. The movement toward a "catholic" canon is located between the narrow exclusiveness of Marcion and the more indiscriminate inclusiveness of gnosticism.

Marcion and Gnosticism

Marcion (ca. 140 CE) developed a collection that excluded the OT and included only his edited Gospel of Luke and an edited selection of Pauline Epistles. The result reflects Marcion's extreme form of Paulinism with gnostic tendencies marked by a dualism that distinguished a morally inferior creator God (of the OT) from the God and Father of Jesus. Unlike Marcion, gnosticism generally showed itself to be inclusive in its use of Scriptures because it developed an esoteric hermeneutic that allowed it to find a gnostic interpretation in texts of diverse origin. Thus, the Gospel of John and the Pauline Epistles became favored gnostic texts. Though the Epistle of James is not a choice, the figure of James is used in the fourth-century gnostic Nag Hammadi library, which contains three texts attributed to James: *Apocryphon of James, First Apocalypse of James*, and *Second Apocalypse of James*. These texts became known with the discovery and publication of the Nag Hammadi library in the mid-twentieth century (see Painter 1997a; 2004, 159–81).

The emergence of the catholic canon presupposes the recognition of the four-Gospel canon and the collection of thirteen Pauline Epistles. The canonical process in the larger church was partly a response to Marcion's exclusive collection and the inclusiveness of the Scriptures of the broad movement that came to be known as gnosticism. Instead, appeal was made to the church found everywhere throughout the empire, giving weight to the churches whose traditions could be traced back to the apostles. Under this apostolic criterion, evidence for recognizing the authenticity of James was dubious.

Eusebius (Hist. eccl. 2.23.25) on James and the Catholic Epistles

Following his account of the martyrdom of James the brother of the Lord, Eusebius concludes,

> Such is the story of James, whose [epistle] is said to be the first of the Epistles named Catholic. Admittedly its authenticity is denied, since few of the ancients [tōn palaiōn] quote it, as is also the case with Jude's [epistle], which is also one of the seven called Catholic. But the fact remains that these two, like the others, have been regularly used in most churches. (Hist. eccl. 2.23.25; see Painter 1997a; 2004, 142, 234–39)

Denial of the authenticity of James arises from uncertainty concerning its apostolic authorship by James the brother of the Lord. Eusebius notes that James (the brother of the Lord) is "said to be" the author of the first of the Catholic Epistles. This is the first explicit identification of the brother of the Lord as the author of James, but the idiom ("said to be") expresses uncertainty about the reliability of this identification. Thus its authenticity is denied. The reason for uncertainty is that "few of the ancients quote it." Quotation by the ancients is the primary criterion of authenticity (see Hist. eccl. 3.24.18, where doubts about the status of the Apocalypse are based on the lack of testimony of the ancients). It implies the ability to trace the work back to the generation after the apostles. That few of the ancients quote James is confirmed by modern scholarship, which can find no early specific quotation of James before Origen and few early possible indirect references or echoes.

In saying "first of the Epistles named Catholic," Eusebius provides the first known reference to the Catholic Epistles, though two of these epistles are mentioned individually in earlier sources (1 Peter and 1 John by Papias and Irenaeus). Later, Eusebius says that Clement of Alexandria, in his Hypotyposeis, "has given concise explanations of all the covenantal [endiathēkou] Scripture, not passing over even the disputed writings [tas antilegomenas], I mean the Epistle of Jude and the remaining Catholic Epistles, the Epistle of Barnabas, and the so-called Apocalypse of Peter" (Hist. eccl. 6.14.1). Bruce Metzger (1987, 131) confirms that Clement's extant writings contain no citation of James. This does not rule out some reference to James in his lost

Echoes of James 2:23

It is often argued that *1 Clem.* 10 (perhaps ca. 96 CE) and Irenaeus, in *Haer.* 4.16.2 (ca. 180 CE), betray knowledge of and use of James 2:23: "And the Scripture was fulfilled which says, 'Abraham believed God, and it was reckoned to him for righteousness,' and he was called friend of God." Three things undermine the case. First, the connection between Abraham's loyalty to God and the identification of him as loved of God or friend of God need not come from James, since it is found in the OT and contemporary Jewish literature (2 Chron. 20:7; Isa. 41:8; *T. Ab.* 1.6; 2.3; *Jub.* 19.9; *Apoc. Ab.* 9.6; *m.* ʾ*Abot* 6.1; CD 3.2; Philo, *Abr.* 40 §235; *Leg.* 3.1 §1; *Sobr.* 4 §17). Second, in none of the cases does the material appear in the same order as James. Third, in the case of Irenaeus, the point is Abraham's faith (Gen. 15:6 as understood by Paul) rather than his obedience (see also *Haer.* 4.13.4). These sayings were more widespread than James, as Luke Timothy Johnson notes (2004, 49n21, 69, 77n71).

writings. But since Origen knows James and does not attest the classification of "Catholic Epistles," it is likely that in *Hist. eccl.* 6.14.1 Eusebius introduced this title with his own classificatory language of "covenantal Scripture" and "disputed writings." Eusebius says explicitly that James is the first of this corpus of epistles. Its place as the first of these epistles is not in doubt; its authorship by James is. That authorship is the subject matter of "said to be."

In *Hist. eccl.* 2.23.25, Eusebius identifies by name only James and Jude of seven Catholic Epistles. Does that mean that Jude was second in order in the corpus? James not only appears first; it is said to be first. Jude follows, and it is the only other epistle named. However, *Hist. eccl.* 3.25.3 again lists Jude second after James!

When Eusebius wrote, James and Jude and the rest of the seven were used publically in most churches. Such use does not override the problem of the absent testimony of the ancients. Noncanonical works were used in churches without implying canonical status. There is no hint here of the two unnamed Catholic Epistles that in *Hist. eccl.* 3.25.2 Eusebius receives as authentic.

*Eusebius (*Hist. eccl. *3.25) on Recognized, Disputed, and Rejected Books*

All seven Catholic Epistles are identified by name in *Hist. eccl.* 3.25, on the assumption that 1 Peter and 1 John are part of that corpus. The Catholic Epistles are not classified as a collection but rather are listed as individual books. Eusebius identifies three categories of writings: recognized (3.25.1–2), disputed (3.25.3–6; cf. 6.14.1 [*tas antilegomenas*]), and illegitimate, or rejected (3.25.6–7). Although 1 Peter and 1 John are listed among the recognized books (3.25.1–2), each is attested as a single work by Papias (Eusebius, *Hist. eccl.*

11

3.39.17) and Irenaeus (Eusebius, *Hist. eccl.* 5.8.7; Irenaeus, *Haer.* 4.9.2; 16.5; 5.7.2; also 1.16.3; 3.16.5, 8), not as Catholic Epistles or as part of a Petrine or Johannine collection. Eusebius (3.25.3–6) places James and the rest of the Catholic Epistles among the disputed books. The preceding remarks of 3.24.17–18 make clear that recognition is dependent on attestation by the ancients (cf. 2.23.25). Lacking this, James and the other four Catholic Epistles were "disputed" until the second half of the fourth century. Luke Timothy Johnson (2004, 39) writes,

> Eusebius listed James among the "disputed books," although it was "recognized by most" (*Hist. eccl.* 3.25.3). The Paschal Letter of Athanasius (367 CE) and the council of Carthage (397 CE), however, included James without any hint of indecision.

This statement correctly marks the transition of James from the "disputed books," when Eusebius wrote (ca. 320 CE), to canonical recognition with Athanasius (367 CE). Its main point, however, is misleading. Johnson's use of "although" implies that Eusebius's listing of James as a "disputed book" was unreasonable, given that it was "recognized by most." That implication is unjustified. First, "recognized" implies acceptance of canonical status. Kirsopp Lake (1926–32) translates *gnōrimōn tois pollois* as "known to most," which implies nothing about recognition. Second, "known to most" is a variation of "used in most churches" in *Hist. eccl.* 2.23.25. Use in the churches was not restricted to canonical writings. Popular works were not necessarily canonical. Third, Eusebius's meaning is clarified by the contextual argument. Eusebius listed the accepted books of the NT, naming the four Gospels, Acts, the Epistles of Paul, 1 John, 1 Peter, and less certainly, Revelation (3.25.1–2). His reservations about the authenticity of Revelation emerge only in his discussion of the rejected books (3.25.6–7) but are foreshadowed in *Hist. eccl.* 3.24.17–18, which immediately precedes 3.25.1–2, by reference to the importance of testimony of "the ancients" (*tōn archaion*). Before dealing with the rejected books, Eusebius names "the disputed [*antilegomenōn*] books that are . . . known to most." These include the five remaining Catholic Epistles, 1 Peter and 1 John having been accepted as authentic.

> Of the disputed books that are nevertheless known to most [*gnōrimōn tois pollois*] are the Epistle called of James, that of Jude, the second Epistle of Peter, and the so-called second and third Epistles of John, which may be the work of the evangelist or some other with the same name. (*Hist. eccl.* 3.25.3)

Here (3.25.3) implicitly, and explicitly in *Hist. eccl.* 2.23.24–25, James is named as the first of the Catholic Epistles. Here also James is named with Jude, 2 Peter, 2 John, and 3 John, making up the other five of the seven Catholic Epistles mentioned by number in 2.23.24–25, where only James and Jude are named. Because the books are not treated here as the Catholic Epistles, we may assume that 1 Peter belonged with 2 Peter and 1 John with 2 John and 3 John in the Catholic Epistles collection. This implies the following order: James, Jude, 1 Peter, 2 Peter, 1 John, 2 John, 3 John. In 2.23.24–25 only James and Jude are named, so that Jude might also be implied to be second there! Athanasius lists the seven Catholic Epistles by name in canonical order in his thirty-ninth Paschal Letter of 367 CE, that is, beginning with James and concluding with Jude. This placement of the two books attributed to brothers of the Lord highlights or features the beginning and end more or less like bookends.

That four of the seven do not have specific addressees may suggest that "catholic" implies epistles addressed to the church at large. Of these four, James is addressed to Jewish communities in the Diaspora, and 1 Peter is addressed to elect sojourners of the Diaspora in Pontus, Galatia, Cappadocia, Asia, and Bithynia as a regional Diaspora letter. Both are "general" epistles only in a limited sense, being addressed to Diaspora Jewish readers (see "Destination: The Twelve Tribes of the Diaspora" below). More likely, reference to them as "catholic" epistles reflects their struggle to emerge from the disputed writings to be accepted as Catholic Epistles by the Catholic Church. Once that was settled, a transition to understanding them as General Epistles was perhaps inevitable in a church that had lost its Jewish roots and the memory of early Jewish leadership.

The unsuccessful search for evidence of the early use of James confirms the conclusion of Eusebius that "few of the ancients quote it" and explains

Origen (ca. 185–ca. 251 CE)

Origen, the most learned scholar of early Christianity, was also its most insightful, imaginative, and constructive theologian. He grew up in the martyr church of Alexandria, a great center of early Christian learning and witness. In his early twenties he became the head of the catechetical school, in succession of Pantaenus and Clement, during years of aggressive and violent persecution. He was a scholar of deep and wide learning whose reputation was widely known: author of some two thousand works; outstanding biblical scholar; skilled in biblical languages, historical knowledge, and exegesis; philosophically informed and intellectually able. Origen was posthumously declared a heretic, but he was not a proto-Arian, despite the Arian misuse of his theology. Many of his works have not survived. His greatest works were biblical: his commentaries and his Hexapla, the latter providing multiple columns of the OT in Hebrew and the various Greek translations. Theologically, his work *On First Principles* displays a sophisticated philosophical mind committed to understanding and expounding the essential Christian theology, of which he was a master, and to responding speculatively to the pervasive issues and dilemmas confronted by people through the ages.

its struggle to achieve recognition as authentic. It was known to and used positively by Origen. He quoted the work more than thirty times, showing that he believed he was quoting Scripture when quoting James 5:20 (*Hom. Lev.* 2.3), but he also was aware that his view did not enjoy universal support (*Comm. Jo.*, fragment 6; see Brooke 1896, 2:216). In *Comm. Matt.* 10.17, Origen deals with Matt. 13:54–56 on the subject of "the brethren of Jesus" (Patrick 1969, 424–25). There he mentions Paul's reference to James as the Lord's brother in Galatians and James's reputation for righteousness. Origen then refers to Jude, "who wrote a letter of a few lines, and said in the preface, Jude the servant of Jesus Christ and brother of James." No mention is made here of any letter written by this James. This is surprising because, as Patrick Hartin (2003, 8) notes, Origen included James in his NT writings (*Hom. Jes. Nav.* 7.1), identifying the author of James 4:7 as "James the Apostle" (*Hom. Exod.* 3.3), and the author of James 4:4 as the "brother of the Lord" (*Comm. Rom.* 4.8; cf. also Johnson 1995, 93).

The Catholic Epistles and the Canon

Eusebius, writing around the time of the Council of Nicaea in 325 CE, makes quite clear that James was not among the accepted (canonical) works because, lacking early attestation, its status remained disputed. The case for inclusion was given a decisive boost when Athanasius, in his thirty-ninth Paschal Letter of 367 CE, included the Catholic Epistles and set out what was to become their canonical order: James, 1 Peter, 2 Peter, 1 John, 2 John, 3 John, Jude. It is likely that the order of the first six was determined by the reference to James, Cephas (Peter), and John, the Jerusalem pillar apostles named in Gal. 2:9. The intent seems to have been to have a Jerusalem collection bounded by writings attributed to brothers of the Lord. The first of these writings was attributed to the first of the three pillar apostles, leader of the Jerusalem church in succession to Jesus and known as "the brother of the Lord," James the Righteous. The status of the pillar apostles reinforces the authority of the collection of Jerusalem Epistles alongside the Pauline Epistles.

The place of the corpus in the New Testament. Contrary to the order of English Bibles, in almost all Greek manuscripts of the NT, the *Catechetical Lectures* (4.36) of Cyril of Jerusalem (ca. 350 CE), the fifty-ninth canon of the Council of Laodicea (360 CE), and Athanasius's thirty-ninth Paschal Letter (367 CE), the Catholic Epistles follow the four-Gospel collection and Acts and come before the Epistles of Paul (see Metzger 1987, 295–96). Tensions between James and Paul are evident within the NT, especially in Gal. 2 and Acts. James 1:22–25 and especially 2:14–26 are intelligible in this context. This order suggests that Paul's Letters should be understood on the basis of the Jerusalem corpus.

James and Alexandrian influence. The views of Alexandria (Athanasius) were adopted in Caesarea and found champions in the Cappadocians, especially Basil of Caesarea and Gregory Nazianzus. In 379 CE Jerome visited Constantinople and came under the spell of Gregory Nazianzus. Not only did Jerome include James in his Vulgate translation, but he also quoted from the epistle 128 times. It was adopted in the canon of the Council of Rome (382 CE). Augustine followed the canon of Jerome (*Doctr. chr.* 2.18.13) and attempted to write a commentary on James. He had to make do with an inaccurate Latin translation because Jerome's translation was not published until 383 CE. Augustine quoted from James 389 times, showing his acceptance of its authority. James was included in the canon of the Synod of Hippo in 393 CE, which led to the adoption of the same canon at the third (397 CE) and fourth (419 CE) Councils of Carthage. Thus, through the influence of Origen, Athanasius, and the Cappadocians, the place of James was secure in the Greek churches and in the West by the late fourth century.

The influence extends to Syria. The Syrian church was slower to acknowledge the canonical status of James, a delay inexplicable if the epistle had been known in the lifetime of the brother of the Lord (see Eusebius, *Hist. eccl.* 1.13.1–22; 1.2.1–7; see also Painter 1997a; 2004, 109–17). Recognition eventually came through the influence of the Greek-speaking church of Syrian Antioch. John of Antioch persuaded Rabbula, bishop of Edessa (411–35), to commission a Syriac translation of James, and James became part of the Syriac Scriptures. The leading role of the Greek-speaking churches in this process is clear. Acceptance of James, first at Antioch and then in Edessa, was probably a consequence of the influence of John Chrysostom (died ca. 407 CE). Chrysostom, an Antiochene by birth and resident there until becoming bishop of Constantinople in 398 CE, identified the author of the epistle as James the Lord's brother, "God's brother" (*adelphotheos*), and refers to him as rabbi and bishop of Jerusalem (*Paenit.* 2; *Hom. Gal.* 2.9; *Hom. Act.* 46; see Painter 1997a; 2004, 236). While this may reflect the Greek tradition of Antioch, it could be a consequence of awareness of a long association of the epistle with Antioch. Thus James finally achieved clear canonical status in both the East and the West.

"God's Brother"

Chrysostom was probably dependent on Eusebius, who uses this title (*adelphotheos*) of James in *Chron.* 2. Eusebius probably derived the title from Hippolytus (see the fragment of his *On the Seventy Apostles* in *NPNF* 5:255). In this list of the seventy apostles, the first is "James the brother of God [*adelphotheos*], bishop of Jerusalem." This is understandably but unacceptably translated as the more common "the Lord's brother." In both the Hippolytus fragment and the Chrysostom quotation, "brother of God" is combined with "bishop of Jerusalem" (see Painter 1997a; 2004, 106, 236). Chrysostom was a strong advocate of the canonical status of James, and this title shows a heightened description of "the brother of the Lord."

Luther, Erasmus, and modern scholarship on James. From that time, James remained undisputed until the Reformation. Luther questioned its canonicity, referring to it as "an epistle of straw" and as "deuterocanonical" (Kooiman 1961, 110ff., and esp. 226n2). He also rejected attribution of authorship to James the Lord's brother. Luther's views were shared by Erasmus (Rabil 1972, 115). The reasoning of Luther and Erasmus is not consistently persuasive, but modern scholarship has tended to accept their conclusion that the epistle does not come from the hand of James the brother of the Lord. Outright rejection is unacceptable in the light of the tradition that links the epistle with no other author and the recognition of the pervasive presence of Gospel tradition in the epistle that has been evident since the work of J. B. Mayor in 1892. Evidence of the influence of Hellenistic literary and moral traditions implies that the link with James the brother of the Lord is indirect.

Authenticity reassessed. Ralph Martin (1988, lxxii) rightly identifies the lack of early evidence of the use of James as a major ground for doubting its attribution to the brother of the Lord. Martin recognizes that "the attestation of the document is unknown until the time of Origen later than AD 200." The lack of early evidence suggests that the epistle did not enter circulation in the lifetime of James (died 62 CE). Late attestation implies a date after the destruction of Jerusalem and the scattering of the Jerusalem church in 70 CE, perhaps even after the disaster of 135 CE. At the suppression of the Bar Kokhba revolt in 135 CE, the Jews were expelled from Jerusalem, bringing an end to the Jewish Jerusalem church. Such an event might have triggered a reorientation of the focus of James from the Jewish mission in Jerusalem to the twelve tribes in the Diaspora (1:1), where the future of Christian Judaism lay. Such reorientation reflects James's continued focus on the mission to his own people, the Jews (see Acts 21:17–26, revealing the focus of James of Jerusalem on mission to the Jews), but also reflects the new Diaspora reality.

The Name "James" or "Jacob"

The name "James" is derived from the Semitic "Jacob" (*Ya ʿāqōb*) and recalls the third great patriarch of the Jewish people. The Hebrew name is transliterated as *Iakōb* in Greek and translated as *Iakōbos*. In the NT this name is used seventy times of as many as nine different persons. Two are named using the Semitic transliteration (*Iakōb*). The remainder are named using the Hellenized *Iakōbos* (see Painter 2004, 2–3, 270–72). It is possible to reduce this number by arguing that some are to be identified with the same person.

"Iakōb" *and* "Iakōbos"

The transliterated form of "Jacob" (*Iakōb*) is used twenty-seven times in the NT, twenty-five times of the patriarch Jacob and twice of the father of Joseph the supposed father of Jesus (Matt. 1:15–16; in Luke 3:23 the father of Joseph is named "Eli"). The other forty-three references in the NT use the Hellenized form *Iakōbos*, which in English editions is translated as "James." About half of these identify James the brother of John and son of Zebedee. About one fourth of them probably refer to James the brother of the Lord. The remaining references relate to figures often difficult to identify or distinguish.

The Semitic form of the name is used of two figures from Jewish history prior to Jesus. Those from "Christian" history are given the Hellenized form. Translators of the Bible retain "Jacob" as an OT and Jewish name, while using "James" as the name for the "Christian" apostles. This decision is anachronistic because those early followers of Jesus remained within Judaism. It was also based on a very small sample of linguistic evidence. Josephus, more or less contemporary with the NT authors, uses only the Hellenized form (*Iakōbos*), whether of the patriarch or figures contemporary with himself. In addition to the patriarch Jacob, Josephus mentions four other people named *Iakōbos*. The names of these four are translated as "James" in the Loeb Classical Library edition of Josephus. Yet Josephus uses the same Hellenized declinable form of the name for the patriarch Jacob! The other four are James the son of Judas the Galilean (*Ant.* 20.5.2 §102), James the brother of Jesus the so-called Christ (*Ant.* 20.9.1 §200), James the bodyguard of Josephus (*Vita* 18 §96; 46 §240), and James the Idumean leader and son of Sosas (*J.W.* 4.4.2 §235; 4.9.6 §§521–28; 5.6.1 §249; 6.1.8 §92; 6.2.6 §148; 6.8.2 §380). These four are more or less contemporaries of Josephus. This is no justification for translating their names as anything but "Jacob." The text of Josephus exposes the limitations and complications involved in translating

---

The Name "Jacob/James" in the New Testament

In the NT this name is used seventy times of as many as nine different persons:

1. The patriarch Jacob
2. The father of Joseph, the husband of Mary the mother of Jesus
3. The son of Zebedee and the brother of John, one of the Twelve
4. The son of Alphaeus, one of the Twelve
5. James the "less," son of Mary and Clopas and brother of Joses (Joseph)
6. The father (brother?) of Judas, one of the Twelve, who may be identified with Thaddaeus (Lebbaeus)
7. James the brother of Jude, author of the epistle of that name
8. James the brother of the Lord and leader of the Jerusalem church
9. James the author of the epistle of that name

the Hellenized form as "James" in the NT. Like Josephus, Eusebius, the fourth-century historian and bishop, uses only *Iakōbos*, whether of the patriarch or the apostles.

"Jacob" and "James"

The two names in English are related to Latin, where *Jacobus* and *Jacomus* are variants of the same name. Similar variants exist in other European languages, in Italian *Jacapo* and *Giacomo*, in Spanish *Iago* and *Jaime*. These variants are of a different order than the addition of a declinable ending as we find in Greek. Further, in English "Jacob" and "James" have tended to be regarded as two different names. The name "Jacob" tends to be used by groups attracted to OT names, including Jews, while "James" has been used by Christians.[1] This practice seems to be implied by the translators of the NT but is unjustified and misleading.

The Brother of the Lord and the Epistle

Reference to "the brother of the Lord" has been variously understood in Christian tradition (see Painter 2004, 198–203, 208–22, 295–308). There is nothing in the Gospels, Acts, and the Epistles of Paul to suggest that those described as brothers and sisters of Jesus are anything but children of Joseph and Mary. Jesus the carpenter (*tektōn*) is known as the son of the carpenter/Joseph, and Mary is named as his mother in the company of those named as his brothers and sisters (Matt. 13:55–56; Mark 6:3; cf. 3:31; John 2:12; 7:3–5; Acts 1:14). Paul refers to James the brother of the Lord (Gal. 1:19). (For a detailed discussion, see Painter 1997a; 2004, 1–102.)

Protevangelium Jacobi *and Jerome*

The narratives of the virginal conception of Jesus by Mary, found in Matthew and Luke, describe it as a sign of the birth of the Messiah. Nothing suggests the sacred purity of virginity, a view found elsewhere in the pluralistic cultures of the Greco-Roman world. It is first known in relation to Mary and the siblings of Jesus in *Protevangelium Jacobi*. Joseph appears as an aged widower with children at the time of his betrothal to Mary. Her continuing virginity is attested after the birth of Jesus. But *Protevangelium Jacobi* is not known until the mid-third century, when it was used by Origen, and is attested by its presence in third-century Bodmer Papyrus V. It is going beyond

---

1. The connection between the two forms is preserved in the reference to the seventeenth- and eighteenth-century supporters of the Scottish Stuart Jameses as "Jacobites" and to the period as "Jacobean," showing awareness of the etymological relation between the two names, but this is lost on most people today.

Ya'akōb bar Yōsef aḥui dĕYeshua'

Paradiso/Wikimedia Commons

Figure 1. James/Jacob Ossuary
Inscription. According to one interpretation
of the Aramaic inscription (Ya'akōb bar Yōsef aḥui dĕYeshua'),
this box once contained the bones of James the brother of the Lord (Jesus).

In October 2002 the discovery of an ossuary (a first-century Jerusalem limestone burial box) inscribed in Aramaic with the words transliterated as *Ya'akōb bar Yōsef aḥui dĕYeshua'* was announced. The association of names in specific relationships led André Lemaire to translate this as "James son of Joseph brother of Jesus." He argued that it is unlikely that there was another "James" in Jerusalem at the time with a brother named "Jesus" and whose father was Joseph. Tal Ilan (2002) notes the small number of Jewish names in use from Palestine and that the three names on the ossuary were among the top ten in that period. Names were perpetuated in families from one generation to another. Jacob the brother of the Lord, whose father was Joseph and grandfather was Jacob (Matt. 1:15–16), had three brothers named after the sons of the patriarch (see Gen. 35:22–26): Joseph, Simeon, and Judah (Matt. 13:55; Mark 6:3). The naming of Jesus after the successor of Moses, *Yeshua'*, was also common (for a full discussion, see Painter 2004, xiii–xv, xvii–xxv, 270–94, 345–55). Because the ossuary was discovered by grave robbers, it lacks precise provenance and other vital data, and there is evidence of tampering with the inscription. Although the ossuary appears to come from the time of Jesus, the authenticity and interpretation of the inscription are disputed.

the evidence to suggest that *Protevangelium Jacobi* may have been known in the late second century (see Painter 2004, 198–203, 279, 297–308).

Around 383 CE Jerome dismissed the story of *Protevangelium Jacobi* as "the ravings of the apocryphal writings" and not derived from Scripture (see Painter 2004, 300). Because he and other leading figures in the West, such as Augustine and Ambrose, were committed to belief in the perpetual virginity of Mary, Jerome needed to find a scripturally based alternative. He developed a new hypothesis, arguing that the apparent siblings of Jesus were cousins, not brothers and sisters (see Painter 2004, 213–23). Although Jerome was ambivalent about aspects of his hypothesis, it was accepted by the Western church, including the churches of the Reformation. In the East, the teaching of *Protevangelium Jacobi* prevailed and was consolidated by Epiphanius, bishop of Salamis (367–403 CE). Jerome's view was effectively criticized by J. B. Lightfoot (1865). Since then, Jerome's view has declined in influence. Lightfoot advocated a reassessment of the more primitive, Eastern view, ignoring the reservations expressed by Jerome and failing to apply the sort of critical analysis that he had used in evaluating Jerome and the Western position (see Painter 2004, 215–18, 279–80, 304–5).

Authorship and Origin

An important argument in favor of attributing this letter to James the brother of Jesus is that no other figure in the early church could expect to be recognized simply by the use of the name "James" (Adamson 1989, 9–11).

James, a Servant of God and of the Lord Jesus Christ

The simplicity of the self-identification of "James, a servant [*doulos*] of God and of [the] Lord Jesus Christ" in James 1:1 (see the discussion there) is taken to support the identification of the author as the brother of Jesus. "If the document had been forged, we would expect a more sophisticated effort to stress his authority" (Adamson 1989, 39). Although "servant" is a seemingly humble description, the Scriptures characteristically refer to the prophets as God's servants, and Israel is ideally the servant of the Lord, an unfulfilled vocation that led Isaiah to portray the ideal servant of the Lord in the celebrated Servant Songs (Isa. 42:1–4; 49:1–6; 50:4–9; 52:13–53:12). The author's reference to himself as "James the servant of God and of the Lord Jesus Christ" is, paradoxically, noble rather than humble. The James of the epistle makes no claims to apostleship, perhaps because in the circles for which the epistle was intended his apostolic status was not in question. Paul's vigorous self-defense in Galatians is in response to hostile challenges. Other aspects of James's persona and status were more important and set him apart from the other apostles. Apostolic claims concerning Paul and this James do not assert that either was one of the Twelve. A broader notion of apostleship applies to them.

Pseudepigraphy in the ancient world is broader than the modern view of forgery. A modified pseudepigraphy is suggested in the case of James, whereby tradition coming from an eminent person is written up by another person in a new and later situation and presented straightforwardly as the work of the eminent person. Something like this has been suggested to explain the relation of the Pastoral Epistles to Paul (Kelly 1963; Barrett 1974) and is proposed here as a way of approaching the puzzle of James. But given significant use of tradition from James in this composition, reference to the epistle as pseudepigraphic may be misleading and inappropriate.

Arguments to the effect that James could not have written such a book are overstated. The book is written in good Hellenistic Greek, but the literary quality is not such that James could not be the author. Greek was widely spoken in Galilee and Judea (see Hengel 1974; Freyne 1980). Both Jesus and James were probably bilingual. However, from what we know of James, this is not the sort of work we would expect him to write, with its use of Greek literary devices and arguments common to the Greek moralists, to the Jewish Diaspora. Nor would we expect to find the ascription "the (our) Lord Jesus Christ" (James 1:1; 2:1) in a document of early Palestinian Christian Judaism. James Adamson (1989, 28) was aware of this problem and notes that *Christos* was used "first as an appellative and then as a proper name." Adamson has to cope with the apparent use of "Christ" as a name in James. Without directly discussing the ascription in James, Adamson argues that in Acts *Christos* is usually a title, not a name, when addressing Jews (1989, 28–29). His intention was to conclude that in James the use is also appellative, not a name. Instead, it seems that James uses *Christos* as a name and that James is a more complex composition than Adamson would like to think.

James's leadership of the Jerusalem church focused on the mission to the Jewish people. After the death of Jesus, the only incident concerning a situation outside Jerusalem involving James occurs at Antioch (Gal. 2:11–14). His intervention was via messengers, and it was to call on Jewish believers to conform to the practice of the circumcision mission of Jerusalem (Gal. 2:2–9). Nowhere is there evidence to suggest that James traveled outside Jerusalem to spread the mission to Jews of the Diaspora or to gentiles. This role seems to have been undertaken by Cephas/Peter, who visited Antioch, probably Corinth, and perhaps Rome. The *Pseudo-Clementines* confirm the NT picture (see Painter 1997a; 2004, 75, 190, 248), depicting James's concentration on the affairs of the Jerusalem church in a way that raises serious questions for a straightforward attribution of the epistle to James himself. The so-called Jerusalem decree is no parallel to James. In the decree (Acts 15:23–29), James establishes the minimum demands of the Jerusalem circumcision mission on gentiles of the Pauline mission. Paul shows no awareness of these demands.

Many modern scholars question the authenticity of James, although its authorship by the brother of Jesus is not without significant defenders (see Pratscher 1987, 209nn2–3). A mediating approach, which has some recent advocates, can be described as the secretary hypothesis (thus G. R. Beasley-Murray, F. F. Bruce, G. Kittel, W. G. Kümmel, B. Mitton, F. Mussner, P. H. Davids, and R. P. Martin). Although Adamson allows that what he has called James's letter to gentile Christians (Acts 15:23–29) might have been composed by Luke while conveying the substance of James (1989, 22–23), he rejects the secretary hypothesis in relation to the Epistle of James, saying that it "raises more problems than solutions" (1989, 37). Adamson has in mind the model of Peter and Silvanus with 1 Peter, which is not useful in relation to James. Yet Adamson (1989, 173–78) shows that there is a significant word statistical relationship between James and Luke-Acts. He demonstrates that the vocabulary of James is closer to Luke than to Matthew or Mark. This evidence supports the recognition of James as a Hellenistic composition by a native Greek speaker, consistent with the view of the use of (Christian) Jewish tradition by a native-Greek-speaking Jewish author.

An Anatomy of Compositional Theories

Theories concerning the situation in which James was written are often closely related to the question of authorship. An attempt to analyze the different positions was made by Richard Prideaux in his unpublished master's thesis (1985, 8–102). What follows builds on my modified summary of his research.

1. *James was originally a Jewish document.* This thesis is found in three forms, from minimal Christian editing to greater interpretative use of Jewish sources.

    a. James is a Jewish document with minor Christianization, such as the insertion of the name of Jesus in 1:1; 2:1. This view was held by Louis Massebieau (1895) and Friedrich Spitta (1896), who apparently reached similar conclusions independently at about the same time. Spitta argued that James is a pre-Christian Jewish work lightly edited by a Christian redactor.

    b. James was written by a Christian author who made use of a Jewish document such as *The Testament of Jacob* between 80 and 90 CE (thus Meyer 1930). This hypothesis was broadly supported by Gerhard Hartmann (1942), Hans Windisch (1951), and B. S. Easton (1957).

    c. James is a Christian midrash on Jewish Scripture such as Ps. 12:1–4 (thus M. Gertner 1962).

2. *James is a very early Christian composition by James or pseudepigraphical.*

    a. The epistle is a composition of pre-Pauline Galilean Christianity (thus Elliott-Binns 1957).

    b. The epistle is the composition of James the Just, from the Jerusalem church (thus Mayor 1892; Adamson 1989; Bauckham 1995; 1999; 2003).

3. *James was written in two stages.* These approaches seek to address two problems: (a) Jerusalem Jewish material expressed in cultured Greek language,

style, and rhetorical devices; and (b) James's single-minded focus on Jerusalem compared with a letter directed to the concerns of the Diaspora and lacking early attestation. Positing two stages allows for authorship of the first stage by James (thus W. L. Knox 1945; Davids 1982; R. Martin 1988). This approach corresponds roughly with the fifth form of authorship that Charles Talbert illustrated from Cicero, where one author, in some relationship to another, writes "as if" being the other (see Talbert 2007, 7–8). With James, some form of earlier draft establishes a strong connection between the first and second authors. The illustration from Cicero provides a recognized example of something like the proposed hypothesis.

4. *James as a pseudonymous composition.* While only category 2b above strictly escapes pseudepigraphical identification, other features determine a scholar's placement in the earlier categories. Further, recognition of a greater degree of authorial composition has led to my placing J. H. Ropes and Martin Dibelius here rather than in category 1, though both see James as a Christian work with a Jewish origin. From the perspective of this category, the following analysis distinguishes approaches on the basis of the supposed place of composition.

a. Palestine (Ropes 1916).
b. Alexandria (Brandon 1957, 238–39).
c. Rome (Laws 1980). Sophie Laws argues for a Roman provenance because of evidence of a connection between James and *Shepherd of Hermas*, for which a Roman context is widely accepted. The major flaw is uncertainty whether the similarities show that *Shepherd of Hermas* knew and used James, because similarities occur in conflicting ways.
d. An undetermined place in the Diaspora where a Hellenistic Christian community had developed out of a liberated Diaspora Judaism. This is the view of Martin Dibelius (1976), who allows for a variation on a two-stage theory involving Diaspora Judaism and Hellenistic Christianity, but without any connection to James. Thus the Epistle of James is pseudonymous.

From J. H. Ropes and Martin Dibelius to a Two-Stage Hypothesis

J. H. Ropes argues that a post-Pauline author in Palestine (perhaps Caesarea or Tiberias) sometime after the Jewish War (i.e., after 70 CE) made use of Jewish devotional and wisdom tradition in writing James. The author was in some isolation from other Christian groups and untouched by controversy over Jewish law. There is evidence, however, of contact with a misunderstanding of the Pauline teaching of justification by faith. Ropes has gathered evidence from within the epistle to show that it moves in a characteristically first-century CE Jewish world of thought, for which *Testaments of the Twelve Patriarchs* provides a relevant example of devotional literature. Absence of important early Christian teaching on the death of Jesus and the Holy Spirit signals James's dependence on Jewish Wisdom literature, where "wisdom" had taken over the role of the Spirit of God. The absence of reference to matters such as idolatry, slavery, and lax moral standards signals the epistle's *Sitz im Leben* in a Jewish community (Ropes 1916, 28–31, 33, 49). Ropes's argument shows both the Jewish and the Hellenistic provenances of James. Location in Palestine, rather than some place in the Diaspora such as Alexandria or Rome, is impressively argued. Jerusalem is ruled out because Ropes sees James as a post–Jewish War composition. This might be modified if a two-stage theory of composition allowed for tradition that came from James of Jerusalem, giving Rope's theory an added dimension. James then would not be strictly pseudepigraphic, having some justification for referring to "James" as its author.

Martin Dibelius asserts that James stands in relation to "an early Christian development, which did not directly derive from Paul"; nevertheless, James is not pre-Pauline, since "*his remarks in 2.14ff are still inconceivable unless Paul had previously set forth the slogan 'faith, not works'*" (1976, 179, italics original). The force of this observation is frequently ignored in the interest of freeing James from a reading determined by Paul and minimizing divisions and conflicts by portraying a harmonious early Christianity.

Ralph Martin (1988, lxxii–lxxviii, cviii) has developed a persuasive outline of the two-stage hypothesis. He suggests that tradition from James, reflecting Jerusalem in the 60s, was subsequently carried by refugees from Jerusalem (during or after the war) to bilingual Antioch. In Antioch the tradition was edited to make it relevant to the new situation, providing the second stage of composition. In support, Martin (1988, lxxii) draws attention to a comment by Jerome in his life of James (*Vir. ill.* 2), to the effect that "James wrote a single Epistle, and some claim that it was published by another under his name."

The tradition carried from Jerusalem to Antioch may have been oral or written. It included James's version of the Jesus tradition (see "James and the Jesus Tradition" below), which was dependent on Israel's wisdom tradition, especially Proverbs, Sirach, and Wisdom of Solomon (see Mayor 1892, cclxiv–cclxv). This process is quite different from the normal secretary hypothesis because the final editor plays a greater role, completing the work after the death of the named author. Thus, while the critique of the wealthy in James makes sense in Judea and Galilee before the Jewish War, the Greek of the epistle and the focus on the Diaspora make better sense later in the Diaspora, where the earlier critique remains relevant.

Diaspora Orientation of James

Three important indications point to the intention to spread James's views beyond Jerusalem. First, the letter is written in Greek, the language most suited to wide dissemination, as is James's use of the LXX as his Bible (see Dibelius 1976, 27). Second, the letter is addressed to "the twelve tribes of the Diaspora." Third, the letter uses a characteristically Greek greeting, *chairein*, rather than a Greek form of the greeting "peace." Helmut Koester (1982, 157) rightly sees the epistle as evidence of the continuing tradition of the Jerusalem church in the Hellenistic world. It is an expression of Jerusalem tradition, coming from the powerful influence of James but issued in a form suitable for the Diaspora some time after the Jewish War and the dispersal of the Jerusalem church.

For the letter to be written as if from James, at least two important transformations had to be made. A focus on Jerusalem was no longer possible in the same way. Hence, the Petrine perspective on the circumcision mission to the Diaspora became a stronger influence in the epistle. The mission, as understood by Peter, was concentrated on "the circumcision," the Jews. There is no sign of the presence of gentiles in James. With Peter, the mission spread into the Diaspora, to Corinth, and probably to Rome. After the Jewish War, it became clearer than ever that any concentration on mission to the gentiles jeopardized the mission to the Jews. In Acts 21:20–26 it is clear that gentile presence was problematic for James. After the Jewish War, the Jamesian perspective was reasserted and became the stance of Christian Judaism. Paradoxically, the name "Peter" became synonymous with the mission of the Great Church, and even the Gospel of Matthew was reinterpreted in these terms rather than as a document from the mission of the circumcision (see Painter 2008, 66–86). The evidence suggests that the same fate befell the Epistle of James, which came to be understood as an epistle to the church at large.

Dating James

Dating the epistle precisely is difficult. Sometime after the Jewish War seems to be demanded, and a date between 80 and 90 CE is possible, though a date after the suppression of the revolt in 135 CE cannot be ruled out, given the absence of early attestation. The later date has the advantage of taking account of the end of the Jewish church of Jerusalem, giving added weight to the orientation of James to the Diaspora. According to Eusebius, after the siege of Jerusalem in 70 CE the apostles and members of the family of Jesus who remained alive regathered in Jerusalem, reconstituting the Jewish church of Jerusalem (*Hist. eccl.* 3.11.1; 3.12.1). Though it did not regain its leadersip role, the succession of Jewish bishops, fifteen in all, continued until the time of the second siege in the reign of Hadrian, ending in 135 CE, and with it the Jewish church of Jerusalem (*Hist. eccl.* 4.5.1–4). On either date, the letter should be seen as the bequest of James to the Diaspora.

Destination: The Twelve Tribes of the Diaspora

Two of the three longer Catholic Epistles (James and 1 Peter) are addressed to the Diaspora. Is their use of Diaspora part of a metaphor for believers generally living as aliens in the world, making these two writings General Epistles?

James is addressed to "the twelve tribes of the Diaspora." This expression is not found elsewhere in early Christian writings or in contemporary Jewish literature, though aspects of the address are found in the LXX and early Christian literature. Reference to the "twelve tribes" is rare in the LXX, but see Matt. 19:28 = Luke 22:30; Acts 26:7; Rev. 7:4–9; 21:12. In the NT the word "Diaspora" is found only in John 7:35; James 1:1; 1 Pet. 1:1; and the verb *diaspeirō* only in Acts 8:1, 4; 11:19. The unprecedented expression "the twelve tribes of the Diaspora" has been understood broadly in three ways. James Adamson (1989, 11n64) lists five ways, making two separate categories each: for unconverted Jews from the Jewish nation (which are included here under category 1) and for gentile Christians from the church as the new Israel (which is included here under category 3).

1. All Jews (in the Diaspora)

This is broadly the position of Arnold Meyer (1930), who argued that the epistle was pseudonymously attributed to the patriarch Jacob and that the name "Jesus Christ" in James 1:1; 2:1 was inserted later in an attempt to Christianize a Jewish document. J. B. Mayor (1892, cxliii) proposes a more straightforward address to the Jewish nation. This seems to be the position taken by James Adamson (1989, 29): "James is addressing Jews in Jerusalem and throughout the Dispersion, converted and unconverted, at a time when Christianity was still simply a Jewish sect." Against this view, Martin Dibelius (1976, 66n15) correctly observes that Diaspora "is a technical expression, and it is not really possible to interpret it as a reference to the situation of the Jewish people in general." Perhaps aware of this, Adamson (1989, 33) changes his view: "It is addressed to the Christian Jews of the Diaspora, and we suggest that here is evidence of their attitude to Christianity in the early Apostolic Age." But this places Adamson in the second classification. If Dibelius is right, all Jews can be addressed only if James is dated after 135 CE, when all Jews were more or less in the Diaspora. Earlier, Jews of the Diaspora retains an exclusive sense.

2. All Believing Jews in the Diaspora

This is the view of Ralph Martin (1988, 8–10). The prima facie case for this position is weak because the address makes no such limitation. Nevertheless, effective circulation might well have been largely limited to Diaspora Jews who were followers of Jesus. The reference in 1 Pet. 1:1 to the "*elect* exiles of the Diaspora" seems to specify believing Jews. Further qualifications in 1 Peter restrict the Diaspora reference geographically to Pontus, Galatia, Cappadocia, Asia, and Bithynia. There are no geographical limitations in the Diaspora address of James. At the time of the Jewish War, the Jerusalem church was scattered, and the address might be considered to include all believing Jews, especially if sent after 135 CE. But the address makes no restriction to *believing*

Jews, and we should perhaps distinguish the audience of address from the audience of effective reception.

3. All Believers, Jews and Gentiles

This so-called symbolic understanding of "the twelve tribes" is the position of Martin Dibelius (1976, 20, 66–67). The early church probably assumed this view in recognizing James as apostolic and canonical, the first of the Catholic Epistles. Yet, as James Adamson (1989, 13) recognizes, it presupposes a very late date because there is no early evidence of the symbolic use of "the twelve tribes of the Diaspora" as an image of the church. This view has little in its favor. It is more likely that the epistle, like the mission of the historical James, was oriented toward the Jewish people, but unlike the mission of James, the epistle is directed to the Diaspora.

Jacob as Patriarch

The address "Jacob, servant of God and [the] Lord Jesus Christ, to the twelve tribes in the Diaspora: Greeting [*chairein*]" takes on greater depth than is usually accorded it because Jacob is represented as addressing his scattered children, the twelve tribes. In what follows, for "James" we should read "Jacob" because the patriarchal connection is obvious, connecting the brother of the Lord with the power of emerging patriarchy of the time. Thus James has been understood as a development of Jacob's blessing of his children (Gen. 49), featured in *Testament of Jacob* and by Philo. The role of James in the Jerusalem church and in the broader mission as described by Paul (Gal. 1:19; 2:1–11) and Acts is best understood in terms of emerging patriarchy in Judaism.

Jacob Neusner on the Patriarchate

The work of Jacob Neusner (2002a; see also 2002b; Neusner and Chilton 2002), which I made use of in my 2004 study (Painter 2004, 310–14), throws light on the authority of James in the early Jerusalem church. Neusner referred especially to the work of David Goodblatt (1994). Neusner distinguishes his form-critical analysis of the theology or ideology of the patriarchate from the specific role of any patriarch, whether Gamaliel I or Gamaliel II. Although the traditions in the Mishnah concerning Gamaliel have been shaped by the social world of its framers, the trajectory of the patriarchate reaches back from Judah the Prince to Hillel. The authority of the patriarchate and of the collegium of sages is grounded in *m. 'Abot* 1–2. There the lineage of both the patriarch and the sages is traced back to Moses and Sinai, grounding the teaching of the Mishnah in the authority of the oral law stretching back to Sinai. While this firmly grounds the authority of the Mishnah, the bifurcation of authorities reveals a tension in the contemporary authority structure between the collegium of sages and the patriarch. The resolution of such a conflict is depicted in *m. Roš Haš.* 2.7–9, which could express the view of the sages in coming to terms with the authority of the patriarch. Here Joshua submits to the ruling of Rabban Gamaliel, who greets him with the words "Come in peace, my master and my disciple—My master in wisdom, and my disciple in accepting my rulings." What this and other stories outlined by Neusner indicate is that, according to the sages, "the patriarch exercises his authority despite the acknowledged superior knowledge of the sage. But he does so in humility and with grace, acknowledging the sage's mastery in wisdom, even while affirming his own authority over the sage, by the Torah's own decree" (2002a, 8). At one level, the sage's submission to the authority of the patriarch can be a reasoned decision. At another level, it is reluctantly acknowledged because it is backed by Roman power. Neusner attributes both views to the influence of the sages.

Neusner finds the perspective of the patriarchate in the domestic *ma'ăśîm* (deeds) of the Mishnah. These predominantly concern the teaching and its demonstration in the exemplary behavior of the patriarchs, especially Gamaliel. The domestic *ma'ăśeh* derives from the patriarchal setting, and the name of the patriarchal authority imposes coherence on the data. It excludes disputes (between equals) and reports the rulings of a single unchallenged authority, that of the patriarch. The example of the patriarch was sufficient to illustrate the normative ruling. Nothing suggests that the patriarch was less in knowledge of the Torah than was the collegium of the sages or dependent for authority on the power of the Roman army. Rather, he was the exemplar of rigorous moral behavior, whose mastery of Torah was marked by physical weakness and intellectual power. His distinctive mastery of Torah was grounded in his ancestry, bound up with the ancestry of the Torah itself (Neusner and Chilton 2002, 58).

Thus, in the Mishnah there is an agreement on the superior authority of the patriarchate but a dispute about the superior wisdom of the collegium of sages. While the sages might have conceded superior authority to the patriarch out of practical expediency, the inner theology of the patriarchate is grounded in the tradition from Sinai embodied in the patriarchate.

Jewish Patriarchate as a Model

What does all of this have to do with James the brother of the Lord? First, the patriarchate is developed on a hereditary basis. Over half a century ago, Ethelbert Stauffer (1952) suggested a hereditary basis for the leadership of James in the Jerusalem church. The model that he chose to illuminate this was the caliphate. Not only is this model anachronistic, but it also ignores the obvious Jewish model that was developing in and around Jerusalem during the lifetime of James and Jesus. While the patriarchate developed a hereditary line from Hillel to Judah the Prince, the intertwining connection with Moses on the one hand and the Torah on the other was crucial. It is also evident that the line reaching back from Judah the Prince (*nāśî'*) to Gamaliel was the royal line of the house of David. For James, too, an intertwining of the Davidic line via his distinctive relationship as the brother of the Lord underpins his leadership of the Jerusalem church. According to Eusebius, the influence of the family of Jesus continues through to the reign of Trajan (98–117 CE), where it is identified with the line of David (*Hist. eccl.* 3.19.1–3.20.7; 3.32.1–6). This tradition illuminates the references to the throne of James, the first bishop of Jerusalem, whose throne was preserved and used by his successors (see Eusebius, *Hist. eccl.* 7.19.1). Eusebius does not mention the *thronos* in relation to any other bishop. (On the Davidic line of the family of Jesus and the throne of James, see Painter 1997a; 2004, 147–58, 308–14.) Hegesippus notes that James was also the exemplar of rigorous moral behavior, and tradition indicates that he was called "James the Just/Righteous" (Eusebius, *Hist. eccl.* 2.23.3–7). He is depicted as scrupulous in law observance and of remarkable intellectual power in resolving difficult problems. His own giftedness was important, but the source of his authority was his relationship to Jesus in the royal succession of David. (On the Davidic line of the Jewish patriarchate, see Levine 1979; Goodblatt 1994).

The Authority of James in Acts 15 and the Patriarchate

The role of James depicted in Acts 15 is described by an author who shows no desire to elevate his authority. Luke-Acts nowhere names the brothers of the Lord, thus the James of Acts 15 is not identified as the brother of the Lord. We make this identification in other ways:

1. The death of James the brother of John is noted already in Acts 12:2, before the mention of this James in 12:17.
2. No other James can possibly fit this role.
3. The explicit identification of James the brother of the Lord in Jerusalem (Gal. 1:19) is soon followed by reference to the Jerusalem assembly in Gal. 2:1–10, making the identification of James explicit.
4. The correlation with Acts 15 implies the identification of James the brother of the Lord in both places and elsewhere in the NT (1 Cor. 15:7; Gal. 2:11–14).
5. The extracts collected by Eusebius and his commentary on them confirm these identifications and the reputation and authority of James the brother of the Lord (see Painter 1997a; 2004, chap. 5).

The authority of James is grounded in his relation to Jesus. He is described as *the* brother of the Lord even though Jesus had three other brothers. The early tradition also asserts that James the brother of the Lord was replaced by another kinsman of the Lord, Symeon, the cousin of the Lord and of James.

A hereditary principle is clearly in view at this time in the leadership of the Jerusalem church. The depiction of the leadership of James at the Jerusalem assembly (Acts 15:13–29) is similar to the leadership of the patriarch. The status of gentile believers is first challenged. Acceptance of their place is then argued, first by Peter and then by Paul. When their argument concludes, James delivers his ruling in authoritative terms (15:19–21), introduced by the words *dio egō krinō*, "Wherefore, I judge." The "I" is emphatic in the Greek. There is no further discussion or dispute of his finding, which involves the acceptance of gentile believers but directs their observance of four requirements. The apostles and elders and the whole assembly gave their assent to James's ruling (15:22), thus mirroring the authority of the patriarch in relation to the sages.

Dissent and Tension in Galatians 2

In Gal. 2:11–14 Paul also depicts the same unquestioned authority of James in relation to the mixed church in Antioch. There Cephas, Barnabas, and the rest of the Jews ate with believing Jews and gentiles until the coming of messengers from James. Then Cephas and the other Jewish believers, apart from Paul, withdrew from table fellowship. The authority of James was recognized without dispute by figures such as Cephas and Barnabas, even when James was not present.

Only Paul asserts his dissent (Gal. 2:11–14), and in retrospect he expresses dissatisfaction in his description of the leadership group in Jerusalem (Gal. 2:2, 6, 9). The use of the verb *dokeō* (e.g., "those who *seem* to be pillars," 2:9) in each of the three verses signals that Paul does not consider the three pillar apostles to be superior to him. But because others did, Paul grudgingly acknowledges the authority of this group and of James in particular as the first of the three pillars, to whose judgment the others submit. The tension is like that between the patriarch and the sages in the Mishnah. Paul obviously did not think himself to be inferior in any way to James or to the three pillars collectively. Nevertheless, the reality was that Paul needed to go to Jerusalem to lay his gospel and mission before the pillar apostles under the patriarchy of James.

Acts 21, Eusebius, and Patriarchy

In Acts 21, at the end of his narrated series of missions, Paul returns to Jerusalem and reports to James. Even for Paul, James and the Jerusalem church play a significant role in the church at large. Eusebius describes the role of James as the first bishop of the Jerusalem church. The role of patriarch better fits what we know of his wider role. His authority reaches out beyond Jerusalem to take in all established believing communities. The Eastern churches came to use the term "patriarch" to describe the leadership of the church in those great metropolitan seats. Jerusalem was the foundational metropolitan seat and for some time gave leadership to the early Christian movement. In time it was followed by Antioch, Alexandria, Constantinople, and Rome. While the Eastern church maintained the use of "patriarchy," the Western church developed a nomenclature that includes "episcopacy," using the term found in early tradition about James as the first bishop of Jerusalem.

The forces that were shaping the patriarchate in Judaism were also at work in the Jerusalem church. Here too, wisdom and knowledge of the Torah were crucial and were manifest in James. What separated him from the other sages of the Jerusalem church was his lineage, being of the family of David and brother of the Lord. This was the basis of his authority, which was also grounded in wisdom, knowledge, and righteousness. His life, like the lives of the patriarchs according to the Mishnah, was an exemplary demonstration of his authoritative teaching. If we are looking for a model for the leadership of James in the early church, we need look no further than the evolving patriarchate, reinforced by the tradition of the appearance of the risen Lord, appointing him as leader of the Jerusalem church.

Here we need to keep in mind successive situations. First, there is the actuality of the leadership of James in Jerusalem until his death in 62 CE. This was shaped by the forces at work within Judaism in Jerusalem at the time. Following the destruction of Jerusalem, these forces would bear fruit in the emerging patriarchate. Those forces were clearer when the Acts account of the Jerusalem church was written toward the end of the first century. That this perspective had a bearing on the image of James in the epistle written in his name is argued in this commentary. "James (Jacob) to the twelve tribes in the Diaspora" has a patriarchal ring to it, coming, as it does, as if from James, making use of tradition from James some time after the destruction of 70 CE, perhaps after the crushing of the subsequent revolt in 135 CE. Evidence for this later date gives more weight to the view that this epistle was sent forth as if from the new patriarch Jacob. This later and more explicit theology of the patriarchate builds on the reality of James's leadership of the Jerusalem church, which under James played a leading role in the early Christian movement. Of course, recognition of the leading role of James and the Jerusalem church does not depend on the evidence of the emerging patriarchate. Rather, that evidence makes the reality of the leadership of James more intelligible in its Jerusalem context, especially when viewed through the eyes of a later period, certainly after 70 CE, and even more clearly after 135 CE.

Scripture and the Mission to the Jewish People

The Epistle of James, like the mission of the historical James, is addressed to the Jewish people. Whereas James himself remained in Jerusalem, the epistle was addressed to the Diaspora. Ultimately, the symbolic interpretation aided the inclusion of James (and 1 Peter) in the canon as an epistle for the whole church. But this was a failure to read James in its own terms, as addressed to Jewish readers in the Diaspora.

Adding to the Old: Adding James to the Scriptures

As long as the Jewish character of the early Christian movement was dominant, it was possible to think of James as a new authoritative writing of the Jewish Scriptures. The process of accumulation was driven by the need to understand new movements as part of the continuing work of God, begun with the creation of the world and the call of Abraham. James is intelligible as a flowering of Israel's wisdom tradition as perceived through the lens of the wisdom of Jesus. James's dependence on wisdom is attested by J. B. Mayor (1892, cclxiv), who says that James "seems to have paid special attention to the sapiential books, both canonical and apocryphal." He particularly notes dependence on Proverbs, Sirach, Wisdom of Solomon, and from the OT Pseudepigrapha, *Testaments of the Twelve Patrarchs* (1892, cxiii, cxvi–cxxi; see also Bauckham 1999, esp. chap. 2; Wall 1997; Hartin 1991; 2003). But the majority of Jews rejected the new movement and disowned the new story. A major reason for this is that after 70 CE the new movement became predominantly gentile in composition and direction. Rather than continuity, some tension emerges in the understanding of law and gospel.

A New Canon: Gentile Christianity and Marcion about 140 CE

All the writings that came to make up the distinctively Christian Scriptures assume a positive relation to the Jewish Scriptures. Yet, in the second century, it was possible for gentile Christianity to repudiate the old. In the first known Christian exclusive collection, Marcion accepted only expurgated editions of Luke and ten Epistles of Paul. Marcion recognized a complex relationship between the law and gospel in the writings of Paul, but his solution was hardly Pauline. He identified two different and unrelated gods at work, one in the Jewish Scriptures and the other in the Scriptures that he adopted. Neither his rationale nor the consequent exclusions were acceptable to the early Christian movement. They were certainly incompatible with James.

Two Testaments: Old and New Testaments

Neither by simple addition nor by an exclusive new body of Christian Scriptures was the early Christian movement to establish itself. A new conceptual formulation arising out of the old Scriptures would do justice to the new story of Jesus. Already in the Gospels (especially Matthew) the relationship between prophecy and fulfillment provided a partial understanding of the relationship, and it is found widely in early Christian writings, including Justin and Irenaeus. Irenaeus also gave expression to a more comprehensive formulation, referring to the writings of the Old Covenant (Testament) and the New Covenant. He refers to the dispute over divorce, where Jesus asserts that Moses "permitted you because of the hardness of your heart" (see Matt. 19:7–8).

> And accordingly they received from Moses the precept of divorce suited to their hardness. And why say we this of the Old Testament? Since in the New also the Apostles are found doing the same for the aforesaid cause [refers to 1 Cor. 7:12]. . . . If then even in the New Testament we find the Apostles allowing certain precepts, in a way of indulgence, because of the incontinence of certain persons, lest such persons, becoming hardened, entirely despair of their salvation, and fall away from God; we must not wonder, if in the Old Testament also the same God would have something of the same sort practiced for the good of his people. (*Haer.* 4.15.2)

Here, although Irenaeus recognizes two covenants, two Testaments, Old and New, he affirms the consistency of the one God in both.

Eusebius also picks up the idiom of Old and New Testaments in his account of the early Christian writings: "At this point it seems reasonable to summarize the writings of the New Testament which have been quoted" (*Hist. eccl.* 3.25.1 [cf. 3.31.6]). (See also his account of Origen on the canon, listing first the books of "the Old Testament" before turning to a list of the books of "the New Testament" [*Hist. eccl.* 6.25.1–3]; see also "James and the Canon" above.) Origen may have used this language; Eusebius certainly did.

This covenantal language is derived from Jer. 31:29–34, in which God promises,

> "Behold the days are coming," says the LORD, "when I will make a new covenant with the house of Israel and the house of Judah, not like the covenant which I made with their fathers. . . . But this is the covenant which I will make with the house of Israel after those days," says the LORD: "I will put my law within them, and I will write it upon their hearts, and I will be their God, and they shall be my people." (Jer. 31:31–33)

Jeremiah does not use this language of the Scriptures. In one of the earliest Christian writings, Paul deals with the tradition of Exod. 34:29–30, where Moses comes down from the mountain bearing the tablets of testimony, with his shining face reflecting the glory of God. Moses covers his face so the Israelites will not see this.

> Since we have such a hope, we are very bold, not like Moses, who put a veil over his face so that the Israelites might not see the end of the fading splendor. But their minds were hardened; for to this day, when they read the old covenant [*epi tē anagnōsei tēs palaias diathēkēs*], that same veil remains unlifted, because only through Christ is it taken away. Yes, to this day, whenever Moses is read a veil lies over their minds; but when a person turns to the Lord, the veil is removed. (2 Cor. 3:12–16)

33

This strange use of the veil tradition from Exodus may owe something to contemporary Jewish interpretative traditions. The veil explains the Jewish failure to believe in Jesus, but paradoxically, only turning to the Lord removes the veil. What does Paul have in mind in saying "when they read the old covenant [testament?]"? It is hard to find any alternative to a reference to reading the Scriptures now commonly referred to as the Old Testament, especially the first "five books of Moses." And if the Scriptures of Israel are called the "Old Testament," does this not imply that the writings of the new movement are the New Testament, the second part of the two-part canon? The emergence of the two-testament canon affirmed continuity with difference between the two. The new became the key to understanding the old, without distorting its historical meaning. Certainly this is true of James.

James and the Jesus Tradition

James embodies an interpretation of the Jesus tradition, opening up Jesus's interpretation of the Torah. James appears to be based not on an independent treatment of the Torah but rather on Jesus's interpretation of the Torah as found in M and the text of Q as found in Matthew (Q^{Mt}). James does not explicitly cite Jesus as a source but does utilize Jesus tradition as a resource in dealing with the issues of the time. This handling of tradition is consistent with the transmission of tradition prior to the recognition of copyright and plagiarism.

A Shared Galilean Theology

Jesus was a Galilean Jew. His distinctive creation theology is shared by James (1:17). According to Séan Freyne (2004, 24–38, esp. 26–27), it is a product of Jesus's Galilean heritage. I develop my understanding on the basis of Freyne's observations. In Mark 10:17–18 Jesus combines the theme of Genesis (Gen. 1:4, 10, 12, 18, 21, 25, 31), that God saw that everything God created was "good" (*ṭôb*), with the psalmist's acclamation "O give thanks to the Lord, for God is good, for God's steadfast love endures forever" (Pss. 100:5; 106:1; 107:1; 118:1–4; 136:1, and the explicatory refrain throughout; see also 1 Chron. 16:41; 2 Chron. 20:21) and the Shema (Deut. 6:4). Affirmation of one God, the creator of all things, binds creation to the Creator, so that the creation participates in the goodness of God. God's goodness is bestowed on the creation, not only at the beginning but also continuously in God's loving care of it (see the teaching of Jesus in Matt. 6:25–34//Luke 12:22–31; Matt. 7:7–11//Luke 11:9–13). These Q passages give Jesus's response to his disciples' anxiety about the uncertainty of life. Jesus did so with an appeal to the beauty of the creation and God's evident care of it as a basis for the recognition of God's care for humans, Jesus's disciples. That the beauty of the creation is an aspect of its goodness is supported by the diverse meanings of *ṭôb* and the cluster of Greek words used to translate it in the LXX, not only by *agathos* and *chrēstos* but also by *kalos*, which can convey the aesthetic sense of "beautiful." The argument presupposes the intrinsic worth of the creation to God and his special care of humans, specifically the disciples of Jesus. James has grasped this in his powerful portrayal of God in creation and providence, "Every generous act of giving and every perfect gift is from above, coming down from the Father of lights, with whom there is no shadow caused by turning" (James 1:17; cf. Lam. 3:22–23: "The steadfast love of the LORD never ceases, his mercies never come to an end; they are new every morning; great is your faithfulness"). For the generosity of the gift-giving God, who gives the gift of wisdom freely to every one who asks, see James 1:5–6 (see the discussion on 1:5–6, 17).

James and the Sayings Sources of Matthew

Various studies have shown a relationship between James and the teaching of Jesus through traditions unique to Matthew (M) and shared with Luke in Q^{Mt}, especially in the Sermon on the Mount. In the delineation of M it is necessary to distinguish it from the final redaction of Matthew, which modifies the Jamesian tradition in a Petrine direction (see Matt. 16:17–19). Although the M tradition shaped the use of Q in Matthew (Q^{Mt}), the final shape of Matthew is Petrine. James draws on the sayings sources used by Matthew rather than final Matthew.

The teaching about the benevolence of God in creation (cf. Matt. 5:45; 6:26–32 with James 1:17) is linked to the demand for greater righteousness in law observance (cf. Matt. 5:17–48 with James 1:25; 2:8–12; 4:11). Both Matthew and James show a concentration on the inner moral demand of the law, but neither repudiates the ritual and purity requirements of Torah. Note James 1:27, which in one breath combines ethical and purity requirements. The unique connection between the prohibition of oaths in James 5:12 and Matt. 5:33–37 provides a basis for recognizing more links between the teaching of Jesus in Matthew and the teaching of James.

Over one hundred years ago, G. Currie Martin (1907, 176) observed that where James addresses his readers as "brothers" (or "my brothers" or "my beloved brothers"), this form of address accompanies words closely paralleled by sayings of Jesus in Matthew. James has fifteen such uses of "brothers" (1:2, 16, 19; 2:1, 5, 14; 3:1, 10, 12; 4:11; 5:7, 9, 10, 12, 19). Currie Martin rightly sees James "as a Storehouse of the sayings of Jesus," especially in their Matthean form. Yet he does not argue for direct dependence of James on Matthew or the reverse. Rather, he argues for the recognition of the independent use of Jesus tradition. Thus we should expect to find resonant echoes rather than exact quotations.

For good reason the NRSV avoids references to "brothers" in James, but they are important rhetorical markers. Currie Martin also draws attention

35

to parallels with possible *agrapha* in the Letters of Paul, and evidence from *1–2 Clement* and the Epistles of Ignatius, where the address "brothers" seems to signpost quotations from Scripture or the words of Jesus. In James, resonant echoes may be expected in a subtle and pervasive way consistent with the use of the Jesus tradition for the author's purpose rather than as quotations.

More recently, James M. H. Shepherd (1956) has developed a thesis arguing that Matthaean Jesus tradition provides the core of the eight homiletic-didactic discourses in James, which correspond fairly closely to my analysis of James. He agrees that James uses, rather than quotes from, this Jesus tradition. Unlike Currie Martin, he does not connect the presence of Jesus tradition with the address of the readers as "brothers." This article is noted with approval by Jesper Svartvick (2008, 34–35), who argues that James is in a way a Matthaean epistle. But he does not think that James uses the Matthaean tradition as Scripture like the LXX. Contrary to this view, I am inclined to think that James reads the *torah* in the light of the Jesus tradition.

Verbal Echoes of Matthew in James

James's presentation of God and religion is nearer to Matthew than the other Gospels (Adamson 1989, 188). James Adamson has interpreted this point of contact in terms of an understanding of the true fulfillment of the law. He notes vocabulary and content links between James and Matthew:

Table 1. Vocabulary Shared between James and Matthew

	James	Matthew
"perfect"	1:4	5:48; 19:21
"righteousness"	1:20; 3:18	3:15; 5:6, 10, 20; 6:1, 33; 21:32
beatitudes on the poor	2:5	5:3
the merciful	2:13–14	5:7
ambitious teachers	3:1	23:8
the peacemakers	3:18	5:9
anxiety for tomorrow	4:13–14	6:34
"parousia"	5:7	24:3, 27, 37, 39
"oaths"	5:12	5:33–37
"church"	5:14	16:18; 18:17

Adamson insists that such similarities need to be carefully evaluated for differences within broad similarities. James is hostile to the rich, while Matthew is more conciliatory. Matthew is hostile to Judaism, while James promotes a form of Christianity uncritical of and firmly grafted onto Judaism (Adamson 1989, 189–90). There is evidence of tensions between tradition used in Matthew and the final redaction of Matthew. From this evidence, it appears to be right to conclude that James and Matthew independently use something like the same tradition but in different situations.

Martin Dibelius (1976, 28–29) contends that parallels with the Gospels show only James's familiarity with the Jesus tradition rather than any knowledge of the Gospels themselves. J. H. Ropes (1916, 39) argues, "James was in religious ideas nearer to the men who collected the sayings of Jesus than to the authors of the Gospels." James is to be compared with the collections of the Jesus tradition known as Q and M. While James has drawn on the Jewish wisdom tradition, including the tradition of the righteous sufferer, the Jesus tradition—especially as drawn together in what is now Matthew's Sermon on the Mount (Matt. 5–7)—has made a manifest impact on James, such that James may be drawing on the wisdom tradition through the wisdom of Jesus.

Ralph Martin also sees a relationship between James and the tradition found in Matthew, drawing attention to twenty-three allusions, while Patrick Hartin concentrates on James's relation to Q. Table 2 builds on the list given by R. Martin (1988, lxxiv–lxxvi) and another from Hartin (1991, 141–42). Hartin notes twenty-six points of contact between James and the Synoptics, mainly Q^Mt.

Table 2. Themes Shared between James and the Synoptic Gospels

	James	Matthew	Source (Q in Luke) and Mark
1. Joy in trial	1:2	5:11–12	Q (Luke 6:22–23)
2. Call to perfection	1:4	5:48	M
3. Asking and being given	1:5, 17; 4:2–3	7:7–8, 11	Q (Luke 11:9–10, 13)
4. Faith and doubting	1:6	21:21	Mark 11:23–24
5. Enduring and being saved	1:12	10:22; 24:13	Mark 13:13 (Luke 21:19)
6. Against anger	1:20	5:22	M
7. Doers of the word	1:22–23	7:24, 26	Q (Luke 6:46–47, 49)
8. Blessing of the poor	2:5	5:3, 5; [11:5]	Q (Luke 6:20; [7:22])
9. Warning against the rich	2:6–7	19:23–24?	Q (Luke 19:24)?
10. Law of love	2:8	22:39–40	Mark 12:38–44 (Luke 10:27)
11. To work sin (lawlessness)	2:9	7:23	Q (Luke 13:27)
12. Royal law of love of neighbor	2:10–12	22:36–40	Q (Luke 10:25–28)
13. Obligation to keep whole law	2:10	5:17–19	M Q (Luke 16:17)
14. Do not kill	2:11	5:21–30	M
15. The merciless will be judged	2:13	5:7; 6:14–15; 7:1	M Q (Luke 6:36)
16. Against lip service	2:14–16	7:21–23	M
17. Help to the poor	2:15–16	25:34–35	M
18. Fruit of good works	3:12	7:16–18	Q (Luke 6:43–44)
19. In praise of meekness	3:13; contrast 4:6, 16	5:3, 5	M
20. Meek . . . peacemaking	3:17–18	5:5, 9	M

	James	Matthew	Source (Q in Luke) and Mark
21. Against divided loyalty	4:4	6:24	Q (Luke 16:13)
		12:39	Q (Luke 11:29)
22. Pure in heart	4:8	5:8	M
23. Mourn and weep	4:9		L (Luke 6:25)
24. Humility and exaltation	4:10	18:4; 23:12	Q? (Luke 14:11; 18:14)
25. Against slander	4:11	5:22; 7:1–2	M Q (Luke 6:37–38)
26. Weep	5:1		L (Luke 6:24–25)
27. Against hoarding	5:2–3	6:19–21	Q (Luke 12:33–34)
28. Do not condemn	5:6	(7:1)	Q (Luke 6:37)
29. Eschatological imminence	5:9	24:33	Mark 13:29 (Luke 21:31)
30. Example of the prophets	5:10	5:11–12	Q (Luke 6:23)
31. Prohibition of oaths	5:12	5:33–37	M
32. Elijah as example	5:17		L (Luke 4:25)
33. Relation to sinful brother	5:19–20	18:15	Q? (Luke 17:3)

A comparable list provided by Peter Davids (1982, 47–48) draws on the work of W. D. Davies, J. B. Mayor, and Franz Mussner. Nothing compels acceptance that James knew and used Matthew. Rather, allusions to common words, themes, and motifs show that Matthew and James are independently working out of a common pool of tradition that can be identified as the wisdom tradition of Jesus. Patrick Hartin (1991, 214, 233, 240, 243) thinks it is likely that James had some contact with Q^{Mt}. Importantly, when dealing with Q, Hartin quotes John Meier, who asserts that "M was the living sea of oral tradition in which Mark and Q floated and were steeped" (Brown and Meier 1983, 55). Hartin (1991, 233) continues,

> M would exert an influence upon Mark and Q before Matthew began the writing of his Gospel. I have argued consistently that the Q source, once accepted into the Matthean community, underwent a development through the incorporation of other Q sayings as well as the insertion of the M material. This was evident in the development of the Sermon on the Mount and, in particular, in the growth of the Beatitudes. Ultimately a written form of Q, which we term Q^{Mt}, emerged within the Matthean community and was used by Matthew in the construction of his Gospel.

Hartin (following Meier) thinks that Q^{Mt} influenced James, that is, Q floating in and saturated by the living sea of oral tradition M. I am more inclined to accept a modified form of B. H. Streeter's position (1956, 486–87, 511–16). The core of M is tradition emanating from James and Jerusalem, which may well have attained written form after the death of James. Whether written or oral, this body of tradition, more than any other, shaped the ideological position of Matthew. This means that the orientation of Matthew is determined to a large extent by M, even when Q material is being used. Q brought to

Matthew an openness to mission to the gentiles, which was accepted on terms appropriate to the ideology of M.

> For a Gentile convert to become a member of the Q community probably meant, in effect, a Christian Jew, following the Jewish law and customs like the rest of the community. It is precisely this kind of Gentile mission that Paul was adamantly opposed to but one which the Q community could hardly have conceived in any other way. (Havener 1987, 103)

What Ivan Havener has expressed in terms of the Q community I take to be true of Q^{Mt}. In all probability, both Q and M emanated from the Jerusalem church. M may well emanate from James, while it is likely that Q is a Petrine tradition. If in Matthew Q was modified by M, the final redaction of Matthew is oriented to the mission to the nations on the terms of the circumcision mission (Matt. 28:19–20 indicates a law-observant mission: "teaching them to observe") of which Peter was the figurehead (Gal. 2:7–8). What distinguishes the Epistle of James from final Matthew is its orientation toward Jewish believers in the Diaspora, not toward the nations. The epistle, like James of Jerusalem, remained oriented toward the Jewish people—the man himself serving those in Jerusalem, and the epistle directed to the Diaspora (see Painter 1997a; 2004, 73–78, 83–102).

Jewish and Greek, Jerusalem and the Diaspora

The Greek of James the Epistle

The epistle was directed to Jews in the Diaspora, and it reveals a duality. It embodies Palestinian Jesus tradition but is expressed in a more polished Greek than almost any other NT work. As Luke Timothy Johnson (2004, 18) says,

> James is Hellenistic first of all in every dimension of his literary composition. Much of James's diction derives from the Septuagint, but it is far from "translation Greek" in its complex rhetorical effects produced by pleonasm (3:6–7), alliteration (see 1:2–3), parachesis (1:24), and paronomasia (2:4, 20; 4:14). His subtle word-play involving *krisis/eleos/aneleos* in 2:13, his frequent use of word-linkages (1:12–13; 1:26–27; 3:17–18), and his construction of a *sorites* in 1:2–4, make it virtually certain that James was not a translation from a Hebrew or Aramaic original [see R. Martin 1988, lxix–lxxvii], but was thoroughly Greek from the start. In terms of composition, furthermore, the letter's use of elements of diatribe, and the paraenetic-protreptic form of his deliberative rhetoric—not to mention his remarkable capacity for *brachylogia* [condensed expression]—locate James's writing within the world of Greco-Roman literature.
>
> James also shares the sensibility of Greco-Roman moralists on any number of small points (the testing of the wise, the unity of virtue, the mirror as a source of self-reflection, the tongue as venomous, the charioteer and pilot as images

of self-control), and fundamental convictions (that virtue must be tested, that speech must be controlled, that friends correct each other, that wars arise from disordered passions, that speech must be translated into action). More than that, James uses the *topoi* of Greco-Roman moral instruction in order to develop his argument: in 3:13–4:10 he employs the *topos* on envy, in 4:4 and 2:23 the *topos* on friendship, and in 1:19–20, 1:26, and 3:1–9, the *topos* on taciturnity. (For a more detailed treatment, Johnson refers to his 1995, 16–24.)

In spite of this evaluation, Johnson sees no ground for doubting that the author was James of Jerusalem, brother of Jesus. He appeals to important works by Martin Hengel and Gerard Mussies (Johnson 2004, 17n34) to show that Hellenistic culture permeated Judaism, both in the Diaspora and in Palestine. In principle, it is difficult to disagree with this conclusion.

Peter Davids (1982, 18–19) concludes, "One needs a great deal of information about an author . . . to determine from a work's content whether or not a certain piece of writing could have been produced by him at a certain time. In the case of James one does not have that information." First, a decision against the direct authorship by James is based, not on content, but rather (contrary to Johnson) on the character and quality of the Greek in which it is expressed. Second, there is no sense of Jerusalem in the epistle. Third, the sense of Diaspora is pervasive. Fourth, Davids does not attribute the epistle directly to James, and the literary evidence is responsible in large part for this.

The Jewishness of James the Person

Hellenism did not influence every person or every group to the same extent. Although Jewish attitudes to Hellenization varied, whether in Jerusalem or the Diaspora, the Qumran sect was not found in the Diaspora, and James remained centered in Jerusalem, focused on the mission to his own people—a view supported by Acts, Paul, the *Pseudo-Clementines*, and early tradition. This observation is especially important for James of Jerusalem. According to Acts 21:17–26, when Paul returned to Jerusalem to report to James and the Jerusalem church, they emphasized how successful the mission to the Jewish people had been, with many Jews zealous for the law becoming believers. They urged Paul to do nothing that would jeopardize the Jewish mission. This incident provides some specific evidence in support of the recognition that James and the Jerusalem church were resistant to the adoption of Hellenistic culture, supporting a Jewish affirmation of Hebraic culture if for no other reason than that to do otherwise would jeopardize the Jewish mission. When Paul sought to gain a hearing from the "mob" in Jerusalem, he spoke to them in "Hebrew" (Acts 21:40). The Hellenistic character of the Epistle of James is incompatible with what we know of James of Jerusalem. Further, the lack of testimony of the ancients makes it unlikely that the epistle was known before 62 CE, when James was martyred.

The Epistle of James: Jewish and Greek

James manifests two streams of evidence pointing in different directions. In one stream of evidence in James there is Jesus tradition best known to us in the Jewish traditions identified as Q^{Mt} and M. The other stream is found in the evidence that the epistle belongs to the world of Greco-Roman literature, addressed to the twelve tribes of the Diaspora. The Hellenistic character casts serious doubt on the identification of James as a direct composition of the brother of the Lord. The lack of any early evidence of the use of James casts doubt on the circulation of the epistle during the lifetime of the brother of the Lord, and the address to Jews in the Diaspora marks a shift in time, at least to the period following the Jewish War in 70 CE.

It is sometimes argued that the language of James is strongly Jewish because of its broad correspondence with the language of the LXX. But the broad scope of the vocabulary of the LXX and the character of readers for whom it was produced (non-Hebrew-speaking Jews of the Diaspora) lead to a different conclusion. The LXX makes use of a rich and diverse vocabulary representative of Hellenistic Greek of the time, much broader than the vocabulary of the NT. That most of the vocabulary used in the small Epistle of James occurs in the LXX is hardly surprising. It was, after all, a book for Diaspora Jews. What is surprising is that sixty-three words in this epistle are not found elsewhere in the NT. Given that this is a relatively short writing, this number is much larger than I expected, suggesting a distinctive place for James in early Christianity. Fifteen of these words are not found in the LXX, of which ten are first known in James. The epistle's place was within the early Jewish messianic movement, which increasingly lost its influence in the early church after the death of James. The subsequent siege of Jerusalem marked the end of the Jerusalem church's leadership of the Christian movement and the emergence of the dominant church of all nations, leaving little evidence of Jerusalem's once-dominant role. The epistle itself gave up James's Jerusalem focus in the interest of a role of influence in the Diaspora, and it was eventually interpreted as the first of the Catholic Epistles addressed to the church of all nations.

James and Jerusalem

For James, the mission to the Jewish people was to succeed or be lost in Jerusalem, and he remained centered there until his death in 62 CE. In the epistle, the shift of focus to Jews in the Diaspora reflects a time subsequent to the brother of the Lord. The suggestion that there is precedent for the epistle in the letter from the Jerusalem assembly to gentile churches of the Pauline mission (Acts 15:19–29) is mistaken. That letter embodies the judgment given by James (Acts 15:19–21) and asserts Jerusalem's oversight over the terms of the gentile mission (see also Acts 8:14; 11:22, where the Jerusalem church oversaw developments in Samaria and Antioch, sending emissaries to approve and report on developments). The decision to send a letter of requirements to the gentile churches established by Paul and Barnabas by the hands of emissaries Judas and Silas is comparable to the earlier expansion of the mission (Acts 15:22–29). The epistle, like James himself, remains oriented to the Jewish people but is now addressed to those dwelling in the Diaspora and lacks any sense of Jerusalem and the urgency of the mission to the Jewish people that we see in Acts 15; 21:17–22:5. Rather, it is concerned with everyday life in the Jewish community of faith in the Diaspora. This looks more like the adaptation of the teaching of James to conditions in the Diaspora, possibly after 135 CE. Nevertheless, the epistle shows intimate awareness of the early Jesus tradition, especially the sayings traditions embodied in Matthew.

Genre and Character

A Quasi-Encyclical Letter

The epistle can be seen as a "quasi-encyclical" letter to Jews (effectively Christian Jews) of the Diaspora, just as the so-called Jerusalem decree can be seen as part of a "quasi-encyclical" letter from James and Jerusalem (Acts 15:23–29) to Christian gentiles. James Adamson provides a summary analysis of the 230 words of Acts 15:23–29, making a comparison with the Epistle of James. Adamson (1989, 18, 19n111) concludes that the affinities are too numerous and nuanced to be coincidental. His conclusion is that both letters come from the hand of James the brother of Jesus. There are some problems with this view.

1. Some of his comparisons fall outside Acts 15:23–29, suggesting that the comparison is between James and the author of Acts.
2. The letter is said to be not from James but rather from the apostles and elders (Acts 15:23). It does, however, embody the judgment given by James expressed in 15:19–21, and it could be argued that James wrote on behalf of all.
3. It could be that the author of Acts is more responsible for the wording of this speech/letter than the supposed author(s). This could be so even if the author of Acts composed in what he supposed was the idiom of James, as Adamson (1989, 23, including n112) argues:

> Luke may have composed the version of the speech James doubtless made on this occasion; but we think that the style is that of James himself; . . . we definitely see James of the Epistle of James. . . . We believe that Luke may have been like, e.g., Thucydides, who put speeches in the mouths of his generals and politicians, as he himself says: "Keeping as far as possible the general tenor of what was actually said" (*Peloponnesian War*, bk. 1, sec. 22).

Adamson wishes to maintain that in both the substance and language of the speech in Acts "we definitely see *the* James of the Epistle of James."

4. Such a view opens up another possibility concerning the authorship of James. Could it be that James owes something of its present form to the author of Acts? Certainly Luke has an interest in a wider mission to the Diaspora.

The Role of Luke

That the author of Acts had a hand in the shaping the speeches of Acts is not in question, but the relationship of the language of that speech to the language of James is less clear. If James was written using Jamesian tradition, perhaps from Antioch after the Jewish War, it is possible to allow that two hypotheses can be accepted. Luke was responsible for James's speech in Acts and perhaps was the editor of James. This takes account of the similarities between James and Acts found outside the speech and letter from Jerusalem. Luke was capable of writing the kind of Greek that we see in James.

The author of Acts, however, did not advocate the position of Christian Judaism. Acts shows some sympathy for the Jerusalem church, but it assumes the mission to the nations without the demand of circumcision and submission to the law of Moses. While insisting on some continuity between Judaism and the church—part of which may be seen as a concession, if Luke is responsible for the fiction of "the Jerusalem decree"—Luke has no doubts where the future lies and about the centrality of the gentile mission. On the other hand, Gal. 2:11–14 implies that although James did not demand law observance from gentiles, it was necessary if they were to enjoy full table fellowship (and all that implies) with Jewish believers (see Painter 1997a; 2004, 48–56, 67–73).

A Native Greek-Speaking Jewish Author

The final author of James was a person who, like Luke, spoke Greek as his first language. Nevertheless, like James, this author was Jewish and committed to the continuing mission to the Jewish people. At the time of writing, this issue had ceased to be controversial among continuing Christian Jews because they could see, as James had much earlier, that an unencumbered gentile mission threatened the survival of the mission to the Jewish people. The crisis of the war, with the destruction of Jerusalem and the temple, left the Jews struggling to find the marks of their Jewish identity. Although the experience of a long history of Diaspora helped with this task, it was not sufficient, since it was no longer possible to look to Jerusalem and the temple, let alone travel there on pilgrimage at the festivals. Because of this sensitive situation, Christian Jews concerned to maintain their own identity as Jews and to develop a mission to other Jews could not even consider developing a mission to the gentiles.

The final author of James was a Jew of the Diaspora whose "mother tongue" was Greek and who made use of paraenesis and of the characteristic Greek greeting *chairein*. Martin Dibelius stresses that the author of James "writes Greek as his mother tongue," employing rhetorical devices (1976, 17, 34–38), and that the epistle is to be understood in terms of paraenesis, using elements of diatribe (1976, 1–11). The epistle is made up of a series of sayings loosely strung together, using literary techniques such as catchwords (*Stichworte*). This favorite device is observed in "1.4 and 5; 1.12 and 13; (1.15 and 16–18?); 1.26 and 27; 2.12 and 13; (3.11f and 13f?); 3.17 and 18; 5.9 and 12; 5.13ff, 16ff and 19f" (Dibelius 1976, 7). Catchwords are used frequently, and they depend on being written in Greek, ruling out the possibility that the epistle was composed in any other language. The author uses the Greek Bible, confirming that the author was a native Greek speaker.

Dibelius asserts that his analysis of the epistle as paraenesis implies that "*the entire document lacks continuity in thought*" (1976, 2), stringing together admonitions of a general ethical content, "addressing themselves to a specific (though perhaps fictional) audience" (1976, 3, cf. 26–34). Thus "even those warnings and admonitions do not reveal a specific occasion for the letter" (1976, 2). The paraenetic analysis is persuasive, but there is significant thematic coherence in James. This is not achieved via consistent logical argument. Rather, James proceeds via a series of analogical images, placed side by side for mutual illumination, and alongside collections of aphoristic sayings that develop by association and build progressively as themes reappear from time to time.

There is also reason to think, with Ralph Martin (1988, lxvii–lxviii), that the tradition in James is best understood against the background of the issue of poverty within the Jerusalem church before 66 CE, but with relevance for the Diaspora at a later time. Patrick Hartin (1991, 20) also argues that paraenesis arises in a specific community *Sitz im Leben*. Dibelius argues that James presupposes a context in literary history: "Through the agency of Judaism, nascent Christian paraenesis was subject to Greek and Hellenistic influence. In this respect Christianity is also the heir of a long literary development" (1976, 4). It is also described as "a pervasive *eclecticism* . . . [in] the transmission of an ethical tradition," where the transmission is more important than any creative composition by the author (1976, 5). Dibelius's analysis is consistent with the transmission of Christian Jewish tradition by a native Greek-speaking Jewish editor. The Epistle of James may lack a continuous train of thought, but it does not lack what might be called "associational coherence." It is the coherence not of a single picture but rather of a series of pictures that "hang together" actually and metaphorically.

Historically, we are faced with the question of whether James was concerned with the mission beyond Jerusalem and Judea. The evidence is ambiguous. Acts portrays James as leader of the Jerusalem church but gives hints of his concern to regulate the participation of the circumcision mission in situations with gentiles (cf. Gal. 2:11–14) and the terms of the gentile mission. The letter from the Jerusalem church to gentile churches of the Pauline mission can be understood in these terms (Acts 15:19–29; cf. 7:14; 11:22). *Apocryphon of James* 16.5–11 implies James's overall responsibility for mission, depicting him as sending the other apostles to various destinations while he remained in Jerusalem. A similar picture is given in the *Pseudo-Clementines*, where there is more stress on the mission. James directs the strategy from Jerusalem, while Peter is the chief exponent of mission beyond Jerusalem. But the epistle was directed to Jewish readers in the Diaspora. The transition of the tradition of James from Jerusalem to the Diaspora proved to be the means by which the Epistle of James became an epistle for the whole church.

Text and Translation

The translation used in this commentary is based on the critically reconstructed Greek text shared by NA[27] and UBS[4]. Barbara and Kurt Aland et al. (1997) provide the manuscript evidence for the reconstructed text, and Bruce Metzger (1992; 1994) sets out the critical textual methodology for the reconstruction of the text.

The complete text of James is preserved in the great fourth-century codices Vaticanus (B) and Sinaiticus ($\aleph$) and in the fifth-century codices Alexandrinus (A) and Ephraemi Rescriptus (C [for James 1:1–4:2]). There are also Greek manuscripts from the ninth century and papyri fragments of parts of the epistle from the third to the sixth centuries. A number of the versions—including the Old Latin, Vulgate, Armenian, Coptic, Ethiopic, and Syriac—provide important testimony. Perhaps because the epistle was not known early, relatively few variants occur in the critical apparatus of the UBS[4] text of James. Variants for only 1:3, 12, 17, 19; 2:3, 19, 20, 25; 3:3, 8, 9, 12; 4:4, 5, 12, 14 (3x); 5:4, 7, 14, 20 (2x) are noted (for evaluation, see Metzger 1975, 679–86; 1994, 608–15).

The variants listed in UBS[4] differ slightly from UBS[3]. Though a total of six additional variants appear in UBS[4], one variant with a B rating (1:27) from UBS[3] is omitted. Of the twenty-three variants now listed, seven of the adopted readings have an A rating (indicating a consensus among the editors), twelve have a B rating (indicating indicating a dissent), and the remaining four have a C rating (indicating two dissenters). None of the adopted readings in James has a D rating (indicating great uncertainty about which reading is original).

An alternative to using a critically reconstructed text, which agrees with no single surviving manuscript, is to adopt the text of James from one of the great fourth-century codices. Against this course of action is the conflicting textual evidence even at that time. The critically reconstructed text gives weight to the earliest independent textual evidence, making use of the accumulated awareness of common scribal errors and ideological/theological tendencies of the time. The rule of giving weight to the most difficult reading, especially if variants look like attempts to overcome the difficulty, is also helpful. Variants in James do not constitute a serious problem.

Structure and Train of Thought

James addresses his readers as those who are subject to passionate desire and live in a world that is often hostile. At the same time, they are to know themselves in relationship to God, who is the source of generosity and every perfect gift. This understanding of God arises from the recognition of the goodness

---

An Outline of James

Address/salutation (1:1)
Epitome of the exhortation of James (1:2–27)
  Faith, wisdom, and testing (1:2–8)
    Joy in enduring testing (1:2–4)
    The request for wisdom, and the prayer of faith (1:5–8)
  Reversal of fortunes of rich and poor (1:9–11)
  Enduring trials, wicked desires, and God's gift (1:12–18)
    Enduring trials, and the crown of life (1:12)
    Epithymia the source of temptation (1:13–15)
    God the source of goodness (1:16–18)
  The use of the tongue: Hearing and receiving (1:19–21)
  Faith and works: Hearing and doing (1:22–27)
Warning against partiality (2:1–13)
  An example of discrimination (2:1–4)
  God's choice of the poor, and human discrimination (2:5–7)
  The sin of discrimination, and the triumph of mercy (2:8–13)
Faith and works (2:14–26)
  Faith: Two questions, an example, and a conclusion (2:14–17)
    Faith: Two questions (2:14)
    Faith: An example (2:15–16)
    Conclusion 1 (2:17)
  Diatribe on faith and works (2:18–20)
    Diatribe (2:18–19)
    Conclusion 2 (2:20)

Justification: Two examples with successive conclusions (2:21–26)
Abraham (2:21–23)
Conclusion 3a (2:24)
Rahab (2:25)
Conclusion 3b (2:26)
The tongue (3:1–12)
The tongue and teachers (3:1–2a)
The tongue and self-control (3:2b–5a)
The tongue as a deadly power (3:5b–12)
God and the world (3:13–4:10)
Wisdom from above and wisdom of the earth (3:13–18)
Friendship with the world is enmity with God (4:1–10)
The passions and the world (4:1–3)
Friendship with God or friendship with the world (4:4–6)
Exhortations (4:7–10)
Admonitions and warnings (4:11–5:6)
Warning about judging a brother/sister (4:11–12)
Warning against boasting (4:13–17)
Warning to the rich (5:1–6)
Concluding pastoral advice (5:7–20)
Patience and the compassion of God (5:7–11)
Above all, no oaths (5:12)
Prayer and other advice (5:13–16)
Elijah as prayer exemplar (5:17–18)
Restoring a sinner from the way of error (5:19–20)

of God's creation, grounded in Gen. 1:4, 10, 12, 18, 21, 25, 31. Yet the world expresses hostility to God, reinforcing human desire in its propensity for sin and error. Faithfulness to the compassionate God is expressed in the prayer for wisdom from God, who gives generously to all who ask faithfully. This is the way to overcome sin and error. God has chosen the poor. Those who choose friendship with God rather than friendship with the world are committed to the poor. True religion is expressed in action to aid those in need and distress. Faithfulness to God is expressed in compassion for the poor and needy rather than in the satisfaction of passionate desire, which uncontrolled is the source of sin and evil. It is also a goal to turn sinners from the error of their way to a relationship of friendship with God.

James 1:1

Address/Salutation

Introductory Matters

Early in the twentieth century, Adolf Deissmann (1910, 218–46) made a distinction between the everyday letter of the Hellenistic period and the literary epistle. The absolute distinction is often blurred in reality. This is true of James and most of the Pauline Epistles. Like many everyday letters of the time, James has a standard form of address: "From A to B: Greeting." Most ancient letters also have a closing, though the form of this is more variable. Thus, although James lacks a usual closing, it qualifies as a letter and has a suitable conclusion if not a farewell. Yet "Jacob, servant of God and the Lord Jesus Christ" is an unusual and more formal self-identification than expected in a common, everyday letter. The recipients are identified in the address "to the twelve tribes in the Diaspora." This is no ordinary letter from one person to another. Reference to the named recipients resonates with the twelve sons of Jacob (Israel), who gave their names to the twelve tribes. The English translation of the author's name as "James" is nowhere more unfortunate than here in 1:1. James is addressed to the children of Israel scattered throughout the Diaspora. They do not belong to an identifiable locality but rather are identified as Jews outside Judea, wherever else they may be scattered.

From the earliest references to the epistle, it was attributed to James the brother of the Lord, though its authenticity was doubted because there is little, if any, evidence of it prior to the time of Origen (see Eusebius, *Hist. eccl.* 2.23.24–25; see also "James and the Canon" in the introduction). This may be because the epistle was sent out in the name of James, after his death, using Jamesian tradition (see "Authorship and Origin" in the introduction).

Tracing the Train of Thought

1:1a. The epistle purports to be from Jacob (see "The Name 'James' or 'Jacob' " in the introduction), whose name is used to identify this epistle.

James 1:1 in the Rhetorical Flow

▶ Address/salutation (1:1)

Unlike the Pauline Epistles (and Hebrews), which are named after their recipients, the remainder of the epistles in the NT (the Catholic Epistles) are named after their supposed authors. The name "James/Jacob" may look ordinary enough, and according to available evidence, "Jacob" was one of the ten most common Jewish names for Jewish men in Palestine at the time. As many as nine persons named "Jacob" may be referred to in the NT. Of these, only the brother of the Lord has been seriously identified as the named author. It is an irony that the Hellenized Greek form of the Hebrew/Aramaic name was translated as "James," obscuring its relationship to Jacob, the eponymous patriarch of Israel. The Gospels identify James as the first of four brothers of Jesus (Matt. 13:55; Mark 6:3). The other three are named after the sons of Jacob. The brothers are found in the company of Jesus and his disciples during Jesus's ministry (Matt. 12:46; Mark 3:31; Luke 8:19; John 2:12; 7:3–5; see Painter 1997a; 2004, chap. 1); they were part of the company of believers from the beginning of the early Christian movement, and James emerged as the first and preeminent leader in Jerusalem (Acts 1:14; 12:17; 15:13–21; 21:17–36). Paul describes James as "the brother of the Lord" and as the first of the three pillars of the Jerusalem church (Gal. 1:19; 2:2, 6, 9). The tradition about James collected by Eusebius adds weight to this picture of his eminence and leadership. Eusebius gathers tradition from Hegesippus, Clement of Alexandria, and Origen, who also knew the testimony of Josephus to James. (On later alternative views of the brothers, see "The Brother of the Lord and the Epistle" in the introduction.)

In this commentary, the Jacob named as author is identified as the brother of the Lord and son of Joseph and Mary subsequent to the birth of Jesus. Though James (Jacob) is named as author, there are reasons to think that this epistle embodies tradition from him but was completed and sent after his death (see Davids 1982, 12–13; for a detailed discussion of the historical James, see Painter 1997a; 2004).

The Jewish name "Jacob" reminds the reader immediately of the Jewish character of the author and of the letter he has written. The epistle uses the Hellenized form of the name (*Iakōbos*), not the transliteration (*Iakōb*), signaling the duality of its Jewish and Greek origin. The substance of the epistle comes from James the brother of the Lord, but the finished letter was published subsequent to his death and the destruction of Jerusalem in 70 CE, perhaps even subsequent to 135 CE. The Jewish name "Jacob" reflects the deeply Jewish tradition found in this letter, drawn from the Wisdom literature and the teaching of Jesus found in two strongly Jewish strands of the Jesus tradition known to us as Q^{Mt} and M (see "James and the Jesus Tradition" in the introduction). The use of the Greek form of the name, *Iakōbos*, reflects the good mastery of the Greek language and literary conventions as well as familiarity with the language of the Greco-Roman moralists found in the letter (see "Jewish and Greek, Jerusalem and the Diaspora" in the introduction).

1:1b. Jacob identifies himself with words in this order in Greek: of God [*theou*] and of Lord Jesus Christ, servant [*doulos*]. The placement of the word "servant" at the end of the identification makes clear the inseparable connection between the two coordinates "of God and of Lord Jesus Christ." Although both *theos* and *kyrios* are used to refer to God in the LXX, the latter has a broader range of meaning, from "sir" (in the vocative) to "master" or "Lord." Here "Lord" refers to Jesus Christ. In James, Jesus is mentioned by name only in 1:1; 2:1. In both cases he is referred to as "Lord Jesus Christ," once without "the" (1:1) and once with "the" and "our" (2:1 [in this case "the," present in the Greek, is absorbed by "our" in English translation: "our Lord Jesus Christ"]).

In Greek, word order is used flexibly to convey emphasis. The first word following Jacob's own name is "God," the genitive case attaching the word "God" to the last word in the phrase, "servant": "God's servant." The word order in Greek puts the emphasis on God. This is entirely appropriate for this epistle. Just as God (the kingdom of God) was the central message of Jesus, so God is the primary focus of the Epistle of James (Jacob). The distinctive understanding of God that emerges has deep connections with aspects of the teaching of Jesus found in strands of the Jesus tradition (see below on 1:5, 13, 17–18, 20, 27). The priority, character, and concentration of this motif in the opening and epitome imply that James's understanding of God underlies the entire epistle.

1:1c. This understanding of God is bound up with the other defining relationship, **servant of God and servant of Lord Jesus Christ.** The God whom James serves is made known in the person and teaching of "Lord Jesus Christ." The absence of the definite article ("the") in this phrase may be intended to balance with "God," which likewise lacks the definite article: "servant of God and Lord Jesus Christ." Reference to Lord Jesus Christ sounds anachronistic on the lips of James of Jerusalem in 62 CE or earlier. The later the publication, the more easily we can accept the use of "Jesus Christ" as a name prefixed by "Lord."

This is not a matter of serving two masters: "No one can serve [*douleuein*] two masters [*dysi kyriois*]; . . . You are not able to serve God and mammon" (Matt. 6:24//Luke 16:13 [Q]). Rather, the understanding of God revealed in the Jesus tradition, upon which James draws, is deeply rooted in a strand of tradition found in the Scriptures of Israel. The two sets of genitive cases define the servanthood of Jacob ("*of* God" and "*of* Lord Jesus Christ") and are to be read as a unity. The latter clarifies the former. The understanding of God and of serving God drawn upon here is given in the teaching of Jesus.

Servant of God

In Luke 4:16–21, Jesus quotes from Isa. 61:1–2a to announce his mission to Israel. He uses "servant" language to describe his mission, suggesting a relationship between this passage and the servant poems of Isa. 42:1–4; 49:1–7; 50:4–11; 52:13–53:12 in the minds of first-century Jewish readers, especially in the light of 42:1, where God speaks of his servant, "Behold my servant, whom I uphold, my chosen, in whom my soul delights; I have put my Spirit upon him, he will bring forth justice to the nations." Then in 61:1–2a the servant says, "The Spirit of the Lord GOD is upon me, because the LORD has anointed me to bring good tidings to the poor; he has sent me to bind up the brokenhearted, to proclaim liberty to the captives, and the opening of prison to those who are bound, to proclaim the year of the LORD's favor." If God announces, "I have put my Spirit upon him," the servant affirms in words used by Jesus in Luke, "The Spirit of the Lord is upon me." In the poems, we hear different voices: the voice of God announces the mission of the servant (42:1–4); the voice of the servant describes his mission, grounded in the words of God's commission (49:1–7); the voice of the servant testifies to the sustaining help of God in fulfilling his mission followed by testimony (50:4–11); God's assessment of the work of his servant is followed by the voice of witnesses (52:13–53:12). With this progression of voices, 61:1–2 sounds like the response of the servant to the commission of God in 42:1–4, "I have put my Spirit upon him."

Jesus describes his mission in terms of service. See especially Mark 10:45 in the context of 8:27–38; 9:30–37; 10:32–45. Note the synonymous parallelism of *doulos* in 10:44 with *diakonos* in 10:43, and the function of *diakonēsai* in 10:45. James, as the servant of Lord Jesus Christ, is the servant of the Servant of God, who is nevertheless designated Lord. James's servanthood is defined not only by the servants of the old scriptural tradition but also by the Servant of God par excellence.

This language of servanthood overlaps the meanings of servant and slave. Nevertheless, "servant of God" describes an exalted relationship, with a rich tradition, which affirms deep devotion and obedience to God, underlying a vocation and mission of great significance. This use of the Greek *doulos* is embedded in the Hebrew *'ebed*, which is used in the plural to describe Israel as God's servants (Deut. 32:36) and in the singular of individuals such as Moses (1 Kings 8:53, 56), David (1 Kings 8:66), and particular prophets (Jer. 7:25; Amos 3:7). Most notably, Isaiah not only refers to Israel collectively as God's servant (Isa. 44:1–8) but also names the role of the ideal servant of God in this way (Isa. 42:1–4; 49:1–7; 50:4–11; 52:13–53:12).

1:1d. **To the twelve tribes of the Diaspora** (see "Destination: The Twelve Tribes of the Diaspora" and "Jacob as Patriarch" in the introduction). Although

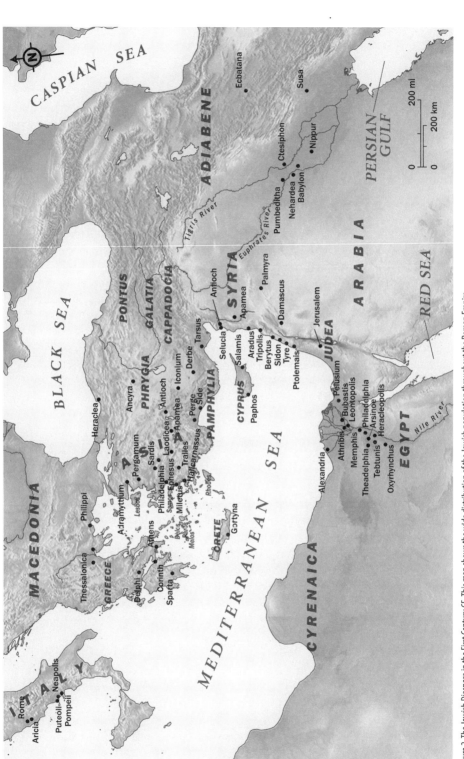

Figure 2. The Jewish Diaspora in the First Century CE. This map shows the wide distribution of the Jewish population throughout the Roman Empire.

"Jacob" was a common name, it is no ordinary name, especially when used in association with "the twelve tribes." This association reminds the reader that the patriarch Jacob was given the name "Israel" and that the twelve tribes of Israel take their names from the twelve sons of Jacob, including the names of the three brothers of James and Jesus. The significance of the Diaspora increases following the destruction of Jerusalem in 70 CE, and even more so following the crushing of a second uprising in 135 CE. The lack of early attestation, supported by internal evidence, suggests that the epistle was circulated after James's death (62 CE) and uses Jamesian tradition, which embodies the wisdom of Jesus. The failure of the second Jewish revolt brought an end both to Jerusalem as the Jewish capital and to the Jewish Jerusalem church. From then on, Judaism became a phenomenon of the Diaspora until the mid-twentieth century.

The address implies an awareness of something like the patriarchal authority of Jacob the brother of the Lord, at least for Jews of the Jesus movement in the Diaspora. The evidence of his authority can be seen in events described in Acts 15 and 21 and in the Letters of Paul, especially Gal. 2 (see "Jacob as Patriarch" in the introduction; also Painter 1997a; 2004, chaps. 2–3). Like the patriarch, James was of the line of David, and he adopted a form of exemplary moral leadership that was not autocratic but rather operated from within a circle of peers, equal in wisdom but not in final authority (cf. Acts 15:19–21). Even Paul found it necessary to bend to the authority of James, though debating with him as an equal.

The addressees were Jewish readers outside of the land of Israel, whether in the eastern Diaspora in Babylon or the western Diaspora. The letter comes, as from the patriarch Jacob, as a Diaspora letter. If the letter embodies traditions coming directly from Jacob of Jerusalem, that may have been enough to lead to the use of his name, even though its application to a later situation was the work of others.

1:1e. The single verb *chairein* (**Greeting**) is the characteristic Greek greeting. It is used elsewhere in the NT in this way in the letter sent out from the Jerusalem church to believing gentiles (Acts 15:23) and in the letter of the Roman tribune Claudius Lysias to the Governor Felix (Acts 23:26). Luke was certainly aware of what was appropriate in a gentile context in the Roman Empire. It is not the type of greeting we would expect from James of Jerusalem to other Jews. For them, the Jewish greeting "Peace," used by the risen Jesus in John 20:19, 21, would be expected. It also differs from the Pauline greeting "Grace and peace." While this greeting may link the characteristic Greek greeting with the traditional Jewish greeting, the combination expresses a more Jewish ambience, as does the Johannine use of "grace and truth," behind which lies the later LXX translation of the Hebrew *ḥesed we'ĕmet*. We have no evidence that the vocabulary of grace was part of the normal repertoire of James or John. The only use of "grace" in James (4:6) is derived from the LXX.

Elsewhere, where "grace" language might be expected, James speaks of the goodness of the gift-giving God (1:5, 17). In this, James shares the vocabulary of Jesus rather than of Paul. James has followed the form of a characteristic Hellenistic letter, and this greeting (*chairein*) forms a linguistic connection with the link word *chara* in 1:2, which begins with the words *pasan charan*, so that *chairein* and *chara* make a formal connection between the opening address and the substance of the letter.

Theological Issues

That the author of the epistle is traditionally identified as Jacob the "brother of the Lord" reminds us of indications elsewhere (e.g., Mark 3:31–32; 6:3; John 2:12; 7:3–4; Acts 1:14; 1 Cor. 9:5; Gal. 1:19) that Jesus had brothers and sisters. The most natural inference is that these were children of Joseph and Mary, though the official teaching of some Christian churches holds otherwise. Here it suffices to recognize the importance of "the holy family" in the early Christian movement. The authority of this letter is grounded in its connection to the family of Jesus.

The quasi-patriarchal authority of Jacob, the author of this letter, highlights a number of theological and ecclesial issues. As distinct from the Petrine model of leadership, which has led to a centralized monarchical form of leadership, the Jacobean model was more collegial, while allowing for real leadership and decision making to break a stalemate. This model may have more potential in contemporary ecclesial situations than the Petrine model.

The role of James in the Jerusalem church and the mission beyond Jerusalem raises still unanswered questions about the relationship between Christianity and Judaism. Some of these have been raised by Paul Van Buren in his multivolumed work *A Theology of the Jewish Christian Reality* (1980–88). Had James survived to give leadership to the church beyond the Jewish War of 66–73 CE, and had a Jewish Jerusalem church survived beyond 135 CE, we might not have needed to wait until the 1980s for these questions to be raised, and Christianity might well have retained a more Jewish character. Although there has been some redress following the Holocaust, only in recent years has the reminder that Jesus was a Jew ceased to surprise and shock some people. Considerable work remains to be done before we can be satisfied with an accepted Christian theology of the people of Israel. Blind support for the State of Israel no matter what, which seems to be the position of many conservative Christians and has been the effective practice of United States foreign policy, will not do theologically if Paul's views in Rom. 9–11 and James's call for impartiality are taken seriously. No significant work has been done to develop the implications of James's theology of mission to the circumcision. The same is probably true with regard to Jesus's mission to Israel. Perhaps it was necessary for the Christian movement to establish some distance between itself and Israel before such a theology could emerge. Certainly this did not happen in the Epistle of James, which is addressed to Israel in the Diaspora. The distance created by Paul's mission to the nations opened up the necessity of a Christian theology of Israel. The problem is that the distance became an unbridgeable chasm with a breakdown of relationship and communication.

James 1:2–27

Epitome of the Exhortation of James

Introductory Matters

The body of the opening chapter (1:2–27) introduces all of the main themes of the epistle, though not in the order of the later chapters. The order of the epitome is closer to a reverse of that order.

Table 3. Intratextual Relationships in James

Passage in James 1	Theme	Related passage in James
1:2–8, 12	faith, wisdom, and testing	5:7–18
1:2–4, 12	joy in enduring testing	5:7–11, 12
1:5–7, 8	wisdom and the prayer of faith	5:13–18
1:9–10, 11	reversal of fortunes of rich and poor	2:1–6; 4:13–5:6
1:12–18	enduring trials, wicked desires, and God's gift	3:13–4:10
1:19–20, 21	the use of the tongue	3:1–12
1:22–27	faith and works	2:7–13, 14–26; 4:11–12

The outline reveals a rough chiastic structure based on the order of the epitome, which is repeated, roughly in reverse, by the following "essays." The structure is clearer if 1:2–8 and 5:7–18 are treated as units. The address in 1:1 forms an inclusio with the conclusion in 5:19–20. In addition to this approach, developed on the basis of Luke Timothy Johnson's analysis (1995; 1998), I note that the structural diagram given by Peter Davids (1982, 27–29) paves the way for the analysis given here.

Figure 3. Structural Diagram of the Epistle of James
(Davids 1982, 29)

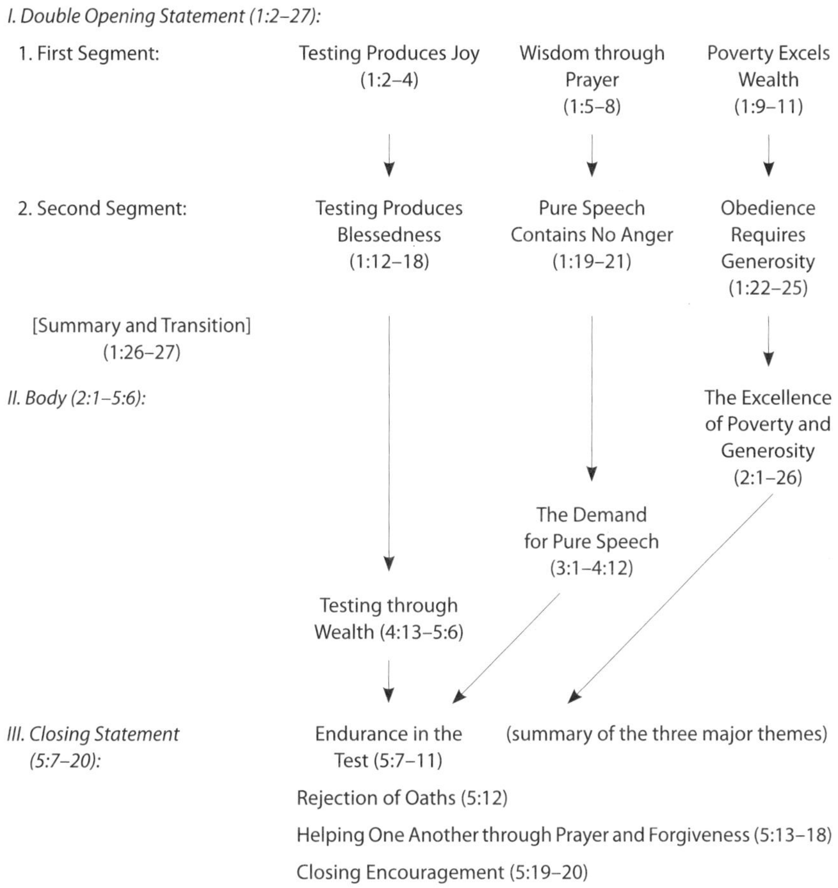

I. Double Opening Statement (1:2–27):

1. First Segment:	Testing Produces Joy (1:2–4)	Wisdom through Prayer (1:5–8)	Poverty Excels Wealth (1:9–11)

↓ ↓ ↓

2. Second Segment:	Testing Produces Blessedness (1:12–18)	Pure Speech Contains No Anger (1:19–21)	Obedience Requires Generosity (1:22–25)

[Summary and Transition] (1:26–27)

II. Body (2:1–5:6):

The Excellence of Poverty and Generosity (2:1–26)

The Demand for Pure Speech (3:1–4:12)

Testing through Wealth (4:13–5:6)

III. Closing Statement (5:7–20):

Endurance in the Test (5:7–11)   (summary of the three major themes)

Rejection of Oaths (5:12)

Helping One Another through Prayer and Forgiveness (5:13–18)

Closing Encouragement (5:19–20)

There is a loose relationship between the themes of the various parts of James 1, which are developed in the following chapters. The resulting composition lacks any tightly knit argument running through it. At the same time, James is no random collection of tradition. Rather, it follows what might be called "associational logic," in which it captures a vision of God and the appropriate human response in a life of faithfulness in a world that, though it is God's creation, is hostile to and incompatible with God's will and purpose for the people of God. This vision has three clearly defined and related parts: (1) underlying all is the vision of the generosity of God as the giver of all that is good and perfect; (2) in tension with this is the understanding of the "world" in the light of this vision; (3) God's will and purpose for the people of

God in the world flow from the vision but take the reality of the "world" with utter seriousness. James makes use of an abundance of associated metaphors that illuminate each other and build a vision of the way of God in the world. The use of *holoklēros* ("complete") in James 1:4 is the first of nineteen examples of words found only in James and Paul in the NT. In Paul it is found only in 1 Thess. 5:23. One of the nineteen words is not found in the LXX or pre-Christian Greek corpus. This exclusive common use by James and Paul is an early reminder that in spite of tensions between them, they share much distinctive language and a common essential theology, even when they adopt different language. They share a view of the indiscriminate graciousness of God, where there is partial linguistic overlap in a broader theological agreement (see James 1:5, 17; 2:1, 9; 3:17–18).

Of the sixty-three words found only in James in the NT, ten are first known in James, not being used in the LXX or the pre-Christian Greek corpus, a further two are not found in the Hebrew books translated in the LXX or the pre-Christian Greek corpus, five are not used in the LXX, another five are not used in the Hebrew books translated in the LXX, one is not used in the pre-Christian Greek corpus, and forty are found only in James in the NT. James reveals a distinct stream in early Christianity, deeply rooted in the Jesus tradition and reflecting both linguistic and theological connections and tensions with Paul.

In 1:2, James addresses the readers as "my brothers" and the like for the first time. Clearly, there were also sisters among those addressed, and explicit reference to the appropriate action if a "brother or sister" (*adelphos ē adelphē*) is in need (2:15) implies a loose and nondiscriminatory form of address. It seems appropriate to translate uses of *adelphos* in 1:2, 9, 16, 19; 2:1, 5, 14, 15; 3:1, 10, 12; 4:11 (3x); 5:7, 9, 10, 12, 19 as "brother and/or sister" because the context suggests that there is no reason to think that a discriminatory reference is implied. The use of "brother or sister" in 2:15 is almost like a rubric: "for brothers, read brothers and sisters." Placing the reference to "sisters" in square brackets where James addresses the readers as "brothers" acknowledges the absence of "sisters" from the text but implies the correctness of assuming it. The brackets remind us of the insensitivity of the time to the presence of women, though their presence is clearly assumed.

From the list of references to the use of "brothers" in the previous paragraph, only 1:9; 2:15; and two of the three in references in 4:11 are not used in direct address to the readers. G. Currie Martin (see "James and the Jesus Tradition" in the introduction) argues that in the fifteen remaining cases, James uses "brothers" five times (1:2; 4:11; 5:7, 9, 10), "my brothers" seven times (2:1, 14; 3:1, 10, 12; 5:12, 19), and "my beloved brothers" three times (1:16, 19; 2:5) in direct address as a signal to the presence of Jesus tradition. Rather than adopt the NRSV practice of translating "brothers" as "beloved," here I show that "brothers" is understood as "brothers [and sisters]." Where the author addresses the readers as "*my* brothers [and sisters]," any distance between

The Language of Command

The Epistle of James has a high concentration of verbs in the imperative mood, plus four uses of other forms of the verb to express command—in all, 57 uses in five relatively short chapters, an average of over 11 uses in each chapter. Because chapter 3 has only 4 imperatives, the concentration is higher in the rest: 12 in chapter 1, 14 in chapter 2, 12 in chapter 4 (10 in 4:7–10), and 17 in chapter 5. These verbs are used in the second- and third-person singular and plural. The language of direct command is clear in the second-person forms, where the person or persons are addressed directly. In the third person, the language has a more hortatory function. Of the 22 singular uses, 14 are third-person hortatory uses. Of the 37 plurals, only 1 is a third-person hortatory use (5:14). Given that the readers do not change, the move from singular to plural forms of address is primarily rhetorical. While the third-person singular use has just under twice as many instances as the second-person singular direct command, the third-person plural hortatory use is almost nonexistent—only 1 out of 37 uses of the plural, 36 being in the second-person plural language of direct command. This remarkable change of balance is explicable because James characteristically addresses all readers authoritatively as a group, so that accounts for 37 of the 57 imperatives in James. The second-person singular uses occur in dialogue between characters in examples given in the text (2:3 [3x], 18; 5:1), as does the only third-person plural use (5:14), and the third-person singular imperatives concern individuals in hypothetical situations (1:5, 6, 7, 13; 5:12, 13 [2x], 14). The dominant form is the language of command addressed to all (readers/hearers), expressing the self-conscious authority of James.

author and readers vanishes, and imperatives (the language of command), which dominate James, are softened and backed by persuasion rooted in the Jesus tradition. Yet the pervasive use of the imperative gives expression to the author's strong sense of authority, even if James shows awareness of the need to persuade his readers. This is consistent with the patriarchal authority of James that was exercised in a context where the claimed equality of wisdom among colleagues was recognized.

The opening theme of enduring testing is taken up at the end of the epistle in 5:7–12, forming a kind of inclusio, framing the letter. From the beginning, the aggressive character of the "world," in which the life of faithfulness is to be lived, makes its mark. Thus faithfulness encounters *peirasmos* ("testing").

Tracing the Train of Thought

The epitome (1:2–27) is made up of a series of seven paragraphs that can be comprehended in five main thematic developments, forming an associational

**James 1:2–27
in the Rhetorical Flow**

Address/salutation (1:1)

▶ **Epitome of the exhortation of James (1:2–27)**

Faith, wisdom, and testing (1:2–8)

Joy in enduring testing (1:2–4)

The request for wisdom, and the prayer of faith (1:5–8)

Reversal of fortunes of rich and poor (1:9–11)

Enduring trials, wicked desires, and God's gift (1:12–18)

Enduring trials, and the crown of life (1:12)

Epithymia the source of temptation (1:13–15)

God the source of goodness (1:16–18)

The use of the tongue: Hearing and receiving (1:19–21)

Faith and works: Hearing and doing (1:22–27)

unity rather than a logically developed argument, favoring metaphor over logic.

Faith, Wisdom, and Testing (1:2–8)

Although the paragraph (1:2–8) is coherent, there is a marked change of focus from the beginning to the end that justifies a minor division to ensure that the emphasis on joy at the beginning is not weakened, and the complexity of faith and the role of wisdom are appreciated at the end.

Joy in enduring testing (1:2–4). The uncommon theme of joy is introduced immediately following the address. In the Greek text underlying "consider it all joy," the verb follows the object "all joy," which is placed at the beginning of the sentence for emphasis. This linguistically connects the greeting (*chairein*) to the opening of the first major theme, "joy" (*charan*), and gives priority to the theme of joy.

The opening is marked by this linking style where the word/motif at the end of a sentence or clause is repeated and developed in the next. Thus "testing" at the end of 1:2 is picked up and developed at the beginning of 1:3; likewise, "endurance" at the end of 1:3 and at the beginning of 1:4, "lacking" at the end of 1:4 and at the beginning of 1:5, "asking" in the second part of 1:5 and at the beginning of 1:6, "doubting" at the end of the first part of 1:6 and at the beginning of the second part of 1:6. This simple literary technique has a rhetorical power, persuasively carrying the reader step by step.

1:2. Consider it all joy, my brothers [and sisters] when you fall into manifold testings [*peirasmois*]. Although not the first words addressed to the readers after the address itself, the identification of the "readers" as "my brothers [and sisters]" comes at the beginning and characterizes what James has to say to them. It is oft repeated throughout, occurring for the last time at the end, in 5:19, at the very beginning of the closing sentence of the epistle, forming an inclusio.

Though addressed widely to the Diaspora, this letter—James implies—will be read in communities among those considered to be brothers and sisters. Thus, although the letter is not addressed to the churches of the Diaspora, it is addressed to communities, not individuals.

Godly and Worldly Joy

The use of *chara* is spread thinly (only 59x) and unevenly throughout the NT: 6 times in Matthew, 1 in Mark, 8 in Luke, 9 in John, 4 in Acts, 22 in Paul (3 in Romans, 6 in 2 Corinthians, 1 in Galatians, 5 in Philippians, 1 in Colossians, 4 in 1 Thessalonians, 1 in 2 Thessalonians, 1 in Philemon), 4 in Hebrews, 2 in James, 3 in the Johannine Epistles (1 time in each of the three epistles). Despite this thin and uneven use, there is something about its use in Paul and John (both Gospel and Epistles) that implies the importance of the motif of joy for believing life and thought. Its place at the beginning of James, where it introduces the initial theme, is impressive. We may suspect that it lays the foundation for the message of the epistle. Linguistically, joy (*chara*) is linked to the initial greeting (*chairein*), drawing attention to the use of *chairō* in the sense of "to rejoice" (occurring 74x in the NT, *chairō* is used in this latter sense 64x, but not so in James 1:1) (*synchairō* occurs 7x in the NT; *agalliaō* occurs 11x in the NT, not in James or in the pre-Christian Greek corpus, but commonly in the LXX; *euphrainō* occurs 14x in the NT, not in James but 8x in Luke-Acts). The sense of joy overlaps the meaning of the language of boasting (*kauchaomai, kauchēsis, kauchēma*), which alerts the reader to a certain ambiguity about the character and ground of joy and rejoicing, since there is a worldly joy as well as a godly joy (1:2; 4:9).

Many of the paragraphs and sentences introduce an ethos of command, with a verb in the imperative mood in the second or third person (see 1:2, 4, 5, 6, 7, 9). With the verb ("consider," 1:2) in the imperative mood, the ethical and hortatory character of the epistle is immediately evident. The force of the imperative is moderated by the use of "my brothers [and sisters]" to identify those addressed in an egalitarian manner. Nevertheless, the second-person plural imperative used here expresses direct command and James's sense of authority even when addressed to brothers and sisters (see the sidebar "The Language of Command"; see also "Jacob as Patriarch" in the introduction).

The first words following the address in the Greek text are "all joy," followed by the verb "consider." This placement as the very first words of the substance of the epistle gives great weight to this theme, belying its rarity of use in James. That rarity of use may signal the complexity of joy. Joy in the face of serious testing is an ambiguous entity, rooted in knowledge and hope (1:3, 12). The second-person plural imperative "consider" (*hēgēsasthe*) exhorts the readers directly to the conscious adoption of an attitude. Clearly, the author does not think that the circumstances described are likely to produce a spontaneous response of joy. Rather, it is precisely such circumstances that are normally antithetical to the experience of joy. Yet an awareness of another perspective or reality may release joy even in unpromising circumstances.

1:3. Though anything but joyous in themselves, these circumstances, when grasped (understood) in the right way, are an opportunity to grow in faith and resilient endurance, **knowing that the testing of your faith produces endurance.** Yet James nowhere suggests that God is the source of negative testing circumstances (see 1:13). Rather, the reference to manifold testing situations is the first indication of the hostile character of the world in which we live. There is nothing good in such aggressive testings per se. When they are used as an opportunity to exercise faith, faith is strengthened, and by enduring, the believer is perfected, lacking nothing.

1:4. Because this positive outworking is not an automatic consequence of testing, James further exhorts, **Let endurance have its perfect work, that you may be perfect and complete, lacking nothing.** Those who are tested are exhorted to cooperate with God in bringing good out of evil.

Only when testing circumstances are evaluated in a particular way can they become an opportunity for a joy. Thus, although God is not the source of testings, the testing situation is an opportunity to develop character, understood as the commitment to God and God's values. Faithful endurance may involve a rejection of worldly joys. There is a worldly joy (4:9 in the context of 4:1–10) as well as a godly joy (1:2). For James, worldly joy is the enjoyment of the pleasures of this world in a way that is self-centered and insensitive to the need of the other, the neighbor. Godly joy is more precarious and, at the same time, more secure. It is precarious because it is known by those who remain faithful in the testing of faith amid life's fiery trials. Such trials have the potential to destroy faith, but for those who endure, faith is purified and strengthened, perfected. The key is in endurance, faithfulness in the face of opposition. The exhortation "consider it all joy" presupposes that the person facing such testing will know that the outcome of enduring is the perfecting of faithfulness. It is more secure because there is in this a certain ground for joy that has nothing to do with a masochistic delight in self-inflicted pain and suffering. The joy of which James speaks is in the present, but also it has an eschatological ring to it. James shares this theme with Paul: "And we boast/rejoice [*kauchōmetha*] in the hope of the glory of God. And not only this, but we boast/rejoice in afflictions, knowing that affliction produces/works endurance, and endurance testing, and testing hope. And hope is not put to shame, because the love of God has been poured out in our hearts by the Holy Spirit who is given to us" (Rom. 5:2–5). This string of consequences is much like James 1:2–4, except that James lacks reference to the work of the Spirit. What Paul attributes to the Spirit, James implicitly attributes to God.

Where James exhorts the readers as "brothers [and sisters]" (1:2), Jesus tradition lies close to the surface. James exhorts the readers to "consider it all joy," knowing that Jesus pronounces the blessedness of those who are persecuted for righteousness' sake, as in Matt. 5:10–12 (note esp. the last verse):

Blessed are those who are persecuted for the sake of righteousness, for
theirs is the kingdom of heaven.
Blessed are you whenever they insult you and persecute you and say all
manner of evil against you because of me.
Rejoice and be glad, for your reward is great in heaven.

The interpretative expansion of the beatitude of Matt. 5:10 in 5:12 makes the
future reward in heaven a basis for rejoicing in the present. There is something
of this also in reading James 1:2 in the light of 1:12: "Blessed is the person
who endures testing, who, having stood the test, will receive the crown of life,
which [the Lord] has promised to those who love him." This understanding
of the crown of life in 1:12 echoes Rev. 2:10 (cf. 1 Pet. 5:4). The connection
between 1:2–4 and 1:12 is hardly to be missed (see the table "Intratextual
Relationships in James").

James 1:2–4 introduces the theme of testing/trial/temptation, all of these
meanings being possible in the use of *peirasmos*. This word is used in the Lord's
Prayer, variously translated as "temptation" ("Lead us not into temptation")
and "trial" ("Save us from the time of trial"). It appears in James 1:2, and
again in the epitome in 1:12, along with *dokimos*, the neuter form of which is a
variant for *dokimion* in 1:3. While the theme of testing in 1:2–4 mainly relates
to the external circumstances, in 1:12 it is linked to and introduces the theme
of temptation rooted in inner desire (*epithymia*) in 1:13–15. Given that 1:2
refers to many different kinds of *peirasmoi*, 1:2–4 probably is an introduction
to the whole range of testings and temptations, though 1:2–4 is focused on
trials of a more aggressive physical character. The themes are taken up again
in 1:12–15 and are amplified with variations at the end of the letter (5:7–12).
The vocabulary of the key associated themes of testing/trial/temptation, linked
with the prayer for wisdom (1:5), echoes Sir. 4:11, 17; Wis. 5:1–14; 7:7; 8:21;
9:6. The similarity of this concatenation of vocabulary and theme in James
1:2–4 with 1 Pet. 1:6–7 and Rom. 5:3–5 suggests the use of a widespread literary device rather than literary dependence (see Dibelius 1976, 74–77).

How then is perfection conceived in 1:4? It is expressed in terms of completion and wholeness. Endurance needs to be sustained if it is to have its perfect
work (*ergon teleion*), making the faithful whole, complete, lacking nothing.
Perhaps we should say that it is endurance only if it is sustained and thus has
its perfect work. For the use of "complete" (*holoklēroi*) in 1:4, see 1 Thess.
5:23, which has the only other occurrence of *holoklēros* in the NT. It is one of
the images of perfection that James piles up. Such wholeness/completeness is
of an ethical and spiritual nature rather than a reference to unlimited possessions ("lacking nothing") or physical wholeness. The epistle does not promise
riches to the faithful, nor does it promise bodily wholeness and length of days.
This is not a promise of the Deuteronomic kind, of prosperity and long life
to the faithful. Rather, it concerns the complete equipment to endure testing.

If testing/trial/temptation is the opportunity to develop endurance, James exhorts, "Let endurance have its perfect work," which lays responsibility on the hearer/reader to live and be faithful in order to be "perfect and complete, lacking nothing." James pronounces a blessing on the person who endures (*hypomenei*) testing/trial/temptation, since this person will receive the crown of life (1:12). Endurance is not the inevitable outcome of testing. Only those who endure are blessed with a crown of life.

The request for wisdom, and the prayer of faith (1:5–8). The person facing testing needs to persevere, to endure, and this requires the gift of wisdom from God.

1:5. If any one of you lacks wisdom, let that person ask [*aiteitō*] of the God who gives to all generously and without reproaching, and it will be given to that person. James is clear: asking God is the one essential condition to be fulfilled to receive wisdom from God, because God gives, without discrimination, to all who ask. Paul says, "There is no discrimination [*prosōpolēmpsia*] with God" (Rom. 2:11). Though James does not use *prosōpolēmpsia* here, he embraces this view without using the word. Rather, James characterizes God as the one who gives to all generously (*pasin haplōs*), without reluctance or argument, without rancor (*mē oneidizontos*) or hesitation (cf. 1:17). Asking God is the sufficient fulfillment of any condition: "Let that person ask, . . . and it will be given." This is a character reference for God in the understanding of James, to which he returns and which he develops. Later James asserts that human discrimination (*prosōpolēmpsia*) favoring the rich is irreconcilable with faith in the Lord Jesus Christ (2:1). To discriminate (*prosōpolēmpteite*) in this way is to commit sin (2:9). Unlike Paul, James surprisingly fails to ground the use of this vocabulary in the way God acts.

Following the first address of the readers/hearers as brothers and sisters in 1:2, the theme of asking God resonates with the centrality of asking God in the teaching of Jesus according to Matthew, especially in Q material of the Sermon on the Mount (5:42; 6:8; 7:7–11; cf. Luke 11:9–13; see also John 14:13–14; 15:7; 16:24). The Jesus of Matthew, like James, makes asking the only condition for receiving: "Ask and it shall be given you; . . . for every one who asks receives." Interestingly, where Matt. 7:11 says that God will give good things to those who ask him, Luke 11:13 says that God will give the Holy Spirit to those who ask. In James, no specific request is indicated. God's gift is a response to the reliance expressed in asking. Jesus's reference to the gift of good things in Matt. 7:11 resonates with James 1:17: "Every generous act of giving [*dosis agathē*] and every perfect gift is from above, coming down from the Father of lights, with whom there is no shadow cast by turning." Such generosity of giving is characteristic of God in the teaching of Jesus. It is God who causes the sun to shine and the rain to fall on all, both the just and the unjust (Matt. 5:45; cf. 6:25–34//Luke 12:22–32).

In the context of testing, James asserts that what is needed is wisdom. The one who lacks wisdom is exhorted to ask the generous God. Though the content of the request is unspecified, it is implied that the request to God is for wisdom. If so, there is an echo of the tradition of Solomon. At the beginning of Solomon's reign, God asks him what gift he seeks. In effect, Solomon asks for wisdom, and God gives him a wise and discerning heart (1 Kings 3:5–12). At the end of 1 Kings 3, after Solomon had judged a case between two women, each of whom claimed that a surviving child was hers, the chapter concludes, "And all Israel heard of the judgment that the king had rendered; and they stood in awe of the king, because they perceived that the wisdom of God was in him to render judgment" (3:28). The same theme is picked up in Wis. 7–9 (see esp. 7:7; 8:21). This implies a contrast between the wisdom from above (from God) and the wisdom of the world, a contrast with which James 3:13–18 resonates.

1:6. It soon becomes clear that genuine asking in faith is a prerequisite, unwavering faith in the God who gives generously every perfect gift. The direction to ask in 1:5 (third-person imperative) is amplified in 1:6, **But let the person ask [*aiteitō*] in faith, doubting nothing.** The prayer/request of faith is contrasted with a doubting response. Genuine asking is the asking of faith. Thus the committed requester is contrasted with the hesitant, doubting requester. **For the one doubting is like [*eoiken*] the waves of the sea, driven and tossed about by the wind.** The doubter is likened (*eoiken* [cf. also 1:23; only in James in the NT]) to an ocean wave, driven and tossed about by the wind, having no stability of its own and thus being taken wherever the wind pushes it.

1:7. **Let that person [*ho anthrōpos ekeinos*] not think that he or she will receive anything from the Lord.** The person (*ho anthrōpos*) described by this image (the wave driven by the wind) should not think (*mē . . . oiesthō* [third-person singular imperative]), that is, expect to receive anything from the Lord

---

Two Negative Images or Metaphors: The Wave and the Mirror

In 1:6 and 1:23 James uses two negative images metaphorically. Each portrays an aspect of the consequences of inadequate faithfulness. James 1:6–8 concentrates on the lack of a firm commitment and portrays such a person as being "like" (*eoiken*) a wave driven by any wind that blows, thus being at the mercy of the wind, having no direction of its own. Such a person is directionless. The second image portrays the person who professes faith but lacks an active way of life that flows from faith as being "like" (*eoiken*) someone who looks into a mirror and immediately forgets the image and thus takes no remedial action to improve the image. The mirror here is an image or metaphor of "the perfect law of liberty" (1:25). This mirror exposes the life of one who looks into it to scrutiny by the standard of the perfect will and purpose of God, revealing the reality of that person's life and providing a basis for action.

(*kyrios*). This is the second use of *kyrios* in James, the first being in 1:1, where James is described as a "servant of God [*theos*] and of Lord [*kyrios*] Jesus Christ," arousing the expectation of a *theos* distinction from *kyrios*. Thus we might expect this reference in 1:7 to be to Jesus. But this seems to be ruled out by 1:5. Anyone who lacks wisdom is bidden to ask God, who gives liberally to everyone who asks, but the doubting asker should not expect to receive anything from the Lord.

The use of *anthrōpos* in 1:7 (cf. 1:19; 2:20, 24; 3:8, 9; 5:17 [7x in James]), and *anēr* (in 1:8, 12, 20, 23; 2:2; 3:2 [6x in James]) is pleonastic and without discernable difference in meaning. It is probably derived from the LXX as a translation of the Semitic *'ādām* by *anthrōpos* or *anēr*. Although this use of language reflects a patriarchal context, in James it is used generically of the human person. The same cultural blind spot is evident in the address of the readers as "brothers." Yet on one occasion the blinders are lifted, and James refers to "a brother or a sister" (2:15). On the whole, it is appropriate to translate *anthrōpos* or *anēr* as "person."

1:8. Such a person (*ho anthrōpos*, 1:7) is also described as a **double-minded person** (*anēr dipsychos*). *Dipsychos* is used in the NT only in James 1:8; 4:8 (the latter without *anēr*) and is first known in James. The *dipsychos* is indecisive and uncommitted, directionless, wavering, and **unstable [*akatastatos*] in every way.** *Akatastatos* appears in the NT only here and in 3:8; a related

Kyrios

Kyrios is used fourteen times in James (1:1, 7; 2:1; 3:9; 4:10, 15; 5:4, 7, 8, 10, 11 [2x], 14, 15) alongside sixteen uses of *theos* (1:1, 5, 13 [2x], 20, 27; 2:5, 19, 23 [2x]; 3:9; 4:4 [2x], 6, 7, 8). Thus *theos* is concentrated early, ten times in the first two chapters, and not used in chapter 5; *kyrios* is concentrated at the end, ten times in the last two chapters, of which eight are in chapter 5. Because *kyrios* is a common translation for the name of God ("YHWH"), there is uncertainty in James concerning whether the use of *kyrios* is a reference to Jesus or God. In the LXX *kyrios* and *theos* are commonly used to refer to God, and this is true in James also, where there are clear uses of *kyrios* to refer to God in 3:9; 5:4. But James also uses *kyrios* to refer to Jesus in 1:1; 2:1. Two references to the coming (*parousia*) of the Lord (5:7, 8) are strong cases to be references to Jesus. Thus *kyrios* is used of both Jesus and God. Ambiguity would be avoided if a thesis advocated by S. M. Barclay (1875, 71–117) and supported by some early church fathers and the Gospel of John could be accepted with regard to James. Simply put, it is that the self-revealing YHWH of the OT is the Logos encountered by the patriarchs and incarnate in Jesus (see John 1:1–18; 8:58). But there is nothing in James to support such a solution. The remaining uses of *kyrios* are probably references to God. (For details, see the commentary at the appropriate place.)

The Image of the *Dipsychos*

The use of *dipsychos* is not known beyond James until its later use in *1 Clem.* 11.2 and in *Shepherd of Hermas* (*Herm. Vis.* 3.4.3; *Herm. Mand.* 9.5–6; 11.2, 4; *Herm. Sim.* 8.7.2; 9.21.1). Interestingly, when this usage emerges, the cognate verb, *dipsycheō* (*Did.* 4.4; *2 Clem.* 11.5; *Herm. Vis.* 3.2.2; *Herm. Mand.* 9.1, 8; *Herm. Sim.* 8.11.3), and noun, *dipsychia* (*2 Clem.* 19.2; *Herm. Mand.* 9.9; 10.1.1; 10.2.2), are also attested. Against this background, James uses only the adjective, though in 4:8 the adjective is used in the plural as if a noun. Does the use in James emerge out of the linguistic use represented by this broader background, or is the broader use directly or indirectly dependent on James? In the extrabiblical references, there is no evidence of dependence on James. The broader linguistic use of noun, verb, and adjective suggests that this is the linguistic context out of which James uses the adjective with the full expectation that hearers/readers will know precisely what is meant. It concerns instability of thinking, commitment, and direction, which is expressed in indecision. In fifth-century christological thought (Cyril of Alexandria) *dipsychos* came to express the belief in Christ "in two souls" or "of two souls."

form, *akatastasia*, appears in 3:16. Such an unstable person does not take God seriously, failing to rely on God's generosity, and should not expect to receive anything from God. But this is not a case of God showing discrimination based on who the person is (cf. the use of *prosōpolēmpsia* in 2:1). Whoever the person is, failure to ask in faith makes that person responsible for the failure to receive.

Reversal of Fortunes of Rich and Poor (1:9–11)

The pairing of the humble (*ho tapeinos*) with the rich (*ho plousios*) implies that *ho tapeinos* here has the meaning of "the poor" brother/sister. The theme of the reversal of the fortunes of rich and poor (1:9–11) is taken up and developed in 2:1–6; 4:13–5:6.

1:9–10. Let the lowly/poor brother [or sister] boast [*kauchasthō*]. In Greek, the third-person imperative *kauchasthō* stands at the beginning of the sentence and continues the hortatory pattern found in 1:4, 5, 6 following the direct address of the second-person imperative in 1:2.

The language of boasting (*kauchasthō*, 1:9) is also found in James 4:16 (*kauchasthe, kauchēsis*), joined by the term *alazoneia* (cf. 1 John 2:16), which describes the characteristic behavior of the *alazōn* (see Rom. 1:30; 2 Tim. 3:2). In Greek comedy, this figure is portrayed as a buffoon, a braggart, whose arrogant boasting is transparently false. From the perspective of James, those who plan their lives without taking God into account are arrogant fools, and their boasting is evil. In the NT, the vocabulary of boasting is frequently found

---

Boasting in James and Paul

James shares with only Paul in the NT three of five cognate words used (all five used by Paul) in relation to the rhetoric and the ethic of boasting: *kauchaomai* (James 1:9; 4:16; 35x in Paul); *katakauchaomai* (James 2:13; 3:14; 2x in Paul), and *kauchēsis* (James 4:16; 11x in Paul). A fourth related word, *kauchēma*, is used only by Paul (10x) and once in Heb. 3:6, while a fifth, *enkauchaomai*, is used only once by Paul (2 Thess. 1:4) and is not found in the surviving pre-Christian Greek corpus (though it is found four times in the LXX: Pss. 51:3; 73:4; 96:7; 105:47). Paul's use of the shared words is much more frequent than James or Hebrews, although, like James, Paul uses *katakauchaomai* twice. The concentration of these words in James and Paul is impressive. Given the limited length of James, compared with the Letters of Paul, James's lesser use of two of the three words common to both of them might seem to be the comparative equivalent of the Pauline use. But James lacks the development of this motif and concentration of use found in 2 Corinthians, complemented and developed in Romans and 1 Corinthians.

---

in Paul's Letters, especially 2 Corinthians. There Paul subverts traditional values by boasting of those elements of his life conventionally considered to be shameful and dishonorable. The same can be said of Jesus's critique of the rich and affirmation of the poor, a theme explicitly taken up in James, making use of the language of boasting, thus, like Paul, explicitly attacking conventional values (see James 4:6, 13–16; 5:1–6).

In Greco-Roman rhetoric, self-promotion was an essential element for establishing one's reputation and influence. Boasting normally drew attention to a person's possessions, achievements, and attributes since excelling in those areas was generally admired. Both Paul and James turn this practice on its head by boasting of what was commonly avoided and despised. This move is related to the great reversal expressed in the teaching of Jesus: "The last will be first, and the first will be last" (Matt. 20:16). It is also relevant to Jesus's critique of the rich and advocacy of the poor in the Beatitudes (Matt. 5:3–12) and the theme of Mary in Luke 1:48, 51–53. The theme of boasting and also its cultural, ethical, rhetorical, and theological relevance and implications are treated by Rudolf Bultmann (1965), C. K. Barrett (1986), and C. H. Dodd (1953b, esp. 73–82). Barrett notes the background of this word group in the comic poets, where the boaster can be turned into a comic character depicted as a loudmouthed braggart. Such a character is a figure of ridicule (see the role of the *alazōn* as described in the *Characters* of Theophrastus, whose account is given in abridged form and discussed in Dodd 1946, 42). Dodd summarizes the character of the *alazōn* as "a conceited, pretentious humbug" who boasts ostentatiously and groundlessly. Although James does not use *alazōn* (in the NT only in Rom. 1:30; 2 Tim. 3:2), *alazoneia* is used in James 4:16 and 1 John 2:16 in a way that is closely connected. "Now you boast [*kauchasthe*] in your *alazoneiais*. All such boasting [*kauchēsis*] is evil" (James 4:16–17). This language (*alazoneia*) is not used in the Hebrew books of the LXX but is common in the pre-Christian Greek corpus, where it is the subject of critique. It is also found seven times in LXX books outside the Hebrew canon (2 Macc. 9:8; 15:6; 4 Macc. 1:26; 2:15; 8:19; Wis. 5:8; 17:7), whose composition reflects greater Greek influence. From the time of Aristotle (*Eth. nic.* 4.7.2) there was a critique of "justifiable boasting" and, in the Greek moralists and the comic poets, a tradition of critique of the *alazōn* and the practice of excessive and groundless boasting. This critique has similarities to and differences from the Pauline critique, which is rooted in the LXX in texts such as Ps. 5:12 (5:11 ET); Prov. 27:1; Jer. 9:22–23 (9:23–24 ET; this last text is quoted twice by Paul: 1 Cor. 1:31; 2 Cor. 10:17). Both James and 1 John stand with Paul in identifying the values of this world with empty and groundless boasting because it leaves God out of the question. But there is an appropriate boasting that overlaps godly rejoicing, as in Rom. 5:3–4 and perhaps James 1:9. James, 1 John, and Paul do not take account of the Hellenistic critique of the *alazōn* because it comes from within the worldview that they criticize. Instead, they identify *alazoneia* with love of, or attachment to, the world and the things of the world, which are transitory and pass away (James 4:16; 1 John 2:16).

The exhortation to boast (*kauchasthō*) is addressed first to a representative poor person and then to a representative rich person in a sentence covering 1:9–10. **Let the humble/poor brother [or sister] boast in his high position, and the rich in his humble state.** The pairing of *ho tapeinos* with *ho plousios* makes clear that in this case the two groups addressed are the poor and the rich, addressed in representative figures. The background for this overlap is the Hebrew word *ʿānāw* (pl. *ʿānāwîm*), corresponding to James's use of the Greek *ptōchos* (pl. *ptōchoi*). The association with the humble poor is found in the use of *ʿānāwîm* in Zeph. 2:3 to designate those who follow God's laws and seek *ʿānāwâ*, which seems to mean "humility." This association is presupposed by James 1:9 and resonates in James's use of the traditional language of poverty.

Nevertheless, there is a kind of reversal of roles but without a change of economic status. First, the poor brother or sister is exhorted to boast in his or her exalted position (see 1:12; 2:5). Following the verb of command, the Greek word order has "brother" (*adelphos*) first, in the position of emphasis, before "humble/poor" (*tapeinos*), recognizing the humble/poor as brother or sister. Then the rich person (*ho plousios*) is characterized simply by wealth and is exhorted to boast in his or her humble state (*en tē tapeinōsei autou*). While the humble/poor person is explicitly exhorted as a "brother [or sister]," the rich person is not. Because the verb "to boast" occurs only once at the beginning of the paragraph but exhorts both poor and rich to boast, the single use of "brother [or sister]" might encompass a reference to the rich also. But the critique of the rich in James 5:1–6 suggests that the author might well have been reluctant to speak of them as brothers and avoids the endearing term where it might have been used.

James expresses a kind of reversal of positions in the exhortation (cf. Matt. 23:12). First, the poor are to boast in their exalted state. The language implies a reversal of roles, but the outcome is not so simple. They do not become the new rich (see 1:12; 2:5). At least, their riches are of another kind, of another world, and this is signaled by the resonance of the opening word of 1:12 with Matt. 5:3–12 and the nature of the blessing that is theirs. Then the rich are to boast in their humble or lowly state, but this does not imply that they cease to be rich (see 5:1–6). An equalizing of positions would be confirmed if the causal comment that follows applied equally to each: "because, as the flower of the grass, each passes away." James would then be giving expression to a central theme of Ecclesiastes (1:4; 2:16–23; cf. Isa. 40:6–8). Yet although, as Ecclesiastes and Isaiah note, the causal explanation applies equally to rich and poor, the application in 1:10b–11 is aimed specifically at the rich person. The rich person is to boast in his (or her) humble state, **because he will pass away like a blossom of grass.** The verb "will pass away" (*pareleusetai*) is singular in Greek and applies explicitly only to the rich person.

1:11. This is confirmed with another metaphor. **For the sun rises with scorching heat and shrivels the grass, and its blossom falls and the beauty of its face is destroyed; so also the rich in their pursuit of wealth will whither away.** Thus the rich person "in the pursuit of wealth will wither away." James ignores the fact that rich and poor alike will wither away. So here we have not a leveling but rather a radical reversal. The rich and powerful are humbled, and the poor and powerless are exalted. James is suggesting, as in Luke 1:52, that God "puts down the mighty from their seats and exalts the humble and meek" (see Luke 1:46–55; note esp. *tapeinōsis* in 1:48 and *tapeinos* in 1:52). That James is using Jesus tradition is likely (see Matt. 19:30; 20:16; and esp. 23:12). "God has chosen the poor in the world to be rich in faith and inheritors of the kingdom that God promised to those who love God" (James 2:5), which might be an elaboration of the promise of "the crown of life" to those who endure testing (James 1:12). Both seem to belong to the future and constitute an element of the future hope. Though the poor, like the rich, shrivel up and die, ultimately the humble poor who endure testing will receive the crown of life (1:12). This language resonates with the motif of eschatological reward (see Rev. 2:10; cf. 1 Pet. 5:4). Likewise, the humbling of the rich is expressed more strongly in 5:1–6, which concerns the eschatological judgment coming on the rich.

What distinguishes the humble poor from the rich is their enduring faithfulness. Poverty alone is not enough. In the biblical tradition, the humble poor are seen as those faithful to God (LXX: Pss. 9:39; 17:28; 33:19; 81:3; 101:18; Isa. 11:4; 14:32). Poverty goes with humility, just as pride is associated with the rich: "God opposes the proud, but gives grace to the humble [*tapeinois*]"

(James 4:6 [quoting Prov. 3:34 LXX, as does 1 Pet. 5:5]). The use of *charis* in James 4:6 and 1 Pet. 5:5 is dependent on the wording of the LXX. The Hebrew text of Prov. 3:34 has "but to the humble he shows favor" (NRSV), but in James 4:6 and 1 Pet. 5:5, *ho theos hyperēphanois antitassetai, tapeinois de didōsin charin* follows the LXX.

The rich are characterized as unscrupulous exploiters of the poor and the weak for the sake of their own comfort and pleasure. They are warned that they will be brought low: "so also the rich in their pursuit of wealth will wither away." The time of judgment is coming on the rich, and they will weep and wail in their distress (5:1–6).

This preliminary treatment of the rich and the poor (1:9–11) is taken up again in 2:1–6; 4:13–5:6. In 1:9–11 it is already clear that James is strongly critical of the rich. The image of the sun scorching the grass (1:10) is applied to the fate of the rich in 1:11. Using two words found in the NT only in this letter, James describes the perishing of the beauty (*euprepeia*) of the flowers of the field in the blasting heat of the sun as a metaphor for the way the rich will wither (*marainomai*) away. James 1:9–11 affirms the poor and develops a strong advocacy on their behalf.

Enduring Trials, Wicked Desires, and God's Gift (1:12–18)

The conflict of values revealed in 1:9–11 is taken further in 1:12–18 and developed in 3:13–4:10. At the same time, 1:12–18 builds on 1:2–4. In 1:12, although the noun *anēr* specifically identifies a male adult, the blessing is appropriate for the faithful person, male or female. This is specifically confirmed by reference to the blessing of the crown of life, which is promised to all those who love God.

1:12. *Enduring trials, and the crown of life (1:12).* James resumes the discussion of enduring testing (1:2–4) and its outcome before introducing the related theme of temptation, its origin and outcome. **Blessed is the person [*anēr*] who endures testing [*hypomenei peirasmon*], because when they have stood the test, they will receive the crown of life, which [the Lord] has promised to those who love him.** *Makarios* is the opening word of this new paragraph. As in the Beatitudes (Matt. 5:3–12), where the blessing is pronounced on those who are persecuted for righteousness' sake (5:10–12), James begins with a blessing (*makarios*), pronounced on the person (*anēr*) who endures *peirasmos* (on the use of *anēr* and *anthrōpos* in James, see the discussion on 1:7–8). Here, as in 1:2–4, hostile and aggressive persecution is indicated by *peirasmos*. Matthew 5:10–12 uses an alternative vocabulary of persecution (*diōkō*; cf. Rev. 12:13) but, like James 1:12, looks forward to the reward for such faithfulness beyond this life: "theirs is the kingdom of heaven" (Matt. 5:10). James 2:5 might echo that tradition in Matthew: "Has not God chosen the poor [*ptōchous*] of the world to be rich in faith and inheritors of the kingdom that God promised to those who love God?" James 1:12, like Rev. 2:10, promises "the crown of life" to those who love God. The blessing promised in James is that those who endure testing will receive the crown of life, the reward for all the faithful, described here as "those who love God." Those who love God in this way fulfill the first and greatest commandment (Deut. 6:4–5; Matt. 22:37–38), which is to love God wholeheartedly, to the death if necessary. The crown of life "promised" to those who love God suggests the martyr's crown and a reward beyond this life (see Rev. 2:10).

1:13. Epithymia *the source of temptation (1:13–15)*. James then turns to temptation, using a negated third-person singular imperative (*mēdeis . . . legetō*): **Let no one say when tempted, "I am tempted by God"; for God is unable to be tempted [*apeirastos*] by evil, and tempts no one.** In refutation of an assertion that God tempts persons, James says that God is incapable of being tempted by evil and does not tempt anyone. The word *apeirastos* ("untemptable") is known to us first in James, not being used elsewhere in the NT, the LXX, or the pre-Christian Greek corpus. If evil is whatever is opposed to God's character, will, and purpose, then it seems self-evident that God cannot be tempted by evil. It also follows that God would not tempt others to be and to act contrary to his character, will, and purpose.

1:14–15. James then provides an alternative account of the source of temptation. **But each person is tempted when they are lured and enticed by their own desire. Then when desire has conceived, it gives birth to sin, and when sin is full grown, it gives birth to [*apokyei*] death.** Temptation arises from desire (*epithymia*). Here James has much in common with Paul's treatment of desire in Rom. 7:7–8, where Paul identifies desire with covetousness. While desire is not essentially evil, it is predominantly so in Paul and James. The roots of this view are found in the Jewish tradition concerning the inclination (*yēṣer*) toward good or evil. These two inclinations, between which a person lives, provide a structure that makes the person free and responsible. But when the evil inclination becomes dominant, the person becomes a slave to the evil inclination, the negative reality of desire (see Davies 1955, 20–27; Urbach 1979, 471–83).

For James and Paul, selfish desire, the desire of the flesh, is the source of temptation. James emphasizes that temptation arises from each person's desires. Such desire can be obsessive, and to realities that are perfectly good in themselves, it gives the power to lure (*exelkō*, used in the NT only by James) and to entice (*deleazō*, used in the NT only by James and in 2 Pet. 2:14, 18) those whose hearts are not fixed on God, so that they capitulate to the world and its values. Then desire gives birth to (*tiktō*) sin. This image implies that sin is born of uncontrolled desire, and its completion gives birth to (*apokyeō*) death. This is vivid imagery. The language portrays desire as a propensity to grasp a baited hook, which lures and entices people, catching the unwary and uncommitted so that they cannot resist being dragged off by desire, with inevitable consequences. The longed-for treasures of the world prove to be full of deception, and sin produces death. The description of the birth of sin, which gives birth to death, uses a powerful organic imagery that captures the way uncontrolled desire gives birth to sin, which remorselessly leads to death. In contrast, God wills to bring about his (new) creation by his "true word" (1:18).

God the source of goodness (1:16–18). James first reiterates the negation of any association of God with evil before affirming the foundational understanding of God as the source of all goodness.

1:16. James begins with a negated imperative (*mē planāsthē* [present passive second-person plural]): **Do not be led astray,** or "Do not be deceived" (cf. 5:19–20; see also 1 Cor. 6:9; 15:33; Gal. 6:7; 1 John 1:8; 2:26; 3:7; 4:6). The notions of error and being led astray have both Jewish and Greek roots, but this language is derived from the latter. If James denies that God is the source of temptation, he does not suggest that the source is demonic or satanic (James 1:13–15; contrast Rev. 2:20; 12:9; 13:14; 18:23; 19:20; 20:3, 8, 10). In the renewed address of 1:16, **my beloved brothers** [**and sisters**] reiterates and expands the initial address of 1:2, adding "beloved" and introducing a transition. The exhortation seems to be a reference back to the rejected claim of being tempted by God (1:13–15). The rebuttal of this claim was crucial because of its incompatibility with God and because an alternative account of the origin of temptation has made clear the human responsibility for sin. There is more to say. The exhortation "Do not be led astray" is addressed to "my beloved brothers [and sisters]," alerting the readers to the use of Jesus tradition in what follows (Matt. 5:45–48; Luke 6:27–28, 32–36 [Q?]; Matt. 7:7–11, esp. vv. 9–11; cf. Luke 11:9–13 [Q?]). Jesus teaches that God is the one who gives good things to those who ask (Matt. 7:7–11; cf. James 1:5–6, 17). James confirms the error of supposing that God is in any way associated with evil, asserting that God is the source of all goodness.

1:17. God is wholly associated with goodness. **Every generous act of giving** [*pasa dosis agathē*] **and every perfect gift** [*pan dōrēma teleion*] **is from above, coming down from the Father of lights** (cf. Matt. 5:45–48). In the Greek text, two parallel phrases, each of three words and joined by *kai* ("and"), provide the opening words. Though the first phrase is grammatically feminine and the second neuter, they may be in synonymous parallelism, using stylistic variations. Certainly *agathos* and *teleios* can cover the same meaning, and both *dosis* and *dōrēma* may mean "gift." But it seems more likely that James uses *agathos* in the sense of "generous" (see Matt. 20:15) and *dosis* in the sense of "giving" (see BDAG 259). This reading is adopted by the NEB and the NRSV. It is supported by James 1:5, which describes God as the one who gives generously "to all" (*pasin*) who ask.

Thus James portrays God as the source of all generous giving and perfect gifts, which is the affirmation of the goodness of God and of all God's gifts. This affirmation arises from the recognition of the goodness of the creation (see Gen. 1:4, 10, 12, 18, 21, 25, 31) and leads to the recognition and affirmation that God is good (Pss. 34:8; 106:1; 107:1; 118:1; 135:3; 136:1). In every case except Ps. 134:3b (where the Hebrew word is *nā'îm*), the Hebrew word is *ṭôb*, which in the LXX is translated as *kalos* in Genesis and Ps. 134:3b (135:3b ET), as *agathos* in Pss. 117:1 (118:1 ET) and 134:3a (135:3a ET), and as *chrēstos* in Pss. 33:9 (34:8 ET; 34:9 MT); 105:1 (106:1 ET); 106:1 (107:1 ET); and 135:1 (136:1 ET). Recognition of the overlapping Greek words enriches the complexity of the goodness of God and God's creation. The instance in Ps. 134:3 (135:3 ET) provides an example of overlapping Hebrew and Greek words reinforcing that richness and complexity. At the heart of this complexity is a firm ethical goodness (strongly in the use of *agathos*). This is nuanced in the direction of kindness and mercy, graciousness (esp. in the use of *chrēstos* and emphasized throughout Ps. 135 LXX [136 ET] by the refrain "for his steadfast love [Heb. *ḥesed*, Gk. *eleos*] endures forever"). In the later books of the LXX, *ḥesed* is translated by *charis* rather than *eleos* (i.e., "grace," not "mercy"). The word *ṭôb* also includes an aesthetic element of beauty, attractiveness (esp. in the use of *kalos*). All of this and more can be found in the use of *ṭôb*. While there is something in the saying "Beauty is in the eye of the beholder," there is more to it than that. The complexity of the creation has produced eyes that can perceive the beauty of the sunrise and sunset and many other natural beauties that have been perceived cross-culturally and trans-temporally. Beauty, like goodness and graciousness, kindness and faithfulness, is embedded in the creation. Of course, that is not the whole story. It is that aspect of reality to which James draws attention here and from it extrapolates the understanding of God that resonates in the tradition in which he was nurtured.

In keeping with this, James characterizes God as "the Father of lights." In the Jewish tradition, the creation of the lights is given pride of place (Gen. 1:3, 14–19; Ps. 136:7) as the most remarkable of all God's creative works. Thus "the Father of lights" draws attention to God's remarkable and benevolent creative work; such is the importance of light for all life on earth. Elsewhere James refers to God as "the Lord and Father" (3:9), a further indication of the importance of God's creative work and recognition of it unlimited by any qualification, even as "the Father of lights," great and spectacular though that aspect of God's work is.

Lest it be thought that God is sometimes like this and at other times quite the contrary, James adds **with whom there is no variation [*parallagē*] or shadow [*aposkiasma*] caused by turning [*tropēs*]**. The words *parallagē, aposkiasma,* and *tropē* are used in the NT only here, and *aposkiasma* is first known in James. These words are known to be used elsewhere in an astrological context, and they tie in with the reference to God as the Father of lights. While the linguistic background of these words is interesting, it is not determinative for their use in James, where this cosmic language is used to affirm the constancy of God's generous goodness. The affirmation echoes the sentiments of Lam. 3:22–23: "The steadfast love of the Lord never ceases, his mercies never come to an end; they are new every morning; great is your faithfulness."

Because the mystery of our world is not wholly consistent with God's generous goodness, James goes beyond the affirmation of God's creative goodness to separate God from what is opposed to and inconsistent with that goodness. God is not at this moment gracious and generous, and in the next spiteful and destructive. God is utterly incompatible with the source of temptation. To attribute temptation to God rather than acknowledging human responsibility for sin in giving way to desire (*epithymia*) is to be led astray into serious error. This is the force of 1:16: "Do not be led astray," or "Do not be deceived." The exhortation looks back to 1:13–15 and forward to 1:17–18, forming a bridge between the two. This portrayal of God as pure beneficence is the basis of the view of the impartiality of God and is contrary to the notion that God is capricious. It is not an expression of the patron-client relationship, where obligations are limited, but rather the expression of the beneficent graciousness of God in creation, which God is renewing.

1:18. It is an expression of God's generosity and perfect gift that **by God's will, God begot [*apekyēsen*] us by the word of truth, that we should be a kind of firstfruit of God's creatures [*ktismatōn*]**. The motif of the divine begetting of humans is here expressed as a mixed metaphor, using the feminine motif of "bearing" (*apekyēsen*) with the masculine instrumental (dative) sense of begetting "by the word of truth." The mixed metaphor is an outworking of the contrasting parallelism between the consequences of sin, which brings forth death (1:15), and the purpose of God in begetting us by the true word, "that we should be a kind of firstfruit of God's creatures [creation]" (see also John 1:12–14; 3:3, 5–7; 1 Pet. 1:3, 23; 1 John 4:7). The motif of divine begetting/bearing is expressed by the image of the direct action of God (John 1:12–13; 1 Pet. 1:3) or of God by the word of God (John 3:3; James 1:18; 1 Pet. 1:23) or by the Spirit of God (John 3:5–6). In all cases, God is the source, even when word or Spirit are God's agents, since they are of God. This motif develops out of Deut. 32:18a LXX; Pss. 22:9; 90:2; Isa. 66:13 and is attested also in the NT references above.

God's purpose (*eis to einai*) in the divine begetting is that humans should be the harbinger (*aparchē*) of the new creation. There is first the Genesis creation of all things as God speaks the creation into being: "And God said" (Gen. 1:3, 6, 9, 14, 20, 24, 26; cf. Ps. 33:6). Related to this is the perception of the *tôrâ* as the word of God. Psalm 119 is a *tôrâ* liturgy in praise of the *tôrâ* as God's word of truth (e.g., Ps. 119:43, 142, 151). *Tôrâ* is also portrayed as Wisdom in both her creative and instructive roles (esp. in Proverbs, Wisdom, and Sirach). Drawing on these traditions, James develops the motif of the godly wisdom from above (3:17–18) and, with other early Christian writers, predicates a new creation of humans by the true word. John 1:13 elaborates: "who were begotten, not of blood, nor of the will of the flesh, nor of the will of a man, but of God." And 1 Pet. 1:23, which is closer to James, speaks of "being begotten anew, not of perishable seed but imperishable, by the living

---

Metaphor: Firstfruit of New Creation

James 1:18 speaks of the renewed humanity as "a kind of firstfruit" (*aparchēn tina*) of God's creatures. The indefinite *tina* signals a metaphorical use of "firstfruit." The metaphor takes its meaning from the firstborn of humans and of the flocks, and the first of the harvest of the fields, offered to God in hope of the full harvest that is to follow. What does it mean when James speaks of reborn humans as a kind of firstfruit of God's creatures? This can hardly be a reference to humans as the culmination of God's creative handiwork in Gen. 1. That would be to take the last as first in the sense of the culmination or crowning creative work of God. Rather, James shares with Paul a redemptive view of reborn humans as the firstfruit of God's creatures. The rest are yet to follow—the residue not only of humanity but also of all God's creatures (see in particular Rom. 8:21–23; 11:16; 16:5; 1 Cor. 15:20, 23; 16:15; 2 Thess. 2:13; *1 Clem.* 24.1; 42.4). This is nothing less than the hope and guarantee of the renewal of the creation or, better, the culmination and completion of God's creative purpose.

---

and abiding word of God." In James, the notion of renewed or reborn humans as the firstfruit of the creation implies the rebirth or renewal of the whole creation, hence the new creation (see the use of *aparchē* in Rom. 8:23; 11:16; 16:5; 1 Cor. 15:20, 23; 16:15; 2 Thess. 2:13; Rev. 14:4). The purpose of the generous gift-giving God is the renewal and completion of the whole creation, a work begun with reborn humans, who are the sign and guarantee (*aparchē*) of the renewed creation. Perhaps it is even implied that the renewed humanity has a role to play in God's purpose of bringing in the transformed creation.

The Use of the Tongue: Hearing and Receiving (1:19–21)

1:19. Another transition is introduced by a command and renewed address to the readers (see 1:16). The abrupt beginning of the adopted reading, **Understand [this], my beloved brothers [and sisters], let every person [*pas anthrōpos*] be swift to hear, slow to speak, slow to anger,** has led to some textual variants. But rather abrupt changes are quite characteristic of James, and a change of subject need not mean that the new subject is unrelated to its context. The adopted reading is strongly supported and has a B rating (see Metzger 1994; also UBS³; UBS⁴). The verb *estō* is a third-person imperative of indirect address, to be understood as "Let every person be . . ." The Semitism "every person" (*pas anthrōpos*) translates the Semitic *kol 'ādām* and is used here rather than the common Hellenistic *pantes*. This alerts the reader to recognize that the use of *anēr* in 1:20 is not gender-specific (see the discussion on 1:7–8). It is not the wrath of only male persons that is under review there, and the exhortation in 1:19 is to every person.

The opening three exhortations echo Israel's Wisdom literature, where three-part sayings are characteristic (see *m. 'Abot* 1.2; 2.10–12; Prov. 30:15, 18, 21, 29). On "swift to hear, slow to speak, slow to anger," see Prov. 15:1; 29:20; Eccles. 7:9; Sir. 5:11; 6:33–35. But the aphoristic form of James 1:19b depends on the author's sensitivity to Greek.

Life appropriate to the firstfruit of the new creation (1:18) is outlined in 1:19: "swift to hear, slow to speak, slow to anger." Note the partial parallel in Sir. 5:11–12: "Be quick to hear, but deliberate in answering. If you know what to say, answer your neighbor; but if not, put your hand over your mouth" (NRSV). "Swift to hear" echoes Jesus's repeated exhortation to followers to "listen" (*akouō*; e.g., Mark 4:3, 9, 12, 15, 16, 18, 20, 23, 24, 33; see Painter 1997b, 76–86). Being swift to hear goes beyond merely hearing the sound to hearing that is attentive, responsive, and retentive—that is listening, the mark of the disciple. "Slow to speak, slow to anger" may seem to be strangely connected. "Slow to speak" is in contrast to "swift to hear," though it is a natural corollary of it. The one who is swift to hear will be slow to speak, and the one who is swift to speak will be slow to hear. The contrast shifts the focus from oneself onto the other, to whom one attends, in contrast to self-assertive speech. Speech may also stand in opposition to action—to have words but not deeds, to be all talk and no action.

1:20. James quickly justifies "slow to anger" (cf. Eccles. 7:9). It is **because human wrath [*orgē andros*] does not produce the righteousness of God.** Thus, "Vengeance is mine, I will repay, says the Lord" (Rom. 12:19; cf. Lev. 19:18; Deut. 32:35). Even this does not go far enough. Rather, "slow to anger" is a repudiation of action arising from anger and seems to be rooted in Jesus's teaching concerning nonretaliation for evil (Matt. 5:38–48). Jesus tradition again lies close to the surface when James addresses the readers as "my beloved brothers [and sisters]" in 1:19 (regarding the translation of *andros* as "human" in 1:20, see the discussion on 1:7–8).

1:21. James signals the summing up of the implications of 1:19–20 with an introductory **Wherefore** (*dio*). Action rather than words is required. Thus James, like the Jesus of Matthew (Matt. 7:24–26), emphasizes the essential connection between hearing and doing (James 1:22–25). Action is twofold: a rejection of certain things, on the one hand, and reception, on the other. **Wherefore, putting away all impurity and abundant wickedness, with meekness receive [*en prautēti dexasthe*] the implanted word [*ton emphyton logon*] that is able to save you [*tas psychas hymōn*].** Here the Greek word that is sometimes translated "soul" (*psychē*) is used in the Semitic sense (*psychē* = *nepeš*, as in Gen. 2:7 LXX) of the whole person, and it could be translated as "you" or "your life." The language of putting aside (*apothemenoi*) is idiomatic of putting aside a dirty garment—a suitable metaphor of ritual impurity, but one that here includes matters of both ritual purity and moral/ethical wickedness. In Christian use, this language became a metaphor of the life-changing renewal of the person. Parallels with Col. 3:8 and 1 Pet. 2:1 strongly emphasize the separation from ethically bad actions. But James retains reference to putting aside both ritual impurity and ethical wickedness, indeed, placing ritual impurity first. Reception of the implanted word harks back to the word of truth (1:18) by which the reader is begotten as a kind of firstfruit of God's creatures. Now the "begetting word" (1:18) is characterized as the "implanted word." Both images are related to the renewal of those who have become the firstfruit of God's creation. The implanted or indwelling *logos* resonates with the Stoic idea of the indwelling *logos*, here not indwelling nature but instead the renewed creation. The rapid change of metaphors, from begetting to implanted, should warn the reader not to take this language as a simple factual description but rather to recognize a symbolic discourse or portrayal of the process of creation's renewal.

Faith and Works: Hearing and Doing (1:22–27)

From asking and receiving in 1:5–8 to hearing and receiving in 1:19–21, the theme progresses to hearing and doing in 1:22–27, and it is developed in 2:14–26 as faith and works. The Hebraic resonance is evident in the association and overlapping meaning of faith, hearing, asking. The lead-up to 1:22–27 makes clear a sequence of thought. Those who seek to live lives obedient to God (asking, hearing) find themselves in a hostile world (1:2–4, 12–13). They also find themselves in relation to the generosity of the gift-giving God (1:17), who gives the wisdom from above (1:5; 3:17–18) without partiality to all who ask sincerely and without wavering (1:5–8). Those who receive are reborn by the word of truth to become the firstfruit of the (new or completed) creation (1:18, 21). Now it becomes clear that believing involves more than hearing and receiving. Believing, hearing, and receiving also involve doing. In 1:22–25 James seems to be at odds with an important theme in the Letters of Paul. James expands the theme further in 2:14–26; 4:11–12 in a way that is often taken to be anti-Pauline polemic.

1:22. Be doers [*poiētai*] of the word and not only hearers [*akroatai*], deceiving yourselves. Paul (Rom. 2:13) and James (1:22, 23, 25; 4:11) agree that those who do (*poiētēs*) the law, rather than those who simply hear (*akroatēs*) or have an understanding of the law, keep the law and thus become "doers." Being and becoming are at one in the act of obeying the word. This Semitizing use of *poiētēs* (see Deut. 28:58; 29:28; 1 Macc. 2:16; Sir. 19:20) is found only in Paul and James in the NT. Acts 17:28 has the only other use of *poiētēs*, but in the unrelated sense of "poet." Thus a significant point of agreement between Paul and James occurs in a context traditionally read as a criticism of Paul. The law can be spoken of as "the word," as in Ps. 119:105 and throughout this psalm, where "word," "precept," "commandment," and "law" appear without differentiation. In James, the word in 1:22 becomes the law ("the perfect law of liberty") in 1:25.

The Jesus of Matthew shares this theme without the same verbal agreement (Matt. 7:26). James 1:22 probably refers to doing the law as expressed in Jesus's interpretation of the law (see Matt. 5–7), the new law. Essential to James and to this teaching is the connection between hearing and doing (cf. Matt. 7:24–27). To hear without doing is to be guilty of self-deception. But what gives rise to self-deception? Presumably, it is a consequence of *epithymia* (1:14), which turns back the hearer from the word of the other to the desires of self. James here reveals the complexity of self-deception as involving a self-justifying rationale that may be believed and used in argument. The use of *paralogizomenoi heautous* in 1:22 to describe this self-deception, rather than one of the other terms used to speak of being led astray in 1:16 (*mē planasthē*) and 1:26 (*apatōn*), may imply this deceptive rationalization. The self deceives the self! Compare the use of *heautous planōmen* in 1 John 1:8. There are strong theological connections between James and 1 John, and the critique of desire/lust (*epithymia*) in 1 John 2:16–17 is related to the critique in James 1:14–15, but 1 John does not go as far as James in rooting the power of temptation in *epithymia*. For James, it is through desire that humans lead themselves astray. Bound up with this is the human inclination to justify even the most inhuman and reprehensible behaviors when such seem necessary for the fulfillment of our desires. Self-deception is willful and culpable, and the further one proceeds with self-deception, the more one becomes a prisoner of the deception and committed to its defense.

1:23–24. Now the focus is on the hearer who is not a doer. **Because [*hoti*] if anyone is a hearer of the word and not a doer, this person is like [*eoiken*] a person [*andri*] who studies his natural face in a mirror; for he studied himself and went away and immediately forgot what he was like.** The connection with 1:22 is signaled by the opening *hoti* in 1:23. Such a hearer is "like" (see also 1:6 for the metaphor of the wave). Here the hearer who does not act is likened to a person (regarding the translation of *andri* as "person" here, see the discussion on 1:7–8) who looks in a mirror and forgets what was seen and takes no action. Such forgetfulness is an alternative way of expressing the process of leading oneself astray, of deceiving ourselves (see 1:22). It suggests that such forgetfulness is willful, a Freudian slip, covered up even to the self.

1:25. The contrast returns to the one who hears and is also a doer. **But the person who looks into the perfect law of liberty and perseveres, not being a hearer who forgets but a doer of work/deed, this person will be blessed in his or her doing.** The image changes from hearing to a careful examination by looking into the law and not turning away from it. Forgetfulness and a failure to obey are excluded. The change of reference from "word" to "law" is characteristic of this tradition. Reference to "the *perfect* law of liberty" is at home in such Jewish sources as Pss. 19; 119; and in the teaching of Jesus concerning the law in Matthew's Sermon on the Mount. In particular, "The law of the LORD is perfect" (Ps. 19:7), and "I will keep your law continually,

Perfect Law of Liberty

Although reference to "the perfect law of liberty" is perfectly at home in Judaism, there is reason to think that this expression owes something to the interaction of Judaism with popular Stoic thought. As Philo's writings show, the view that keeping the cosmic law brings inner freedom was alive and well in Judaism of the time (*Decal.* 1 §1; *Opif.* 1 §3; *Mos.* 2.8 §48; 2.9 §51–10 §52; *Prob.* 7 §45). If it is objected that James of Jerusalem was unlikely to have synthesized the universal *logos* in all living things with the law of Moses, that is probably right. But the view underlying this commentary is that Jamesian tradition was used in the writing of this Diaspora letter sometime after the fall of Jerusalem, when Jamesian tradition was carried into the Diaspora. Judaism of the Diaspora was familiar with this, and James gives every indication of being a letter from the Diaspora and to the Diaspora (see Dibelius 1976, 116–20).

forever and ever; and I shall walk at liberty, for I have kept your precepts" (Ps. 119:44–45; cf. James's reference to "the royal law" in 2:8; see Davies 1955, 402–5). Like James, Paul recognized the role of obedience to God's will as expressed in the law in the believer's ethical life. But there may have been some tension between them over the issue of the relationship of faith and works in salvation (cf. James 2:14–26; Rom. 3:28; 4, esp. vv. 2–4, 6, 22; see Painter 1997a; 2004, 265–69).

James declares that the one who perseveres, who is a "doer of work [*poiētēs ergou*], will be blessed [*makarios*] in his or her doing." To persevere is to be a doer. The future tense, "will be" (*estai*), suggests that the blessing is eschatological, a possibility in line with the blessedness pronounced by Jesus, according to Matt. 5:3–12. The first and eighth of these Beatitudes conclude with "for theirs is the kingdom of heaven," forming an inclusio, and the entire set concludes (5:11–12) with the elaboration "for great is your reward in heaven." Thus in James 1:12, the blessing pronounced on the person who endures temptation declares that "he/she will receive [*lēmpsetai*] the crown of life, which [God] promised to those who love him." Certainly 1:12 should be understood as referring to an eschatological blessing (see Rev. 2:10; cf. 1 Pet. 5:4).

Against this interpretation are the words that follow at the end of 1:25: "Blessed will be this person in his or her doing [*en tē poiēsei autou estai*]." From the full statement it appears that both the action and the blessing belong to the future, from the point of view of the writer, but the action and the blessing are simultaneous. "This person will be blessed *in* his or her doing." What then is the nature of the blessing? Is it the blessing that comes to one who lives in harmony with the will and purpose of God and knows the blessing of friendship with God? Abraham is the model of friendship with God (James

2:23). Such friendship brings enmity with the world, whereas friendship with the world brings enmity (*echthra*) with God (James 4:4).

1:26. From the relationship of faith and action/work, James turns to a more comprehensive treatment of "religion" (*thrēskeia*) and what it means to be "religious" (*thrēskos*). The latter is first known in James. The concept of religion is not native to Judaism, though *thrēskeia* is found four times in the LXX in the later Wisdom literature (Wis. 14:18, 27; 4 Macc. 5:7, 13). It is also found four times in the NT: twice in James 1:26–27, and in Acts 26:5; Col. 2:18. It is also used by Philo (*Spec.* 1.58 §315; *Det.* 7 §21) and Josephus (*Ant.* 4.4.4 §74; 5.10.1 §339; 9.13.3 §§273–74). Clearly, *thrēskeia* is a neutral term for what may be good or bad, true or false religion, from one point of view or another. James provides his own distinctive approach to what it means to be religious, first stating what falsifies any claim to true religion: **Someone who presumes to be religious while not controlling the tongue but [*alla*] deceiving the heart—this person's religion is vain** (1:26). Such religion is vain, empty, useless. It is a failure to do what is needful and instead is a doing of what is opposed to the reality of the goodness of God's creation. Failure to control (bridle) the tongue marks a vacuous religion or a vacuous claim to be religious. This evaluation of religion is rooted in priorities already stated. "Slow to speak," which is a corollary of "quick to hear" (1:19), implies controlling the tongue. Speech should arise as a response after listening to God and the neighbor and not as an expression of desire, *epithymia* (see 1:14). Those who fail to control their tongue deceive their heart and are not pure in heart (see James 4:8; cf. Matt. 5:8). *Epithymia* corrupts the heart, or is the expression of a corrupt heart, which is pure only when devoted to God and the neighbor. Those who deceive their heart deceive themselves, and reference to the heart signifies corruption at the very core of being.

1:27. A more positive statement follows. **Pure religion [*thrēskeia kathara*] that is undefiled [*amiantos*] before the God and Father is this, to visit [*episkeptesthai*] the orphans and widows in their affliction [*thlipsei*], and to keep oneself unstained [*aspilon*] by the world.** Religion is described first of all as "pure." Note 3:17, where the wisdom from above (cf. 1:5) is characterized as "first pure [*hagnē*]." Thus the language of purity is amplified in James and emphasized in 1:27, being reinforced by a second word with meaning in the range of "pure, unstained, undefiled" (*amiantos*). This word is used elsewhere in the NT only in Heb. 7:26; 13:4; 1 Pet. 1:4, in contexts that reinforce the sense of purity. Thus James maintains a view of religion that includes prominent emphasis on purity. If this is not enough, following the emphasis on significant ethical obligations, James returns in the final statement to purity requirements. It is necessary "to keep oneself unstained [*aspilon*] by the world." That this should be the case is not surprising, given the concentration on purity in the Jewish legal tradition (see Neusner 1973; 1974–77). Even Philo of Alexandria combined his assimilation of Middle Platonism with a firm commitment to the law of Moses, including its purity requirements. Those ritual elements that separated Jews from the world remain important in James. The final word in this statement on true religion is "to keep oneself unstained by the world." The world and the faithful community are incompatible. Resistance to the threat of becoming contaminated, stained, by the world (*apo tou kosmou*) dominates James because the world is the agent of contamination. Here James is defensively focused on the protection of the faithful community from a hostile and corrupting world (see also James 4:4).

The ethical requirements of pure religion are focused on the care of the community, to visit the orphans and widows in their affliction (see Isa. 1:17; Jer. 5:28; Ezek. 22:7; Zech. 7:10). James makes no reference to the obligation to strangers, which is prominent, along with responsibility for orphans and widows, in Deut. 10:18; 14:28; 16:11, 14; 24:17–21; 26:12, 13; 27:19; Pss. 10:14, 18; 68:5; 94:6; 146:9; Prov. 23:10; Sir. 4:10; and also Philo, *Spec.* 1.57 §§308, 310; 4.34 §176. The focus on orphans and widows reflects the reality that they were the most vulnerable members of society. James and other evidence from early Christian sources show a concern to care for these vulnerable people.

James asserts that such religion is acceptable to God the Father. Reference to God as "Father" is normal with Judaism (1 Chron. 29:10; Wis. 2:16; 3 Macc. 5:7; Philo, *Leg.* 2.17 §67), and there is no indication that James uses this designation in a trinitarian way. Rather, the use of "Father" reveals God's caring relationship with the children of God. The concern of James does not go beyond the community of brothers and sisters, however.

Theological Issues

Much of the theological discourse of James has a bearing on aspects of theodicy and the effort to reconcile human suffering with belief in a good God. It is the discourse of practical and applied theology. The opening of the epistle turns attention to the central place of joy in the life of faith and obedience, with full recognition that life in the world is often lived in the midst of severe hardships, trials, and temptations. Nevertheless, James affirms that God is the generous giver of every good gift. Faithfulness is encouraged and promised a good outcome in moral and spiritual completeness or perfection through the reception of wisdom from God (1:4–5). God is not the author of trials and temptation, but in God's good purpose some good will come out of them. James's development of this theme (1:2–4) resonates with Paul's treatment in Rom. 5:2–5 and with 1 Pet. 1:5–7. This resonance suggests a common drawing on wisdom tradition and, in James's case, probably via the tradition of Jesus. Though the business of life may be serious, the life of faith, grounded in the presence of God, is characterized by resilient joyfulness.

The primary theological notion of James concerns the generosity of God, who gives to all who ask appropriately. This borders on the theme of the graciousness of God in the Pauline writings, a vocabulary missing from James except in 4:6, where the use of "grace" (*charis*) is derived from Prov. 3:34 LXX. James develops the theme by using the language of Jesus rather than the language of Paul. James's understanding of God shapes the anthropology of the epistle. Human freedom and responsibility are presupposed, but by themselves they are insufficient for the task. Having the gift of wisdom from God, the faithful can negotiate their way in the world, which is not a universal paradise. Rather, the world, with its challenge to the successful negotiation of trials and temptations, is seen as what John Keats called "the vale of Soul-making."[1] For James, the route to moral and spiritual wholeness or perfection is through the successful negotiation of these trials and temptations. James nowhere suggests that this end justifies the trials and temptations, and the notion that God is their source is rejected (1:13). Rather, the generosity of the gift-giving God is able to bring good out of evil. This is God's purpose, which is realized in the lives of those who trust and live in tune with God's purpose, rejoicing in God's presence.

The phenomenon of boasting reflected in discussions by Paul and James opens up the conflicting values of God and the world, a recurring theme in James (see 4:1–10) that he shares with 1 John (2:15–17). One of the conflicting values concerns wealth, the critique of which has never been more crucial than it is today. Not only is the world starkly divided into rich and poor nations, but also even the rich nations are divided into rich and poor, and poor nations have a minority of rich and powerful people. Political, economic, and social structures reinforce the division of wealth and poverty, power and powerlessness, and the disparity between rich and poor continues to grow. Both James and Paul knew that such a world is not sustainable and contains within itself the seeds of its own destruction (James 5:1–6; Gal. 5:13). Yet "desire" makes humans susceptible to the worship of material wealth, even though it often fails to bring happiness to those who possess it, and the accumulation and hoarding of it bring misery to the poor and wreak havoc and destruction on the world of nature, God's creation.

The critique of boasting exposes the confrontation between the values of the world and the way of life grounded in the reality of the bountiful creator God (James 3:13–4:10). Boasting grounded in a view of humans as the masters of all things and careless of the well-being of others is antithetical to the generosity and goodness of God. The reversal of values advocated by James subverts this confidence and redirects self-interest toward the other who is in need. James's distinctive understanding of God (1:5, 17) implies a correlation

1. John Keats in a letter to his brother and sister, George and Georgiana Keats, April 21, 1819 (see Rollins 1958).

with an appropriate way of human life in the world. In Johannine terms it is expressed by loving one another, or loving the brother or sister (John 13:34–35; 1 John 2:7–11; 3:11–18). James asserts a similar view, affirming the necessity of action on behalf of the brother or sister in need (James 2:14–17). The Johannine view of God as the source of generous life-giving love (1 John 4:7–12) has much in common with James's view of the generous gift-giving God (James 1:17). We could say that 1 John and James agree that the person who loves in the way God loves knows God, just as the one who gives generously as God does participates in the life of the gift-giving God, because every generous act of giving and every perfect gift is from above.

James identifies the renewal of humans by the true and abiding word of God as the sign and promise of the renewal of creation in the purpose of God. Those who have received the word in enduring faith and action are the firstfruit of the renewed creation (1:18, 21). They are the beginning, the sign and assurance of the completion. They are taken up into God's renewing activity as a means of God's presence and activity because "every generous act of giving and every perfect gift is from above." In spite of this, the burgeoning human population, coupled with human greed, has produced the global ecological crisis. The global financial crisis has exacerbated this threat by weakening human resolve to meet the costs to deal with it. Human greed, expressed in the will to consume, is a major cause of the ecological crisis and continues to obstruct the remedial action needed to avert ecological disaster. The acceleration of the habitat destruction of other life-forms and the pollution of air, water, and earth—all these have their own destructive consequences and contribute to climate change, threatening all life on the planet. The global economic crisis begun at the end of the first decade of the twenty-first century threatens both to hobble attempts to respond to the ecological crisis and to punish the poor beyond measure. We have need of James's theology of generosity as an antidote to the global greed that has brought the world to the sad state in which we now find it and ourselves. In all of this, little thought has been given to the well-being of the creatures who share the earth with us, including the poor. By "thought" I have in mind consideration that takes action for the poor and for other creatures.

The creative and generative word of God is the key to the purpose of God for the world (1:18). The "implanted word" (*emphytos logos*, 1:21) implies that the word is a seed, or the seed is the word (Mark 4:14; Luke 8:11). The received word is implanted and grows within the new creation. Receptivity to the word of God is clearly in focus, and it may be heard in the voice of the neighbor. Being "quick to hear, slow to speak" (1:19) involves a reorientation from self-concern to concern for others. This radical reorientation is fundamental to the work of the implanted word. Thus be quick to hear, "Listen!" In a modern assertive society, all are speakers with their own agendas and their own stories to tell, and there is much latent anger. "Be slow to anger!"

Actions that arise from anger are seldom just and are often excessive in their violence and are certainly without compassion. The word *orgē* has a range of meanings, indicating anger, wrath, revenge, retribution, and punishment. James rules out the legitimacy of human anger because it is incompatible with the righteousness of God, but what of divine *orgē*? Given the opposition of *orgē* to the righteousness of God, it may be that James also excludes the *orgē* of God. Yet judgment has a place in James (2:4, 12–13; 3:1; 4:11–12; 5:9, 12).

Purity issues in James make clear the threat that the world poses to the faithful community. It has the power to corrupt the community (see John 17:9–17; 1 John 2:15–17). Both James and the Johannine Gospel and Epistles view the world in which the faithful live as a hostile and corrupting force. Hostility and the threat of corruption are evident in the directives "to visit the orphans and widows in their affliction [*en tē thlipsei autōn*]" and "to keep oneself unstained by the world" (1:27). The threat of affliction characterizes the pressures in a hostile world (e.g., Matt. 13:21; 24:9; John 16:33). James and 1 John also note the more subtle threat of corruption posed by the seductive power of the world (James 1:14; 1 John 2:15–17), which has led to a more defensive mind-set and a loss of any sense of mission. Although the Jesus of John was conscious of the corrupting power of the hostile world, Jesus does not lose sight of the mission to the world, that the world may come to believe and to know the love that God has for the world (John 17:18–26). The corrupting power of the world and its hostility to God and the friends of God so dominate James that it has almost totally obscured any sense of God's love and purpose for the world. Almost! Those whom God willed to beget by the word of truth were begotten to be a kind of firstfruit of God's creation (1:18). For the author, this is not some impersonal doctrine. It is the author's self-understanding, inclusive of his readers, "that we should be a kind of firstfruit of God's creatures/creation."

The need to control the tongue is illustrated by the use of the metaphor of the way a horse is controlled by a bridle. So there is the need to bridle the tongue. Use of this analogy illuminates how this small member, the tongue, is both powerful and unruly and in need of effective control if one is to live an ethical life in the presence of God and neighbor. The metaphor of the bridle is used again in 3:2: "For we all fail often. If anyone does not fail in word/speech, this person is perfect, able to bridle the whole body." Here it seems that the ability "to bridle the tongue" (1:26) demonstrates the ability to control the whole body. This connection is made obliquely in 3:3–5a. The bit put into the mouth of a horse allows the rider to control the whole body of the horse; the tiny rudder allows the helmsman to control the whole ship. "Likewise the tongue." What follows in 3:5b–12 illuminates the disproportionate destructive power of this small member, the tongue. Because the tongue is capable of instant retaliation in anger, it has become the most sensitive gauge of human failings, just as in the past a canary was used as the most sensitive gauge of dangerous gases in mines. The uncontrolled tongue exacerbates conflicts and is capable of setting the world aflame. With this view of the tongue, it is not surprising that James gives strong attention to speech ethics.

James has a distinctive treatment of self-deception and sin concentrated in a range of words (*planaō* [1:16; 5:19]; *planē* [5:20]; *paralogizomai* [1:22]; *apataō* [1:26]). In two references, the language is used to express the theme of self-deception (1:22, 26). In 1 John 1:8 the author writes, "If we say, 'We have no sin,' we deceive ourselves [*heautous planōmen*]." Here, as elsewhere, James and 1 John reflect a common perspective, this time in the recognition of the human propensity for self-deception. In James 1:15 it is desire (*epithymia*) that brings forth sin. Hearing but not doing is self-deception (1:22). For the person who knows what is the good/right thing to do and does not do it, it is sin (4:17). Self-deception and sin are closely related, as are desire (*epithymia*) and sin. There is much to suggest that, for James, desire is the root of self-deception as well as sin. We are driven to rationalize and justify what we desire.

James 2:1–13

Warning against Partiality

Introductory Matters

The linguistic evidence of the distinctive character of James in the NT continues to accrue. Three words in 2:1–13 are first known in James: *chrysodaktylios* ("gold ring," 2:2), *prosōpolēmpteō* ("discrimination," 2:9), *aneleos* (2:13). The first two provide examples of the Greek propensity to create a composite word to express a Semitic phrase. The third (*aneleos*) is a negative built on a common biblical (OT) word, "mercy" (*eleos*), and means "merciless, without mercy." God is merciful and calls for those who love God to show mercy. But *eleos* is not common language in the NT (*eleos* occurs only 27x), except in contexts influenced by biblical language. In the Gospels, *eleos* is found only in Matt. 9:13; 12:7 (both echo Hosea 6:6); 23:23 (echoing Mic. 6:8) and in the psalmlike compositions of Luke 1:50, 54 (echoed in 1:58), 72, 78, which echo the language of the LXX. It is also found in the parable of the good Samaritan (Luke 10:37). Elsewhere, *eleos* is found three times in Romans; once in Galatians, Ephesians, Titus, Hebrews, and 1 Peter; once in each of the traditional greetings in 1 Timothy, 2 Timothy (plus 2x), 2 John, and Jude; and once in the farewell in Jude. In this context the three uses in James (2:13 [2x]; 3:17) stand out as less formulaic and more part of the idiom of James, though no less rooted in the biblical tradition. In spite of the small harvest of this language in the NT, even when cognate words are added, mercy has a much more central place than statistics indicate. The importance of showing mercy as God does is clear in such key texts as Matt. 5:7; 6:2; Luke 10:7; and in James 2:13; 3:17. Further, James's depiction of true religion as visiting widows and orphans in their distress is precisely what is meant by works of mercy.

Another four words are used only by James and Paul in the NT: *prosōpolēmpsia* (James 2:1; Rom. 2:11; Eph. 6:9; Col. 3:25), which again is a Greek creation of a composite word to express a Semitic phrase and is unknown prior to their use of it; *kritērion* ("court," James 2:6; 1 Cor. 6:2, 4); *parabatēs* ("transgressor," James 2:9, 11; Rom. 2:25, 27; Gal. 2:18), which is not found in the Hebrew books translated in the LXX; and *katakauchaomai* ("triumph," James 2:13; 3:14; Rom. 11:18 [2x]). Another two words are used only by James and Luke-Acts, works more at home in the Greek literary world than most other NT books: *esthēs* ("clothes," James 2:2 [2x], 3; Luke 23:11; 24:4; Acts 1:10; 10:30; 12:21), a word also not found in the Hebrew books translated in the LXX; and *katadynasteuō* ("oppress," James 2:6; Acts 10:38). One expression, "the good name" (*to kalon onoma*), is used only in James 2:7 in the NT.

The tension between rich and poor reflected in James makes sense in the context of Galilee and Judea in the time of Jesus and leading up to the Jewish War of 66–73 CE. It is also relevant to the situation of much of the Roman Empire in the later first and second centuries CE. As in Galilee and Judea, much of the empire was marked by the swallowing up of small landholdings by an increasingly rich but narrow class of wealthy landowners, creating a mass of urban poor. James is best understood against this double background, reflecting the context of Jesus's mission and message, while addressing the later situation of the epistle. James shows hostility toward the rich (5:1–6), though in the first instance, the letter calls only for impartiality (2:1). The call not to show favoritism toward the rich grows out of the language of the LXX, which translates a Hebrew idiom into a comparable Greek idiom. The two words used by James to identify discrimination based on self-interest, *prosōpolēmpsia* (used also by Paul) and *prosōpolēmpteō*, build on a Semitic idiom (*nāśā' pānîm*), which is translated in the LXX as *prosōpon lambanō* or *prosōpon thaumazō*. These two words (*prosōpolēmpsia, prosōpolēmpteō*) and two other cognate words used in the NT only in Acts 10:34 (*prosōpolēmptēs*) and 1 Pet. 1:17 (*aprosōpolēmptōs*) are not found in the LXX or the pre-Christian Greek corpus. James, Paul, Acts, and 1 Peter show an awareness of the Greek genius for coining a single word to express an idiom, whether as a verb or a cognate noun or adjective.

The first issue to receive more detailed treatment on the basis of the epitome is the place of the poor, first alluded to in 1:9–11, where the humble (*ho tapeinos*) brother (or sister) is contrasted with the rich person (*ho plousios*). The contrast implies the poverty of the humble but varies the image to accentuate the tension implied by the exalted condition of the humble about to be stated in 2:5, where the poor are revealed to be the truly rich. The epitome concludes by addressing the issue of social justice for the most vulnerable members of society—widows and orphans—calling for relief for them in their situation of distress. In the light of 2:14–17, visiting the orphans and widows in their distress can hardly mean simply "wishing them well"; rather, it must involve the provision of relief.

James 2:1–13 in the Rhetorical Flow

Address/salutation (1:1)
Epitome of the exhortation of James (1:2–27)
▶ **Warning against partiality (2:1–13)**
An example of discrimination (2:1–4)
God's choice of the poor, and human discrimination (2:5–7)
The sin of discrimination, and the triumph of mercy (2:8–13)

Tracing the Train of Thought

James 2:1–13 follows naturally after 1:26–27. Yet 2:5–6 also develops out of 1:9–11, which features the reversal of the fortunes of the rich and the poor because God has chosen the poor of this world to be heirs of the kingdom (2:5), a theme rooted in the Jesus tradition of Matt. 5:3; Luke 6:20. The blessing pronounced on the poor in Luke 6:20 is closer to James than the saying about the poor "in spirit" in Matt. 5:3. We may suspect that Matthew has softened and spiritualized the reference by Jesus to the poor in this text. James 1:22–25, on faith and works (see also 2:14–26), turns to the theme of caring for the poor and oppressed (1:26–27), which leads into the theme of impartiality (*prosōpolēmpsia* [2:1], *prosōpolēmpteō* [2:9]) and, by advocating caring for the poor, addresses the problem of showing favor to the rich, thus building 2:1–13 on the foundation of 1:26–27.

In 2:1 James continues to use the language of command that dominated chapter 1, employing twelve imperatives in chapter 2. At the same time, some variation is introduced with the use of examples, as well as a more dialogical approach in the use of leading questions with implied answers. The specific negative form used in the question (*ou*[*k*] or *mē*) implies either a yes or a no answer. Given that the expected answers are implied, the dialogue is more directive than questions imply. James offers an example of discrimination (2:2–3) and seeks to evoke a response from the readers affirming the option for the poor by asking a series of four leading questions in 2:4–7. In each case these leading questions imply a positive, yes answer.

An Example of Discrimination (2:1–4)

2:1. The new beginning is signaled by the reiterated address to the readers as **My brothers [and sisters]**, which was first used at the beginning of the epitome (1:2; cf. 1:16, 19) and is now used to begin the elaboration of the themes introduced in the epitome. Just as "My brothers [and sisters]" in 1:2 is followed by "my beloved brothers [and sisters] in 1:16, so the address of 2:1

89

is quickly followed by "my beloved brothers [and sisters]" in 2:5. In each case, the address that follows signals a transition and, in the case of 2:5, is closely connected to 2:1–4. The human example (2:1–4) is followed by the divine perspective (2:5–7). The form of address signals a transition, narrows any distance between author and readers, and alerts us to the presence of Jesus tradition.

The use of this egalitarian form of address belies the authority that pervades James, with its lavish use of verbs in the imperative mood. Even the form of question often implies the answer expected from the reader by using the negative form of question where *ou(k)* implies an affirmative answer, and *mē* a negative answer. Thus the use of questions is both rhetorical, seeking to draw a response from the reader, and directive, seeking to secure the desired response.

James 2:1 continues the dominant mode of command, which pervades chapter 1: **Do not have/hold with partiality the faith of our Lord Jesus Christ of glory.** Scholars who take James to be a Jewish document treat the whole reference as a Christian interpolation. There is no textual support for such an approach. Given the relationship of the whole document to the Jesus tradition and uniform identification of the author as "the brother of the Lord," this hypothesis lacks sufficient weight of evidence to be taken seriously.

Because James refers to Jesus by name only in 1:1; 2:1, it is difficult to know how to take this reference. The role of James in the early Jesus movement in Jerusalem renders problematic, in any epistle coming directly from him, the use of "Jesus Christ" as a name: "holding the faith of our Lord Jesus Christ." The difficulty is overcome if James is seen as a posthumous publication appropriately edited for Diaspora readers (see the discussion on 1:1). There is also difficulty concerning the precise meaning of the final words of the phrase "of glory." Should "glory" be taken with "the glorious faith " or "our glorious Lord Jesus Christ"? The latter is more likely, given the word order, where a string of genitives follows "the faith," the final genitive being "of glory" (*tēs doxēs*). In 1 Cor. 2:8 Paul refers to Jesus as "the Lord of glory," identifying Jesus with God in glory.

The example of discrimination is drawn from experience in Diaspora synagogues. It is possible that a judicial setting is implied, but a judicial context does not explicitly appear until 2:6, and there is no suggestion that this is the situation of 2:1–4. The reference to becoming judges in 2:4 is a comment on the practice of discrimination in their gatherings and has no judicial implications.

James does not follow Paul in rooting the rejection of discrimination in God's character using *prosōpolēmpsia* and cognates (Rom. 2:11; Eph. 6:9; Col. 3:25). In Gal. 2:6 Paul uses a Greek translation of the Hebrew idiom that underlies the Greek construct. James uses this language only in the rejection of human discrimination, which is unequivocal and without qualification. In general terms, James asserts that discrimination/favoritism is incompatible with "faith *in* our glorious Lord Jesus Christ" (2:1). The awkwardness of the idiom in this statement has led to some editorial corrections that are neither well attested nor credible and persuasive. They attest the awkwardness of the adopted reading. In the phrase "the faith *of our glorious Lord Jesus Christ,*" the italicized words are in the genitive case in Greek and can be read as subjective or objective genitives. A reference to the faithfulness of Jesus is possible, but almost certainly the reference is to faith in our Lord Jesus Christ. An appeal to the faithfulness of Jesus might make clear, on the basis of the example of Jesus, that favoring the rich is unacceptable, but that does not fit the idiom of James 2:1 ("Do not have/hold the faith . . ."). Rather, this is a reference to faith in Jesus as the judge in waiting, who waits in glory but who will come—indeed, whose coming is near, at the door (5:7–9). It makes good sense that reference to faith in the imminently coming judge should be opposed to discriminatory behavior that favors the rich and disadvantages the poor. The call for justice in the Jewish Scriptures was to vindicate the poor against exploitation by the rich. Thus, although no appeal is made to the impartiality of God, that impartiality is assumed in the role of the coming judge, and this awareness is brought against discriminatory behavior (see also 1:26–27).

2:2. For if a man [*anēr*] wearing a gold ring [*chrysodaktylios*] and in fine clothes comes into your synagogue, and also a poor person [*ptōchos*] in shabby clothing enters . . . Chapter 2 now introduces the first of two new elements. First, an example is used to illustrate the nature of the discrimination under critique. A meeting of the local synagogue is described in which two visitors enter. First enters a rich person (*anēr*), characterized by the wearing of a gold ring and fine clothing, who is followed by a poor person (*ptōchos*) in shabby clothes. In this case, the description favors an understanding of *anēr* as an indication that both visitors are men (see the discussion on 1:7–8). The description makes clear that the first person is rich, though *plousios* is not used, whereas the second is called *ptōchos* and described as wearing shabby clothes. Why the rich person is not identified as such is curious. In 1:9 the poor person is not identified as *ptōchos* but is called "humble" (*tapeinos*) and identified as a "brother" (*adelphos*). The parallel description of the rich person (1:10) seems to imply that both are brothers. Thus the presence of the rich person in 2:2 lends no support to the suggestion that reference to the synagogue rather than church (*ekklēsia*) implies that the gathering was not for worship but rather for judgment on a matter of dispute. James 2:2 is not the only verse to use *synagōgē* as a reference to a Christian gathering in the NT, and there is evidence that an interchangeable use of *ekklēsia* and *synagōgē* continued through to the third century CE (see, e.g., Ign. *Pol.* 4.2; Ign. *Trall.* 3; Herm. *Mand.* 11.9, 13–14). Elsewhere James admonishes, "Is anyone among you sick? Let that person call the elders of the church [*ekklēsias*]" (5:14). Why is "synagogue" used in 2:2 and "church" in 5:14? Perhaps because 2:2 describes a gathering together, whereas 5:14 describes the elders coming to the sick person. All are members of the church, but the church is not gathered as such. There is no reason to think that the gathering in 2:2 is to deal with a dispute or disputes between members.

2:3. The rich and the poor persons entering the synagogue may be described as visitors to that local gathering. That need not mean that they are new converts. They do not appear to be regular members of the "congregation" and may be examples of the way visitors from other places are treated: **and if you show respect for the one wearing fine clothes and you say, . . .** The honoring of the rich person and the shaming of the poor are evident in the tone of language used toward each and in the favorable position given to the rich and the lowly position given to the poor. In the adopted reading, the rich person is told **Sit here well** [*hōde kalōs*], that is, close to the speaker in a good seat; the poor person is told **Stand there** [*ekei*] **or sit below my footstool.** One variant changes the placing of "there" (*ekei*) to read, "Stand or sit there below my footstool." Another variant reads, "Stand there or sit here below my footstool." It is not so much a question of overwhelming textual evidence as recognizing some difficulty in a reading that explains the variants. Ambiguity about "here" and "there" in the adopted reading provoked copyists to provide variants as clarifications. If one of the variants had been original, there would probably be no scribal clarifications. The point of the illustration is that the rich person is given a place of honor and addressed with respect, while the poor person is spoken to dismissively and is shamed by being offered a dishonorable place, perhaps a servile position. This is anything but equal treatment.

2:4. Chapter 1 and 2:1–3 are dominated by verbs in the imperative (commanding) mood. Now the first question is introduced, inviting the readers to accept the conclusion implied by the example: **have you not discriminated among yourselves and become judges with evil thoughts/motives?** The question is introduced by the negative *ou*, which in a negative question ("have you not?") expects/implies the answer yes. More rhetorical questions follow in 2:5, 6, 7. The question in 2:4 in no way implies that the meeting was constituted to deal with disputes between members. The discriminatory action was not a formal judgment in a disputation but was rather a favoring/honoring of the rich person and a shaming of the poor. Underlying such favoritism may be the hope that the favor will be returned in some way—something beyond the means of the poor person. Self-interest drives this behavior. The call to impartiality (2:1) apparently involves a refusal to judge/discriminate between brothers and sisters on the basis of power or wealth (cf. 4:11–12). This critique of discrimination in terms of judges with evil thoughts/motives may arise from a vision of Jesus's exaltation to glory as the imminently coming judge of all, whose judgment they will face without favor or prejudice (5:8–9). It does not imply a judicial setting for the gathering in 2:1–4.

God's Choice of the Poor, and Human Discrimination (2:5–7)

2:5. A renewed address to the readers follows the opening imperative: **Listen** [*akousate*], **my beloved brothers** [**and sisters**], which reaffirms and deepens the

Rhetorical Questions

Asking questions is a common rhetorical device, one found often in James. Questions allow an answer to be given, involving some response and progressing the discourse or argument. The form of the question may be straightforward (2:14,16, 19, 20; 3:13; 4:1, 12; 5:13 [2x], 14) or may imply an expected answer, to be taken up and discussed by what follows. Questions introduced by some form of the negative *ou(k)* imply an affirmative answer (2:4, 5, 6, 7, 25; 4:1, 4), while those introduced by *mē* imply a negative answer (2:14; 3:11, 12). Half of the questions in James imply an answer. Thus the rhetoric of questions can be almost as directive as the use of the imperative, though psychologically it may be more persuasive. Questions and interjections are a common feature of diatribe. In James, there are twenty identifiable questions used in a rhetorically skillful manner and carefully arranged pattern. The first question appears in 2:4, with 1:2–2:3 being dominated by the language of command. From 2:4 the weight of imperatives is relieved by the use of rhetorical questions in 2:4, 5, 6, 7, 14 (2x), 16, 19, 20, 25. Ten of the nineteen questions in James occur in chapter 2, which nevertheless also contains twelve imperatives. Questions are concentrated in 2:4–7 and 2:14–25, leaving a gap between 2:7 and 2:14. A reduction in use of imperatives occurs in chapter 3, which contains only three imperatives and three questions (3:11, 12, 13). An above-average use of imperatives is found in chapter 4, which has four questions (4:1 [2x], 4, 12), and chapter 5, which has three questions (5:13 [2x], 14).

relationship expressed in 2:1. As in 1:16, the opening address is deepened by the addition of "beloved." The deepened familial form reinforces the critique of discrimination/partiality in 2:1–4 and marks a transition that introduces an allusion to a significant saying of Jesus. So far, James has argued against showing partiality, exposing the natural inclination to favor the rich. Because this inclination is so strong and was reinforced in the culture of the Roman Empire (as well as in ours), James moves beyond the language of command, appealing to what his readers know, seeking their admission and acknowledgment (2:4). Prejudice favoring the rich is entrenched, reinforced by deeply rooted self-interest. The new paragraph opens, building on the question of 2:4, with a string of three questions showing the faulty logic of their self-interest, each of which suggests that the readers will agree with the answers implied in the questions.

The implied answer to the first of the three questions raised in 2:5–7 leads to a reversed discrimination: **Has not [*ouch*] God chosen the poor in the world to be rich in faith and inheritors of the kingdom that God [through Jesus: Matt. 5:3; Luke 6:20] promised to those who love God?** This negative question introduced by *ouch* implies an affirmative answer, which builds on an awareness of the Jesus tradition concerning the poor. Paradoxically, God has chosen the poor of the world to be rich in faith. It is implied that the rich of the world are poor in faith. Reversal situations such as this (the first will be last, and the last first [Matt. 19:30//Mark 10:31; cf. Matt. 20:8, 10, 16]) are characteristic of Jesus's teaching. James exhorts the poor brother (or sister) to boast in his exalted position and the rich also to boast in their paradoxical reversal (see 1:9). This use of language accentuates the paradox of the poor (*tous ptōchous*) who are rich (*plousious*) in faith. Though the poor are to boast of this, James asserts that it is so by God's choice. It therefore is not a basis for arrogant pride. In this context, the language of boasting may overlap the meaning of rejoicing (cf. 1:2, 9, 12; Rom. 5:2–3; note also Matt. 5:12: "Rejoice and be glad, for great is your reward in heaven"). In their critique of boasting, James and Paul target inappropriate rejoicing.

James implies that the rich of this world are not inclined to be rich in faith or to be citizens of the kingdom of God. This perspective is grounded in the tradition of the teaching of Jesus: "Blessed are you poor, for yours is the kingdom of God" (Luke 6:20; cf. Matt. 5:3). The poor are identified with those who love God and are inheritors of the kingdom. They are blessed because the kingdom of God/heaven is theirs. This affirmation of the poor presumes a strong critique of the rich that is already evident in 1:9–11 and is now developed in 2:1–13 and comes to a climax in 5:1–6. For the roots of this tradition, see the references to Amos below, in the discussion on 2:6.

Wealth, or at least the love of it, is portrayed as a barrier to faith and entry into the kingdom of God. Jesus commented, "How difficult it is for those who have riches to enter into the kingdom of God! Indeed, it is easier for a camel to pass through the eye of a needle than for a rich person to enter the kingdom of God" (Luke 18:24–25//Matt. 19:23–24; Mark 10:23–25). Jesus also warned, "Do not store up for yourself treasures on earth, where moth and rust consume and thieves break in and steal; but store up for yourselves treasures in heaven, where neither moth nor rust consumes and where thieves do not break in and steal; for where your treasure is, there will your heart be also" (Matt. 6:19–21//Luke 12:33–34 [Q]). Note the use of such language in James 5:2–3 in describing what will happen to the riches of the wealthy. Those who set their hearts on riches in this world are unlikely to be rich in faith and, from the perspective of Jesus and James, are unlikely to enter the kingdom of God. If the poor are those who love God, this evaluation gives expression to the conclusion "No one can serve two masters, for either you will hate the one and love the other, or you will be devoted to the one and despise the other. You cannot serve God and money [*mamōna*]" (Matt. 6:24//Luke 16:13 [Q]). For James, those who love God are those who serve God. Thus a case has been built up for honoring the poor as those who serve God. The other side of the critique of the rich is the idealization of the "poor," which becomes an alternative designation of the pious, the *'ănāwîm*.

2:6. To whom, then, does James speak when he says, **But you dishonored the poor?** The accusation apparently distances those who are addressed from the poor. But neither are they the rich! James continues, **Is it not [*ouch*] the rich who oppress you, and is it not they who drag you into courts?** These negative questions introduced by *ouch* expect an affirmative answer: "Yes, the rich do these things to us." While this may be true, there is no suggestion here that those who drag them into court are Christian brothers and sisters. They are identified simply as "the rich." Certainly a person characterized as rich is the subject of 2:2 and is hypothetically present in the synagogue. James seems to gather the rich together in his critique, whether they are "brothers and sisters" or not, and here it seems more likely that they are not.

The logic of the evidence given concerning the rich is "Then why favor them?" But where do the readers fit? Most likely they fit more with the poor than the rich and powerful, and they hope to gain something from the rich, though that hope is unrealistic, as the questions make clear. This critique of the rich stands in a strong tradition that can be traced back to Amos, who scathingly rebuked the rich of Israel who "sell the righteous for silver and the needy for a pair of shoes," "trample on the poor and take from them an excessive amount of wheat," and "trample on the needy and bring the poor of the land to an end" (see Amos 2:6; 5:11–13; 8:4–6).

2:7. Not only do the rich exploit the poor, but also **Is it not they who blaspheme the good name that was pronounced over you?** This language suggests that the name is that of Jesus, pronounced over them in baptism. To blaspheme the name may be to curse the name. Again, the question introduced by *ouk* implies the acknowledgment that this is indeed the case. Such an accusation implies that these rich people are not part of the Christian community, yet some of them apparently visited the synagogue (2:2).

The Sin of Discrimination, and the Triumph of Mercy (2:8–13)

2:8. Alternatively, at the beginning of 2:8–13, *mentoi* signals an approved way in contrast to the way of partiality/discrimination. However [*mentoi*], if you fulfill the royal law [*nomon basilikon*] according to the Scripture, "You shall love your neighbor [*plēsion*] as yourself," you [pl.] do well. The word *basilikos* is used only five times in the NT and in three contexts: twice in John 4:46, 49 to refer to a royal official (from the household of Herod?); twice in Acts 12:20–21 to refer to King Herod's country and robes; and in James 2:8 concerning fulfilling the commandment "You shall love your neighbor as yourself," the royal law according to the Scripture. Those who fulfill this commandment are commended: "you [pl.] do well [*kalōs poieite*]" (for a singular use of this expression, see 2:19).

James identifies the "royal" law as the law of the kingdom (of God) announced by Jesus (Matt. 5:43; 19:19; 22:39; Mark 12:31, 33; Luke 10:27; Rom. 13:9; Gal. 5:14; James 2:8) and expressed in the Levitical command (Lev. 19:18).

The Matt. 5:43 reference to it makes clear the antidiscriminatory character of this command in the teaching of Jesus, because the neighbor is understood in terms inclusive of the stranger and even the enemy (Matt. 5:43–44), a line of interpretation also taken up by the Lukan Jesus (Luke 10:25–37). In this latter passage, in response to a lawyer's question concerning the conditions to be fulfilled to receive eternal life, Jesus replied with his question about how the lawyer read what is written in the law. The lawyer answered by identifying the dual commands to love God (Deut. 6:5) and to love neighbor (Lev. 19:18). This reading involved the construal of two texts to form a coordinated unity, which Jesus approved as formally correct and instructed, "Do this and you will live!" To this the lawyer replied, "And who is my neighbor?" (Luke 10:29). Jesus turns the question on its head in order to delimit the understanding of the neighbor by telling a story of a Jewish (?) man, traveling from Jerusalem to Jericho, who was beaten, robbed, and left half dead only to be ignored by a passing priest and a Levite. By contrast, a Samaritan helped him. Jesus then asked his questioner, "Which of these three do you think proved to be neighbor to the man who fell a victim to thieves?" (Luke 10:36). The answer was unavoidable: "The one who acted mercifully [*ho poiēsas to eleos*] with him." To this Jesus responded, "You go and behave the same way" (Luke 10:37). James is very much in accord with this answer. The commended behavior is in stark contrast to acting with partiality/discrimination against the poor and needy.

2:9. On the contrary, **but if you show discrimination** [*prosōpolēmpteite*; cf. 2:1], **you commit sin and are convicted by the law as transgressors.** To act negatively with discrimination is to commit sin by failing to keep the command to love one's neighbor and to be self-evidently convicted as "transgressors" (*parabatai*) of the law, to be lawbreakers (2:9), because to discriminate is to fail to act justly (Mic. 6:8)—this is to deny justice.

2:10–11. For whoever keeps the whole law but fails in one point has become guilty of all of it. For the one who said "Do not commit adultery" also said "Do not murder," but if you do not commit adultery but you murder, you have become a transgressor of the law. James adopts a common Jewish argument, that to break just one commandment is to be guilty as a lawbreaker, a transgressor of the law, because every commandment is God given and important. Yet Jesus, like the rabbis, recognized the weightier commandments (Matt. 23:23). The weightier matters are evident in the first part of Jesus's answer to the lawyer, quoting the dual love commands (Luke 10:27; see also Matt. 22:37–39; Mark 12:29–31). In Luke, though Jesus begins with the dual commands, the focus moves to the command to love the neighbor and concludes by emphasizing keeping that command. In James also the focus is squarely on that royal command according to the Scripture (James 2:8). Paul too has a high view of this commandment: "Owe no one anything but to love one another, for the person who loves the other [*heteron*] has fulfilled the law." He concludes that all the commandments are summed up in this saying: "You shall love your neighbor as yourself. Love for the neighbor does not work evil; therefore love fulfills the law" (Rom. 13:8–10). The breaking of this royal law is ultimately serious, though the breaking of any commandment makes the person a lawbreaker (James 2:9–11). The formal keeping of any of the commandments counts for nothing if the royal command is flouted or ignored.

2:12. In light of the seriousness of lawbreaking, the turn to the theme of judgment is threatening. So [*houtōs*] **speak and so** [*houtōs*] **act as those about to be judged by the law of liberty.** Speaking and doing/acting make up life, so that this is a way of characterizing the manner and way of life. James calls on the readers to live in the light of the coming judgment. The law was characterized as the royal law and identified with the command "You shall love your neighbor as yourself." What then is the law of "liberty" (*eleutherias*)? On the basis of the discussion of this expression in 1:25 (see the discussion there), it seems clear that this is to be understood in the context of the Jewish law as interpreted by Jesus, but in James, as a Diaspora letter to the Diaspora, the expression occurs in a context where Stoic influence is possible. In this sense, in keeping the law is the freedom of living in harmony with the creation and with one's own being as part of God's creation. What it means to be judged by the law of liberty is hinted at in 2:13. Certainly, 5:7–8 implies that the *parousia*, bringing judgment, is near at hand.

2:13. James returns to language that suggests that keeping the love command moderates the consequence of judgment. **For judgment** [*krisis*] **is without mercy** [*aneleos*] **to the person who has not shown mercy** [*eleos*]; **mercy triumphs over judgment** [*kriseōs*]. Balancing judgment with mercy seems to be as crucial for James as for Mic. 6:8. There the prophet tells the readers that God has shown them what is "good" (*ṭôb*), "and what does the LORD require of you, but to do justice [Heb. *mišpāṭ*; Gk. *krima*], and to love kindness/mercy [Heb. *ḥesed*; Gk. *eleos*], and to walk humbly with your God." In a way, Micah has stated the matter in an ascending order of importance, yet all three elements are interconnected and crucial. Certainly nothing less than justice is required, but with God justice is tempered by mercy, because God is merciful and forgiving (Num. 14:18–19; Deut. 5:10; 7:9). James is built on a characterization of God as gracious, who gives freely to those who ask (James 1:5), and James affirms that every generous (good, gracious) act of giving and every perfect gift is from above (James 1:17). Those who share the goodness of God affirm the generosity of God's way. Consequently, it seems that walking humbly with God involves showing mercy, which is never less than doing justice. In the balance of mercy and justice/judgment, mercy takes priority.

In James, justice/judgment is tempered by mercy because judgment is based on the law of liberty, that is, the law as interpreted by Jesus. "Blessed are the merciful, because mercy will be shown to them" (Matt. 5:7). One aspect of mercy is the willingness to forgive: "Forgive us our debts as we forgive our debtors. . . . For if you forgive people their transgressions, your Father in heaven will also forgive you; but if you do not forgive people, neither will your heavenly Father forgive you" (Matt. 6:12, 14–15; cf. Luke 11:4). Very likely this tradition underlies James 2:13: "For judgment [krisis] is merciless [aneleos] to the person who has not shown mercy [eleos]; mercy triumphs [katakauchatai] over judgment [kriseōs]." The prefix an- in the word aneleos indicates negation, thus "merciless" (an + eleos). This word is first known in James and perhaps was coined to bring out forcefully the opposition to God's mercy. Mercy is of God. Micah claims that God has made known what is good, and James reveals that all that is generous and good has its source in God. That source of goodness means that judgment is grounded in mercy. Certainly justice should never be denied, but mercy goes beyond justice. So it is with God, according to James. There is mercy for the merciful, and the good purpose of God is that humans may live in a generous and merciful way with each other and in response to and relation with the God of mercy. But those who fail to be generous and merciful fall outside the mercy of God.

Theological Issues

James has polarized wealth and poverty so that the rich and their wealth have become identified with exploitation and ungodliness. In so doing, James draws on tradition mediated by Jesus. The scriptural evidence bears witness to a pervasive phenomenon—in the legal material of the Pentateuch, historical narratives, prophetic literature, the Psalms and wisdom tradition—suggesting that poverty and the plight of the poor were pervasive problems in the history of Israel. This is confirmed by the multiplicity of the vocabulary that amplifies and elaborates the literary record of this theme as it bears witness to the inhumanity of human exploitation throughout the history of Israel. With varying shades of meaning, seven different Hebrew words are used to describe the poor in different situations, from the poverty of laziness and begging to peasant poverty, poverty from unjust oppression, and the pious poor. The richness of the vocabulary bears witness to the pervasive reality of poverty. Of the Semitic words, 'ebyôn and 'ănāwîm are important for the period of early Christianity, and 'ănāwîm corresponds to the use of ptōchoi in James to refer to the "humble poor" (1:9–10), or pious poor. Though not used with great frequency, 'ănāwîm is used most often in the psalms of lament, which characterize the relationship of the poor to God, providing a basis for identifying the humble poor as godly. It is also used by Isaiah (11:4; 29:19; 32:7; 61:1) and memorably by Amos to describe the unjust oppression of the poor by the rich (Amos 2:7; 8:4).

Our present world, like that of the first and second centuries CE, is marked by the stark division between rich and poor (see Mark 14:7). The sociopolitical reality is shaped by rich and powerful minorities, whose interests are served by the structured application of power and the exploitation of the great majority by the few. As then, so today the world is divided between rich and poor nations. In our world, some of these nations are desperately poor, though even in the poorest nations, a very small minority of the very rich live well at the expense of the many poor. In a world such as ours, James raises the cry of "justice for the poor." The exploitative nature of the globalism of our time cries out for a vision of justice for the poor of the entire world, and for generosity in place of greed. James's vision of the generous gift-giving God underlies his view of the goodness of the creation and its potential for generosity.

It is the desire to possess and control the earth that leads rich and powerful individuals and nations to seize and control the resources of the earth for their own benefit, while excluding the weak and powerless from a fair share of earth's bounty. Thus earth's bounty is limited by human greed. Greed exploits the resources of the earth so that the earth itself is degraded. The habitat of other life-forms is progressively destroyed; the sea, rivers and lakes, the air, and even the soil of the earth itself are degraded and polluted by waste products created by humans. Against those who deny justice and fail to show generosity, James rails, "Go to now, you rich people, weep and wail for the miseries that are coming upon you" (James 5:1). James had not begun to hear the cry of the earth itself against those who despoil it and limit its ability to sustain life. Destructive human actions cause other life-forms to become extinct every day. Overfishing and the pollution of our oceans threaten to make the oceans barren places within a human lifetime. James's attack on exploitation now needs to be extended against exploitation of the earth, not only because the poor are the first to suffer in any crisis but also because the earth as God's good creation is valuable in itself and needs to be preserved, not unchanged but undiminished.

James 2:14–26

Faith and Works

Introductory Matters

James 2:14–26 returns to the relationship of faith and works, introduced in 1:22–27 under the imagery of hearing and doing, where the sense of the hearing of faith is evident. The opening question in 2:14 uses a word ("profit," *ophelos*) found only three times in the NT, twice in James (2:14, 16) and once in Paul (1 Cor. 15:32). Elsewhere in the NT, the cognate verb (*ōpheleō*) is used to the same effect (Matt. 16:26; cf. Luke 9:25). Use of this language in questions fits in with the dialogical style of James and the style of popular rhetoric.

In 2:19 the textual variants concern word order and the presence or absence of the definite article with "God" (*theos*). In this instance, the adopted reading (*heis estin ho theos*) conforms to the Jewish confession "God is one" and has the strongest textual support. Although "God" comes at the end of the clause, the use with the definite article after the verb "to be" identifies God as the subject.

That James here responds to the Pauline teaching of justification apart from works is confirmed by their common use of Gen. 15:6 (James 2:23; Rom. 4:3, 9, 22; Gal. 3:6), the wording of which suits Paul but not James. There is also their common use (James 2:18, 20, 26; Rom. 3:28; 4:6; cf. 3:21) of the words "apart from works" (*chōris tōn ergōn*), which are not found in Gen. 15:6 LXX. It is not surprising that James appeals to the *Aqedah*, the binding and offering of Isaac, as an example of the obedient "work" of Abraham (James 2:21–22), but there is no support for this view in James's key text, Gen. 15:6 (James 2:23). There can be little doubt that this verse is chosen in order to

---

James 2:14–26 in the Rhetorical Flow

Address/salutation (1:1)
Epitome of the exhortation of James (1:2–27)
Warning against partiality (2:1–13)
▶ **Faith and works (2:14–26)**
    Faith: Two questions, an example, and a conclusion (2:14–17)
        Faith: Two questions (2:14)
        Faith: An example (2:15–16)
        Conclusion 1 (2:17)
    Diatribe on faith and works (2:18–20)
        Diatribe (2:18–19)
        Conclusion 2 (2:20)
    Justification: Two examples with successive conclusions (2:21–26)
        Abraham (2:21–23)
        Conclusion 3a (2:24)
        Rahab (2:25)
        Conclusion 3b (2:26)

---

refute those who (like Paul) use this text to teach justification through faith alone and apart from works.

Tracing the Train of Thought

The theme of 2:14–26 follows naturally from 2:1–13 in that the argument moves from not discriminating against the poor in favor of the rich (2:1–13) to a positive concern for and care of those who are poor and needy (2:14–26). The new discussion of faith and works begins with the example of a destitute brother or sister. This discussion has its roots in 1:22–27 of the epitome. Faith without works is like hearing without doing (1:22–24), and compassion in action for the needy is of the essence of true religion (1:27). James then develops his distinctive view of the essential place of works to complete real faith in 2:18–26.

Faith: Two Questions, an Example, and a Conclusion (2:14–17)

The rhetorical mode of questioning dominates 2:14–17. The theme moves to the relation of faith and works. Initially, the question is whether faith alone can save a person. The question is directed to those whom James addresses as

101

"my brothers [and sisters]." This warm self-identification with the readers is reinforced by drawing them in to give their views. But the authoritative culture of James is such that this is not an "open" question but rather a "leading" one.

2:14. *Faith: Two questions (2:14).* **What is the profit/good [*ophelos*], my brothers [and sisters], if a person claims to have faith but has no works [*erga*]?** James addresses the readers in a way that makes him one of them: "brothers [and sisters]." Coming alongside them, he inquires, "What is the profit [*ophelos*] . . . ?" echoing words of Jesus in which the cognate verb is used: "What will it profit [*ōphelei*] a person to gain the whole world but lose his or her life?" (Mark 8:36 par.). The questions concern the effectiveness of certain courses of action in attaining life/salvation. James makes a case with a series of two questions, the first of which is asked in an open way without prompting an answer: What is the value of faith without works? Lest the readers miss the point, a second question follows immediately. **Surely faith [alone] is not [*mē*] able to save that person, [is it]?** This form of negative question, using *mē*, implies a negative answer from the readers: "No, it is not able to save that person." It is a leading question that does not rely on the reader to come to the right answer. In case the prompt might be insufficiently persuasive, an example is provided to bring home the point of view.

Before turning to the example, we may ask whether it is appropriate to speak of faith as saving anyone. Certainly this is not an expression that we would expect to find in Paul. For Paul, it is not faith that justifies or saves, but God (Rom. 8:33). Of course, James does not affirm the view that faith saves but rather aims to repudiate it as if some people held it. James implies that faith that expresses itself in works does save a person. It may be that James has chosen this rather crude way of expressing the work of salvation to show the scandal of the claim that belief (faith in that sense) without any action can save a person. The problem rebounds on James when the reader follows the implied conclusion that it is faith expressed in works that saves a person because 2:13 already teaches that even those whose faith is expressed in works rely on the mercy of God. And of course, James is right: a living faith involves more than a theoretical belief in God.

2:15–16. *Faith: An example (2:15–16).* **If a brother or sister is naked and lacking daily food, and one of you says to them "Go in peace; be warmed and satisfied" but you do not give to them what is necessary for the body, what is the profit/good [*ophelos*]?** Here James specifically refers to "a brother or a sister" (*adelphos ē adelphē*), though when addressing the readers as brothers, James never mentions sisters. Perhaps in this case women, especially widows, were more commonly in desperate and immediate need than men. At least here women are mentioned without discrimination as a sister alongside a brother, and we may take the failure to address the readers as "brothers and sisters" as a social blind spot of the time. The scene is set with a "brother or sister" destitute of all the essentials needed to survive. Because James is explicitly addressing "brothers" (2:14) when he says, "one of you [pl.] says to them [*autois*]," it is brother speaking to brother or sister. Yet James uses the third-person dative plural (*autois*). This grammatically incorrect move allows James to cope economically with the masculine/feminine problem ("him/her"). Given this precedent, the translation in this commentary may occasionally follow James's own practice.

The example demonstrates what James means by "faith by itself" (2:17; cf. 2:24). Faith without works does nothing to alleviate the desperate bodily needs of the brother or sister. Faith without works is like words without deeds. Instead of action to deal with those needs, faith alone speaks pious words: "Go in peace; be warmed and satisfied." We might ask, "In what sense, if at all, can this be understood as faith?" Perhaps it is implied that the speaker, having faith, expects that what is spoken will be miraculously achieved. After all, Jesus spoke about faith as moving mountains (Matt. 17:20; 21:21; cf. 1 Cor. 13:2). But the main point for James is that such faith leads to no action on behalf of the brother or sister in desperate need. Here James leaves nothing to the reader's imagination or insight, concluding impatiently, as he had begun in 2:14, "What good is that?" (2:16). Thus the end of 2:16 forms an inclusio with the beginning of 2:14. There is nothing more to be done but to sum up in 2:17. Yet the dialogue and debate continues in 2:18–20, and the place of works will be demonstrated by two examples, each with its own conclusion (2:21–26).

2:17. *Conclusion 1 (2:17).* **So also faith by itself, if it does not have works, is dead.** "So also" is James's formula for applying an example (see 1:11; 2:26; 3:5). Here "faith by itself" is explained as not having works; in 2:24 it is "faith alone [*monon*]." By itself, faith alone, without works, is sterile, a lifeless corpse, dead. Perhaps the term "dead" (*nekra*) is chosen because of its resonance with "works" (*erga*). Otherwise, James might have used "vain, empty" (*kenos, mataios*) or some other metaphor. Certainly, "dead" captures the powerlessness of such faith, which is perhaps the point of what follows. But for Paul, faith described in these terms is no faith at all. Thus, although this critique may be aimed at the Pauline language, it misses the mark of the Pauline meaning, which is closer to James than perhaps either of them knew.

Diatribe on Faith and Works (2:18–20)

While the overall argument is clear, the means by which it is expressed is confusing. What appears to be an objection to the mainstream argument of James turns out to be a clarification of that argument.

2:18. *Diatribe (2:18–19).* Use of an anonymous interlocutor is common in Stoic diatribe and is found also in the synagogue homily. The formulaic opening **But [*all'*] someone will say, . . .** implies opposition to the line of argument so far (in 2:14–17). The adversative meaning is supported by every known use of the formula (in Stoic sources, Josephus, Paul, and other Jewish and early Christian sources). Weakening the adversative force of "but" does not seem to be an option. What follows, however, actually supports the argument of James. Alternative interpretations are unpersuasive. The most attractive is the suggestion that the words of the objection have been removed from the text by some unknown circumstance, leaving only the response of James to the anonymous objector. This hypothesis makes good sense of the text as it stands. The problem is that there is no textual evidence to support the theory. If something like this happened, it must have been very early, before copies of the original were made. But James is a circular letter to the Diaspora. Unless this is a fabrication, multiple copies would have existed from the beginning, and without some textual evidence of disruption at this point, this attractive hypothesis remains unpersuasive. Thus an objection is expressed in "But . . ."

Surprisingly, the interlocutor takes up the argument on behalf of James: "You have faith and I have works. Show me your faith apart from [*chōris*] works, and I will show you faith from [*ek*] my works." Some translations (e.g., RSV, NRSV, NIV, NET) restrict the quotation of the interlocutor to "You have faith and I have works." The rest—"Show me your faith apart from [*chōris*] works, and I will show you faith from [*ek*] my works"—is then viewed as coming from James. This makes little difference, because the interlocutor surprisingly does not object to James's view but actually supports it, and James merely spells out the implications for his argument. The problem is that, because the interlocutor speaks from the perspective of James, there is nothing to distinguish the interlocutor's words from those of James that follow. This distinction does nothing to alleviate the adversative "but" that introduces the *objection* of 2:18. The objection cannot be addressed to James, because it is addressed to a second implied interlocutor representing the "faith only" position. The adversative force of the "but" addresses that view, asking, "What tangible evidence is there of faith alone?" At the same time, the first interlocutor, arguing on behalf of James, asserts that works of mercy are tangible evidence of faith, insisting on the inseparability of completed faith and works (see 2:22). What has provoked this internal debate in James is the affirmation of the validity of faith apart from (*chōris*) works, which is found in Paul (e.g., Rom. 3:21, 28; 4:6). Against this view as James understands it, and supported by the first interlocutor, James puts in question the reality of faith without works. But the criticism does not actually address Paul's view, though an accumulation of Pauline language is criticized, suggesting that the Pauline language is the target. James rejects the validity of "faith apart from [*chōris*] works." Can a case be made for faith alone?

2:19. You believe that God is one—well done; even the demons believe and tremble with fear. There is no indication that the voice of James has returned to address the readers/hearers generally. Rather, the voice of the pro-Jamesian interlocutor, explicitly introduced in 2:18, which is also the voice of James, responds to the view of an implied opposition interlocutor, "So you believe that God is one, do you?" Because these voices *in the text* dispute with each other, I treat them as pro- and anti-James voices or interlocutors. The implied response of the opposition interlocutor to the call to demonstrate faith without works is "I believe God is one." Such correct belief might be thought to be valid evidence of faith apart from works. To this the pro-Jamesian interlocutor responds, "Well done [*kalōs poieis*]. . . ." Such a commendation suggests that the evidence is approved (see 2:8, where the keeping of the royal law according to the Scripture is approved with the same words). But in this instance, the words of approval are followed by the somewhat mocking reply "even the demons believe and tremble with fear." In other words, "What good is that?" (see 2:14, 16). The inference may even be that intellectual belief alone, without a life commitment to God expressed in works of mercy, is demonic (cf. the demonic recognition of Jesus in Mark 1:23–25; 5:7–10).

This understanding of faith as an intellectual belief is not the Pauline understanding of faithful and trustful commitment, "the obedience of faith" (Rom. 1:5). The belief that God is one is not wrong or irrelevant, being at the heart of the Jewish daily confession of the Shema (Deut. 6:4–5) and affirmed by Jesus (Mark 12:28–29). Hence the response "Well done." But this is not enough. The first commandment does not end there. It continues, "And you shall love the LORD your God with all of your heart and all of your life and all of your mind and all of your strength." To this Jesus adds a second commandment ("You shall love your neighbor as yourself") and asserts that there is no other commandment greater than these (Mark 12:30–31). It is likely that James draws on this Jesus tradition of the double command, which begins from the confession that God is one and goes on to the requirement of total devotion to God, encompassing total commitment to the well-being of the neighbor (see the overlapping tradition in Matt. 22:34–40//Luke 10:25–28), which, according to James, is the royal law according to Scripture.

James reverses the order of the commandments in dealing first with the royal law according to the Scripture, "You shall love your neighbor as yourself" (2:8), before affirming belief that God is one (2:19). Both receive words of approval: "Well done." Even then, the assertion addressed by the latter comes not from James but rather from the implied opposition interlocutor. Because the belief is not wrong, but even essential, it is commended in the same terms used to commend those who keep the royal law in 2:8: "Well done." Because the commendation of 2:8 is addressed to the readers/hearers, it is plural (*kalōs poieite*), but 2:19 is singular (*kalōs poieis*), being addressed by the pro-Jamesian interlocutor to the implied opposition interlocutor. Thus the two linked commandments featured by Jesus are reversed in order and commended in this way in James. While the commendation of keeping the royal law in 2:8 is unqualified, in 2:19 it is addressed to an implied opposition interlocutor and in the singular, and it is qualified by "even the demons believe and tremble with fear." The commandment commended in 2:8 focused on works of mercy for the neighbor. The assertion of belief that God is one is put forward as evidence of the independent value of faith, faith without works. While such faith is commended in itself, the commendation is quickly qualified in terms expressing irony or sarcasm, given such faith is not expressed in works of mercy.

2:20. *Conclusion 2 (2:20).* The pro-Jamesian interlocutor, who is the voice of James, concludes this phase of the argument with a summary statement addressed to the implied opposition interlocutor: **Do you wish to know, O foolish person [*anthrōpe kene*], that faith apart from [*chōris*] works is useless [*argē*]?** Although framed in the form of a question, the words are addressed in a way that shows no respect for the dialogue partner, who is addressed as "O foolish person" (on this translation of *anthrōpe kene*, see the discussion on 1:7–8). Impatience and frustration with those who think that "faith alone" has some value bristle in the question. The question is ironic or even sarcastic, as if such a person would really wish to know! Such words are not likely to sway those who are characterized as empty-headed and foolish. The person who wishes to separate faith from works of mercy does not wish to know that such faith is useless, which is the implied answer to the question of 2:14, 16. The question "What is the profit/good of faith apart from works?" was answered in 2:17 in these terms: "Faith by itself is dead." Now, after dialogue between the interlocutors, the answer is given in other terms. The value of faith alone is nothing at all, "useless" (2:20). Such a dismissive treatment implies that this view belongs outside the communities to which James is addressed. This form of argument is designed to ensure that it stays that way.

Justification: Two Examples with Successive Conclusions (2:21–26)

2:21. *Abraham (2:21–23).* **Was not [*ouk*] Abraham our father justified by [*ex*] works when he offered Isaac upon the altar?** While the reference to Abraham as "our father" is not impossible in a purely Christian context after Paul, it is more at home in a Jewish context (including Christian Jewish). This observation is strengthened by the choice of the example of the *Aqedah*, the binding and offering of Isaac (Gen. 22). The example is introduced by a leading question. Such a question, introduced by the negative *ouk*, implies an assenting answer. Why then was a question used rather than the statement "Abraham our father was justified by works when he offered Isaac upon the altar"? The purpose of this question is to lead the readers to assent to the conclusion James desires, that Abraham was indeed justified by (*ex*) works. Yet the use of the passive ("was justified") may be taken as a so-called divine passive, implying that God is the real agent of justification (see also 2:25). The use of the passive allows reference to God without naming him, thus avoiding the possibility of taking the name of God in vain. Paul straightforwardly asserts, "It is God who justifies [*theos ho dikaiōn*]" (Rom. 8:33). What then would be the role of works? Does James make them instrumental in justification? If so, who wields the instrument that brings about justification?

The sense of instrumentality is normally expressed by the dative case or by the preposition *en* followed by the dative case. James uses *ek/ex* followed by the genitive case. Moulton and Geden (Marshall 2002, 313) list sixteen different possible uses of *ek* in the NT. Of these, the instrumental, or causal, use is listed as number 6. While this use is not rare, it is less common than various uses of the dative case and seems to be more vague about the process than are the more common idioms of agency and instrumentality. Roughly speaking, agency relates to the person who does something. Goliath's head was cut off by David (agent) with a sword (instrument).

James uses *ek* a total of twelve times. Seven of these occur in 2:16–25. One of these (2:16) expresses a partitive sense: "one of [*ek*] you [a group]." The other six are related to works and might be examples of the instrumental use. The other five uses of *ek* in James occur in chapters 3–5. Only 3:13 is identified by Moulton and Geden as an example of the instrumental use of *ek*, along with the six uses in James 2:18, 21, 22, 24 (2x), 25. In these references, the possible instrumental use of *ek* is in relation to faith or works. If an instrumental use is accepted, who justifies using works as the instrument of justification? The language does not suggest that Abraham justified himself by his works. Rather, Abraham "was justified," an idiom more suggestive of God as the one who justifies. Clearly, for James, works are relevant, but the precise role that they play in justification is unclear.

With the tradition of the binding and offering of Isaac, James has good evidence of Abraham's active obedience to the command of God (works of the law) and can argue that Abraham was justified by works. But is Abraham the agent who justifies himself by his works? James does not clearly say this. In terms of this kind of language, Paul certainly does not assert that believers justify themselves by their faith. "It is God who justifies" (Rom. 8:33), and I strongly suspect that James's regular use of *ek* (or *ex*), which generally means "from/out of," here indicates something more vague than instrumentality. For James, too, it is God who justifies, because all who face judgment need mercy to triumph over condemnation: "For judgment is without mercy for those who show no mercy" (2:13). Thus works of mercy are relevant for those who receive mercy, and it is God who shows mercy.

2:22. You see that faith was cooperating [*synērgei*] with his works, and by [*ek*] works faith was completed/perfected. James continues the dialogical style, "You see," drawing the reader into the conclusion, with which, it is implied, they will agree. That faith was cooperating with works implies that the two, though distinguishable, belong together. Only when working together with works is faith really faith, because it is completed or perfected by works. Without works, faith is incomplete and useless (*argē*, 2:20); it has no benefit (2:14, 16). The kind of works required of faith begin to be described in 2:8, commending the keeping of the royal law according to the Scripture. The command "Love your neighbor as yourself" is in line with the call for works

107

of mercy to those in need (2:14–17). But the works evident in the binding and offering of Isaac, though clearly works of obedience to God's command, can hardly be viewed as comparable to the works of mercy described in 2:15–16. At this point there is some slippage in developing an understanding of the nature and function of justifying works.

2:23. **And the Scripture was fulfilled that says, "Abraham believed God, and it was reckoned [*elogisthē*] to him for/as righteousness," and he was called [a] friend of God.** The quoted text is Gen. 15:6, and it was used by Paul (Rom. 4:3, 9, 22; Gal. 3:6) to argue that Abraham was justified by faith apart from works (Rom. 3:28; 4:6; cf. 3:21). The shared use of Gen. 15:6 and unusual language ("apart from the law") where James's argument presupposes and opposes the Pauline formulation, if not the Pauline meaning, make a case for recognizing a critique by James of some form of the Pauline position. Further, James's use of Gen. 15:6 requires explanation in a way that Paul's use of it does not. A straightforward reading of the text makes the case for the "faith only" position. Paul read it that way. Because this use of Gen. 15:6 was so damaging to James's position, he had to find a way to incorporate it. Had it not been used by the "faith only" supporters, James could have ignored it, using only texts, such as Gen. 22, that give clear support for the role of works of obedience. Of course, if Gen. 15:6 is read from the perspective of the offering of Isaac, then faith and works are united, though this view is not to be found in Gen. 15:6. There its context is in reference to Abraham believing God's promise concerning his descendants. That belief "was reckoned to him for righteousness." But James read the text from the perspective of the offering of Isaac, an event yet to take place from the perspective of Gen. 15:6. Because Isaac was Abraham's heir, the offering of Isaac was a test of Abraham's trust/ belief in God's promise. Because of Abraham's trust and obedience, "he was called a friend of God" (note Isa. 41:8: "the seed of Abraham my friend"; cf. 2 Chron. 20:7). James does not argue, as the later rabbis do, that faith is a work. For him, faith and works are separable, and faith as intellectual belief is completed by works.

2:24. *Conclusion 3a (2:24).* **Take note, a person [*anthrōpos*] is justified by [*ex*] works and not by faith only [*monon*].** On this translation of *anthrōpos*, see the discussion on 1:7–8. Although James has argued that faith and works belong together, they are logically separable. He does not discuss works without faith, but it is clear that faith without works is of no benefit, powerless, useless, incomplete (2:14, 16, 20, 22). If incomplete, it would not be genuine faith, and James asks the leading question "Surely such faith cannot [*mē*] save a person, can it?" (2:14). By the use of *mē* James clearly implies that it cannot. But what about works of mercy without faith? What about those who keep the royal law according to the Scripture, "You shall love your neighbor as yourself"? James has said that if you keep this commandment, "you do well [*kalōs poieite*]" (2:8). If "every generous act of giving and every perfect gift is from above, coming down from the Father of lights" (1:17), it may be that James considers God's grace to be more widely present and effective than some who demand orthodox faith might allow. James's main point, however, is to reject the view that a person is "justified by faith alone [*monon*]." "By faith alone" (Lat. *sola fide*) has become a slogan that encapsulates "by faith apart from works," a slogan repudiated by James. Though James has used the example of Abraham to support his conclusion that "faith alone" is insufficient for justification, he turns to a second example, less impressive than Abraham and more surprising.

2:25. *Rahab (2:25)*. **And likewise, was not [*ouk*] even Rahab the prostitute justified by [*ex*] works when she welcomed the messengers and sent them out another way?** The story of Rahab is told in Josh. 2; 6:17, 22–23, 25. That she should be chosen for mention alongside Abraham, the father of the nation of Israel, at first seems extraordinary. But then, the story in Joshua is itself extraordinary. That the two spies sent out by Joshua should find refuge in Jericho with Rahab, identified as a prostitute (Josh. 2:1), is extraordinary. That she should enable them to complete their task and to provide Joshua with the necessary intelligence to make a successful conquest of the city of Jericho gives her a notable place in the history of Israel. But there is more to it than that. Matthew names just five women in the genealogy of Jesus. The second of these is Rahab (Matt. 1:5), a near ancestor of King David (Matt. 1:6). The first four women are before the exile, and the fifth is Mary the mother of Jesus (Matt. 1:16). Perhaps of more interest is Heb. 11:31: "By faith Rahab the prostitute received the messengers with peace and was not destroyed with those who did not believe / who disobeyed." Interestingly, Hebrews identifies faith as the crucial element, whereas James sees the welcoming of the messengers as the "works" that saved her. Hebrews roots that action in the recognition and acceptance of the two men, not as messengers of Joshua but as messengers of God (Josh. 2:9–11). Both Hebrews and James feature Abraham and Rahab, though Hebrews accentuates the role of Abaham (11:8–17) and deals with Rahab in one verse (Heb. 11:31). The concentration on Abraham is less accentuated in James, which deals with Abraham (2:21–23) and Rahab (2:25), providing single-verse conclusions for each of them. James overlooks the emphasis in Joshua on Rahab's recognition of (belief in?) the role of two men as messengers of the God of heaven and earth, which was the basis of her action in sheltering and assisting them. Because James recognizes the complementary roles of faith and works, the stress on works is not a denial of the role of faith, even if in this brief summary that role is underplayed. The point, no doubt, is "What use would that faith have been if she had not helped them?" Thus, viewed from the perspective of the treatment of Abraham, "Was not [*ouk*] Rahab justified by works?" The implied answer is "Yes! Of course."

As in Joshua, so also in Hebrews and James, Rahab is identified as a prostitute. In Joshua, as a result of the aid provided, she and her extended family were spared when the city was destroyed with its inhabitants. In Matthew, Rahab becomes an ancestor of King David and of the Messiah. In Hebrews, she becomes an exemplar of faith along with Abraham and a great cloud of witnesses. In James, she exemplifies those saved by their works (2:14), justified by (*ek*) her works. For readers today, the incongruity of prostitution and doing the works of God may be more difficult to accept than in ancient times. Certainly, sexual immorality has been singled out as particularly evil since the holiness of virginity became emphasized. The case of Rahab might well be a challenge to rethink our evaluation of moral evil. For James, it seems likely that the failure to show compassion to those in need is a more serious sin: "For judgment will be without mercy for those who do not act mercifully" (2:13).

2:26. *Conclusion 3b (2:26).* **For even as the body is dead apart [*chōris*] from the spirit, so also faith apart [*chōris*] from works is dead.** This conclusion comes at the end of the example of Rahab and sums up its contribution, but it is also the most forceful expression of the progressive summaries found earlier in 2:17, 20, 24. In 2:17 James asserts that "faith by itself is dead [*nekra*]"; then in 2:20 that "faith apart from works is useless [*argē*]." It follows that a person is not justified by faith only, apart from works (2:24). Indeed, this formulation emphasizes justification by works, adding "and not by faith alone [*monon*]." The emphasis falls on the effectiveness of works, though the final words allow faith some role, cooperating (*synērgei*) with works (2:22): "not by faith only" (2:24). Finally, faith without works is like a lifeless body (2:26). It is powerless, useless, good for nothing. In the analogy, faith is like the lifeless body, while works are comparable to the "breath of life," "the life-giving spirit" that animates the living person.

Theological Issues

In the recent past, the debate in James 2:14–26 has been understood in terms of a conflict between the gospel of the grace of God and the social gospel. The modern debate may well be a distortion of both Paul and James, who are sometimes portrayed as representative of these two positions. Recent commentators have worked to show that although there are significantly different emphases in the writings of Paul and of James, the differences are not as great as has often been supposed or even as they themselves might have thought. Nevertheless, two quite distinct positions can be set out. One position finds its focus on bringing people into relationship with God in order that they may be justified (2:21, 23, 25) or saved (2:14). If one's focus and priority in life is to be justified or saved and that others also should be justified or saved, then it is possible to disregard well-being in this life for the sake of the life to come. Well-being in this life is comparatively unimportant if it is in conflict with well-being in eternity. But this may be a false alternative. James recognizes that Jesus connected the two great commandments as foundational for true religion. Love for God and love for the neighbor are not in competition. Love of God involves the command "You shall love your neighbor as yourself." In response to the keeping of each of these commandments, James affirms, "You do well" (2:8, 19). This common evaluation of the keeping of each of these two commandments draws attention to their interrelatedness, their unity.

Although James's position is framed in relation to the teaching of Jesus, his position confronts the Pauline formulation. In doing so, James addresses a breakdown of the connection between faith and works. Such a breakdown has been common in history and may have been aided by a misuse of Paul, for whom the gospel was essentially social in scope and ethical in character (see 1 Cor. 13; Gal. 5:16–26; note esp. Gal. 6:2: "Bear one another's burdens and so fulfill the law of Christ"). The law of Christ may well be what James calls "the royal law according to the Scripture, 'You shall love your neighbor as yourself'" (2:8). For Paul, as much as for James, faith essentially involves action for the sake of the other, especially the other in need. Jesus, James, and Paul understood this social concern to be rooted in the goodness (Jesus and James) or grace (Paul) of God and as a manifestation of the kingdom (kingly rule) of God. The gospel proclaims God's goodwill toward and concern for the creation and all God's creatures, and those who love God will love his creatures as well. Whereas Paul taught that this outworking is an essential expression of the life of faith, James confronted the issue of faith without works. At this point there is a difference between Paul's analysis of the redeemed life of faith, in which works are the expression of a transformed life, and James's view of faith, which belongs with works but is separable from them. But if separable, such faith is not complete, not perfected. This is not so far from Paul, for whom such would not be faith at all. A more apparent difference from Paul is that James lacks Paul's emphasis on the role of the Spirit in the life of faith. Here James speaks rather of the role of the gift-giving God. Is this difference more apparent than real? Does the language of James reflect strong ties with the Jesus tradition and its Jewish roots more than the characteristics of the new movement in the power of the Spirit? Whatever the reason, James helpfully reminds us of the unity of God and God's goodness, which can be overshadowed by a concentration on the role of the Spirit.

James 3:1–12

The Tongue

Introductory Matters

Three words in James 3:1–12 are not found in the LXX and appear only in James in the NT: "boast" (*aucheō*, 3:5), "sea creature" (*enalion*, 3:7), and "gush" (*bryō*, 3:11). Another ten are found only in James: "guide" (*metagō*, 3:3, 4), "forest" (*hylē*, 3:5), "set on fire" (*phlogizō*, 3:6 [2x]), "wheel" (*trochos*, 3:6), "deadly" (*thanatēphoros*, 3:8), "likeness" (*homoiōsis*, 3:9), "ought" (*chrē*, 3:10), "bitter" (*pikros*, 3:11, 14), "salty" (*halykos*, 3:12), and "understanding" (*epistēmōn*, 3:13). Thus, in this short passage (plus 3:13) are thirteen words used only in James in the NT. Another two words are found only in James and Paul in the NT: "how great" (*hēlikos*, James 3:5 [2x]; Gal. 6:11 [the reading adopted by Tischendorf and Westcott and Hort]; Col. 2:1) and "poison" (*ios*, James 3:8; 5:3; Rom. 3:13). Five words found in James are rare uses in Luke, Acts, or Hebrews and not found elsewhere in the NT. These linguistic details continue to build a picture of the distinctive place of James in early Christianity and of its relationship to Paul and the Hellenistic world. Of course, its relationship to Judaism is a given. At the same time, James stands in a closer literary and linguistic relationship to the Hellenistic world than do most other books in the NT.

Tracing the Train of Thought

This treatment of the tongue vividly develops a theme already introduced in the epitome in 1:19, 21, 26. James 1:19 calls on every person to be "swift to hear, slow to speak, slow to anger." The order and relationship of "swift to hear, slow to speak" introduce the need to control the tongue, explicitly noted in the distinctive conclusion of the epitome: "Someone who presumes to be religious while not controlling the tongue, . . . the religion [*thrēskeia*] of this person is vain [*mataios*]" (1:26). Here "vain" has the sense of empty, vacuous, worthless. It is of the sort about which James asks, "What good is that?" (2:14, 16).

The Tongue and Teachers (3:1–2a)

3:1. Do not many of you become teachers, my brothers [and sisters], knowing we will receive the greater condemnation [*meizon krima*]. James opens with a negative command. In the Greek text, the opening negative (*mē*) is separated from the second-person plural present imperative (*ginesthe*), which comes at the end of the clause. The translation into English is awkward: "Do not many of you become teachers." This directive might seem unreasonably harsh, especially because teachers were respected and honored in Judaism and in the early Jesus movement. James addresses these words to the readers as "my brothers [and sisters]," a form that has become familiar (see 1:2, 16, 19; 2:1, 5, 14). Here it announces a new topic and signals the author's use of traditional material, especially Jesus tradition. Used with the imperative, this egalitarian form of address softens the language of command, closing the gap between the writer as a teacher and those to whom he writes as brothers and sisters. At the same time, James identifies himself with teachers, "knowing *we* [teachers] will receive the greater condemnation," a sterner judgment, and a greater penalty or condemnation (*krima*) for those who teach error, because it places those who learn in peril. Thus, with honor comes serious responsibility.

The teacher's role and authority in the community was recognized by Jesus, who directed a scathing criticism at (some) scribes and Pharisees as teachers who failed to live up to their responsibility (Matt. 23:1–36). "The scribes and Pharisees sit in the seat of Moses. Therefore, do and keep whatever they teach you, but do not do what they do" (Matt. 23:2–3). The word order in the Greek text places their position as teachers first for emphasis: "Upon the seat of Moses they sit." That privileged place lays great responsibility on them. Jesus then pronounces a sevenfold woe on the scribes and Pharisees, labeling them as hypocrites (Matt. 23:13, 15, 16, 23, 25, 27, 29) and drawing attention to the disparity between what they say (teach) and what they do. This

---

James 3:1–12 in the Rhetorical Flow

Address/salutation (1:1)

Epitome of the exhortation of James (1:2–27)

Warning against partiality (2:1–13)

Faith and works (2:14–26)

▶ The tongue (3:1–12)

The tongue and teachers (3:1–2a)

The tongue and self-control (3:2b–5a)

The tongue as a deadly power (3:5b–12)

---

is comparable to James's critique of those who speak but do not act (James 2:16–17). But teachers can also err in what they teach, leading others astray. This was not the focus of Jesus, but it seems to have been included by James. Reference to "the seat of Moses" reveals the honored place of the teacher. The Greek word used for "seat" in Matt. 23:1 is *kathedra*. From this word the tradition developed in the church of making a cathedral the seat of the bishop. As "the seat of Moses" was the place of teaching the law, so the practice of the bishop is to sit to teach. That seat became known as a throne (*thronos*). Eusebius (ca. 320 CE) frequently mentions the "throne of James, the brother of the Lord," whom he names as the first bishop of the Jerusalem church. Eusebius reports that the successors of James preserved and treasured his throne (*Hist. eccl.* 2.1.2; 2.23.1, 4; 3.5.2; 3.11.1; 7.19.1; see Painter 2004, 110–13, 118–19, 142–43, 144–47, 154–58, 308–14). Eusebius mentions no other such throne than that of James. The seat (*kathedra*) of the bishop became a throne (*thronos*) and is located in a cathedral.

3:2a. For we all make many mistakes [*ptaiomen*]. Although the tongue is not mentioned in 3:1–2a, the reference to teachers alerts the reader to the role of the tongue. The words "For we all make many mistakes" have many echoes and parallels in Jewish and Greek sources, and they appear to be proverbial and universally applicable. But in context they are applied to teachers. The "we" who make the mistakes are "we" teachers of 3:1b, who will receive the "greater punishment/condemnation" (*meizon krima*). Consequently, James issues a warning to those who would be teachers. This was necessary because the high status of teachers in the Jewish community carried over into the Jesus movement. In addition to those with a genuine divine calling, the role and position attracted the personally ambitious as well as those with social, political, and economic agendas. Thus James cautions prospective teachers about the ethical and spiritual demands of this vocation. He does this, identifying himself with the teachers who will face the more serious penalty because they carry greater responsibility. That responsibility is to be faced knowing that "we all make many mistakes." This description is all-embracing of the failure to act consistently with the teaching (to say but not to do), which was the fault of (some of) the scribes and Pharisees, and the failure to teach the truth, leading others astray.

The Tongue and Self-Control (3:2b–5a)

3:2b. If anyone does not make a mistake [*ou ptaiei*] by word, this person [*anēr*] is perfect/complete and able to bridle/control [*chalinagōgēsai*] the whole body. For the use of *anēr* interchangeably with *anthrōpos* as a generic reference to the human person, see the discussion on 1:7–8. In 3:2b James sets up a hypothetical conditional situation. The discussion is no longer restricted to teachers but instead is expanded by the opening statement. "If anyone makes no mistake by word," then certain things follow. Nevertheless, words are the tools of trade for teachers, so this warning is pointedly applicable to teachers. This hypothetical person, who makes no mistake by word, is "complete" and "able to bridle/control the whole body." Apparently, it is implied that control of the tongue is instrumental in the control of the whole body. Thus *chalinagōgeō* is used of controlling the tongue in 1:26 and of the whole body in 3:2b and is taken up in 3:3 in reference to the *chalinos*, which is linguistically and physically connected to the bridle. According to 3:2b, the ability to bridle/control the whole body is demonstrated by the ability to make no mistake by word. If the same verb had not been used in relation to the tongue in 1:26, we might not have made the connection between control of the tongue and the whole body, although the latter is made conditional on making "no mistake by word." Given that the connection is made clear by 1:26, this seems to imply that to achieve control of the tongue is to control the whole body as well, because control of the tongue tends to be lost first and leads to the loss of bodily control.

The intricate relationship between 1:26 and 3:2b casts doubt on the widely influential view of Martin Dibelius (1976, 21) that James is a collection of traditional ethical material lacking a coherent theological perspective. What operates here on a microscale operates more widely in James also. While James lacks a unity bound by logical rigor, it unfolds an understanding of God and the world in which faithful lives need to be lived. The understanding is built up using associated analogies or pictures. These are placed side by side and interact with each other. The epitome, as a ground plan to be developed in later chapters, reveals the interrelatedness of the smaller units of teaching that work analogically to build a unifying vision. According to James (1:26), any claim to be religious is shown to be vacuous, empty, vain by the failure to control the tongue. In James, words without actions have little value (see 2:14–17). They are like faith without works (2:15–16) or hearing without doing (1:22–25). Thus the consequent control of the whole body, flowing from the control of the tongue, is also crucial.

The significance of the tongue is not restricted to teachers. That is clear in 1:26. Any claim to be religious is falsified by the failure to control the tongue. Appropriate control of the tongue arises out of love for God and for the neighbor (2:5–13, esp. vv. 5, 8, 13). Yet the tongue has special significance for the teacher, which is clear in 3:1–2. For the teacher, to make no mistake by word is the goal, even though "we all make many mistakes." The connection between controlling the tongue and controlling the body is taken further by extending the use of the bridle (*chalinagōgeō*) to include a bit (*chalinos*) placed in the mouth of a horse.

Speaking for all teachers, James says, "We all make many mistakes [*ptaiomen*]" (3:2a). Similarly, the saying of 3:2b has a special relevance for teachers, though it is directed more widely: "If anyone makes no mistake [*ou ptaiei*] by word . . ." But how does this relate to 3:2a, which it directly follows? If to make no mistake "by word" is more limited in scope than to make no mistake at all, this need not be a contradiction. But this seems to be ruled out, because the person who makes no mistake by word is perfect and able to bridle/control the whole body. One way around this apparent contradiction is to observe the hypothetical nature of the proposition: "*If* anyone makes no mistake by word . . ." That being the case, the possibility of so bridling the tongue as to make no mistake by word is the challenge and the goal for both teacher and student, without actually claiming to be free of mistakes. Control of the tongue is essential for a godly life. From the point of view of James, control of the tongue is theologically and ethically necessary, to be "swift to hear, slow to speak, slow to anger" (1:19).

3:3. If we put bits [*chalinous*] into the mouths of horses that they may obey us, we control their whole body. Here, following 3:2b, "we" is not restricted to teachers but includes anyone who uses a horse and bridle. James has argued that if we bridle/control the tongue (1:26; 3:2a), we bridle/control the whole body. To illustrate this, he describes how bit and bridle control the mouth/head of the horse and thereby control the horse completely. The priority that James gives to the analogy of bit and bridle may owe something to the bit being in the mouth of the horse and thus close to the tongue. It may also be because the horse was considered to be the most spirited of animals: "Even the horse, most spirited of all animals, is easily controlled by the bit" (Philo, *Opif.* 28 §86). Similar references to the control of certain four-footed animals as beasts of burden are found widely in the literature of the time (e.g., Sophocles, *Ant.* 342–44; Cicero, *Nat. d.* 2.60.151; Seneca, *Ben.* 2.29.4). Choice of the example of the horse may also have been influenced by the fact that it was the most common means of land travel apart from walking.

Nevertheless, it is not the bit and bridle that control a horse but rather "we" who put the bit in their mouths so that we may control them. Thus the image may really be that of the charioteer who controls the horse. If this is right, with the following example of the helmsman, these two metaphors were common in Stoicism and were used by Philo as metaphors for God as charioteer and helmsman. But this does not fit the examples in James. These analogies imply that humans are the charioteers and helmsmen, and James uses them as metaphors for the human control/bridling of the tongue.

The bit, like the tongue, is small, but it produces a big outcome in controlling the horse. James has a high view of the power of the tongue for (good and?) evil. If, for the teacher who controls the tongue, this is a potential power for good, for all people it is also a threat of dissension and destruction. Everything depends on the control of the tongue for good. The uncontrolled tongue will speak great and proud things, wreaking havoc. Consequently, like the charioteer, who uses bit and bridle to control the horse, all of us need to bridle the tongue (James 1:26).

3:4. See also the ships, being so big and driven by harsh winds; they are guided by a very small rudder where the will of the pilot chooses. Not surprisingly,

Rémih/Wikimedia Commons

Figure 4. Ancient Ship's Rudder. This wall relief from the courtyard of the Temple of Edfu, on the west bank of the Nile River, shows the small rudder used to steer a large ship.

the metaphorical use of guiding a horse by bit and bridle and of a ship by a tonguelike rudder are common in Hellenistic literature because these were common forms of land and sea travel. Association of the tongue with the bit in the horse's mouth and the tonguelike shape of the rudder might also have influenced the choice, but the essential analogy is that the small item, the tongue (bit and bridle/rudder), controls the whole body (the horse/the ship). The analogy of the ship makes clear that the steering of the ship by the small, tonguelike rudder is "where the will of the pilot chooses," just as the rider guides the horse via bit and bridle. These analogies bear out the conclusion drawn in 3:2a, that the person who bridles/controls the tongue controls the whole body, just as the rider, who controls bit and bridle, controls the whole horse, and the helmsman, who controls the rudder, directs the whole ship. For this reason James concludes, "If any think that they are religious, and do not bridle their tongue but deceive their heart, their religion is vain" (1:26).

3:5a. So also the tongue is a small member and makes great and wild claims [*auchei*]. James introduces a transitional conclusion ("So also") that sums up the aspect of the discussion that is to be carried forward in what follows in 3:5b–12. In another way, this conclusion also justifies the initial assertion that the person who controls the tongue controls the whole body, because although the tongue is but a small member of the body, it is powerful, so powerful that it can dominate the body and produce disastrous consequences if it is not restrained, controlled, and directed appropriately. In Greek there is a neat alliteration in expressing the "small member" (*micron melos*) that makes "great" (*megala*) and wild claims. Such a description fits the self-promoting boasting (cf. *kauchasthō*, 1:9; see also the sidebar "Boasting in James and Paul" in the discussion on 1:9–10) of the Greco-Roman world, though even there a limit was recognized beyond which the boaster was perceived as a fool (*alazōn*). But the great and wild claims of the tongue could be more than just "hot air," precipitating conflict and calamity. Bold and brash talk can lead to bold and brash action, and it can provoke others to violent reaction. Thus the tongue is a deadly power. The counter side of this is that the person who can control such a power is in charge of the whole body (3:2b).

The Tongue as a Deadly Power (3:5b–12)

3:5b. See how small a fire sets ablaze a great forest! Those who live in areas prone to bushfires, such as southeastern Australia or parts of California, know how a spark caused by a lightning strike, a carelessly used match, or a tossed cigarette can set a forest ablaze such that, under certain conditions, humans with all their resources are powerless to restrain and control it. This was true of parts of Palestine in the dry season.[1] The analogy of 3:6 is based on the common human experience of devastating fires that, from a spark, have the potential to get out of control, wreaking death and destruction. The myth of Prometheus, who stole the secret of fire from the gods and gave it to humans, reflects awareness of the potential usefulness of fire and, at the same time, expresses the foreboding of the destructive force of fire. The universal experience explains the proverbial character of the saying in James.

3:6. And the tongue is a fire. This identification is an application of the proverbial saying of 3:5a. It reflects the tonguelike form of flames that eat up or consume what is burned. The writer of Acts (2:2–3) depicts the coming of the Holy Spirit with the sound of a mighty rushing wind and the appearance of cloven tongues (*glōssai*) as if of fire sitting on each of those gathered. The point of this reference is to suggest that part of the reason for the association of the tongue with fire is visual. We speak about tongues of flame "licking" at whatever is being burned. Once this association has been made, other less visual similarities become evident, particularly the destructive potential of the tongue and of fire and the potential for a spark to produce a conflagration or

1. Having made this observation, I was subsequently reminded in early December 2010 that although the ancient forests of Palestine are no more, the small areas of modern forest are subject to the threat of uncontrollable fires. The fire of December 2010, which started in the Carmel Range, took forty-one lives, with others unaccounted for, destroyed thousands of acres, and threatened the suburbs of Haifa, causing evacuations there.

of a word to spark a war. There is widespread evidence of this association and imagery of the tongue with fire in the Wisdom literature (Pss. 39:1–3; 120:2–4; Prov. 16:27; 26:21; Sir. 28:13–26, esp. v. 22). There is also widespread evidence of the passions being compared to a flame. The expression "enflamed passions" describes the passions out of control, and James knows something of this (1:14–15). James asserts, "And the tongue is a fire."

The image of the tongue as fire naturally relates it to fiery passions, which are inclined to enslave and control a person. In itself, the tongue is a small and seemingly insignificant member of the body. It may be a small fire, but inflamed by passion, it is capable of setting the world ablaze. Paradoxically, the tongue can be inflamed by passion but is also an instrument with power to inflame the passion of the speaker, who can be carried away by his or her own rhetoric, even as the hearers are inflamed by it.

The rest of 3:6 poses problems: **The tongue is the world of unrighteousness set among our members**

Figure 5. Tongues of Fire at Pentecost. This icon from the Greek Catholic Cathedral of Hajdúdorog, Hungary, was painted around 1810 and depicts the descent of the Holy Spirit at Pentecost. The tongue-like appearance of the flames may explain James's description of the tongue as a fire.

[*melesin*], **which pollutes the whole body and sets on fire the cycle of existence and is set on fire by hell.** Scribes and translators of the early versions sought to clarify the text, leading to variants. None of these make much difference, but they do reveal the difficulties recognized in the text from ancient times. The punctuation adopted here is consistent with the most likely reading of the text. The first decision to be made is whether "the world of unrighteousness" (*ho kosmos tēs adikias*) or "the tongue" (*hē glōssa*) is the subject of the verb "set" (*kathistatai*). Grammatically, either is possible, but the tongue was the subject in 3:6a and logically continues to be so here and in 3:8. But how then is "the world of unrighteousness" to be understood? It seems best to translate

119

it as "the unrighteous world," reflecting James's view of the world. The world (*kosmos*) is defined by unrighteousness. This comes close to the Johannine view of the world as the sphere of darkness, which is evil and antithetical to God (John 1:5, 9–10; 3:19–21; 8:12; 9:5, 39; 12:35–36, 46; 1 John 1:5–7; 2:11, 15–17; 2:15–17). The tongue is that organ (member of the body) through which the unrighteous world takes control of the body and contaminates it, pollutes it. Thus the tongue needs to be bridled in order "to keep oneself unspotted by the world" (James 1:27), and "love of the world is enmity with God" (James 4:4; cf. 1 John 2:15: "Do not love the world or the things in the world. The love of the Father is not in those who love the world" [NRSV]).

Jewish purity observance recognized contamination by contact. James uses purity language analogically of spiritual or ethical contamination in a way similar to the language of Jesus concerning the heart in Mark 7:14–23. The power of the tongue affects the whole body. There is nothing to suggest that James uses "body" in Pauline fashion as an image of the community. Rather, the power of the tongue to corrupt the individual and the impact of the tongue on others is an ethical issue dealt with in terms analogically related to ritual purity. Reference to the pollution of the whole body signifies the total corruption of the person. The agent capable of such corruption is the tongue. Nothing in this treatment suggests that James has abandoned the requirements of ritual purity. Rather, it seems, James insists that ritual and spiritual matters are related.

The consequences of the activity of the tongue do not end there. The discussion turns from the imagery of contamination back to the imagery of the tongue as a fire, which sets on fire the "cycle of existence" (*ho trochos tēs geneseōs*). This expression may be derived from the Orphic description of the cycle/wheel of birth and rebirth, which continues as long as the soul remains unsanctified. If so, James has used it without dependence on its original meaning, probably being dependent instead on earlier Jewish use of the expression, in which the Orphic meaning was lost. For James, it has the meaning that the fire of the tongue spreads destructively throughout the cycle of existence, the course of existence (see Dibelius 1976, 196–98). This suggests that the searing destruction goes on and increases throughout life, being fueled by the fires of hell (*geenna*).

James says that the tongue is set on fire by Gehenna, assuming that the fire of Gehenna was a devilish force, a view somewhat in tension with the view that Gehenna is the place of punishment for the wicked. That Satan dwells in Gehenna is explicitly stated in *Apocalypse of Abraham*. Note especially the reference to "be burned by the fire of Azazel's tongue" (*Apoc. Ab.* 31.5). Martin Dibelius (1976, 198–99) notes that Adolf Schlatter and Werner Foerster, on the basis of references in Revelation (1:18; 6:8; 20:13, 14, using *hadēs*), contest the view that Gehenna is the dwelling place of Satan, but he concludes that James 3:6 should not be read on the basis of these references from Revelation

Gehenna

The notion of the fires of hell may have developed from the Hebrew *Gehinnom* (Gk. *geenna*, Eng. "Gehenna"), the Valley (*Ge*) of Hinnom. In earlier times, this valley was the place where the devotees of Baal and Moloch sacrificed their children in fire. The valley later became the rubbish dump for Jerusalem, where corpses and garbage rotted and burned. In rabbinical and early Christian sources, Gehenna becomes the place of punishment for the wicked. In the NT, there are only twelve references to Gehenna, eleven of them in the Gospels and the other one in James 3:6. In the Gospels, all references are sayings attributed to Jesus. Six involve overlaps between Matthew and Mark and can be reduced to the single saying that it is better to lose one part of the body than to be cast whole into Gehenna (Matt. 5:29, 30; 18:9; Mark 9:43, 45, 47); Matt. 10:28 more or less corresponds to Luke 12:25 concerning whom to fear, the one with power to cast a person into Gehenna; Matt. 5:22 says that whoever calls someone a fool is bound for Gehenna; Matt. 23:15 speaks of the Pharisees making a convert twice as much a child of Gehenna as themselves; in Matt. 23:33 Jesus calls the Pharisees a brood of vipers and asks how they will escape Gehenna. All but Matt. 23:15 refer to Gehenna as the destination of the wicked. Matthew 23:15 refers to Gehenna as the source of the wicked: "a child of Gehenna."

(see Jeremias 1964). Both James 3:6 and Matt. 23:15 seem to presuppose the view that Gehenna is a devilish place and the source of evil and destruction. Compare the reference to demonic wisdom in James 3:15.

3:7. For every kind of beast and [*te kai*] bird, reptile and [*te kai*] sea creature [*enaliōn*] can be tamed and has been tamed by humankind. Reference to "every kind" (*pasa physis*) echoes the Gen. 1 creation story with its reference to the various creatures multiplying each after its own "kind" (1:25). The creation story distinguishes land animals from the birds of the air and sea creatures, and land animals are divided into cattle and creeping things, perhaps a reference to reptiles (1:26; cf. 9:2). It is not surprising that this classification enters Jewish sources such as Philo (*Spec.* 4.20 §110–22 §116). However, in Genesis it seems that sea creatures and winged fowl are linked, as are land animals and reptiles. In James, " beast and bird" form a first pair, and "reptile and sea creatures" form a second pair, each pair linked by *te kai*. For this arrangement, James may be depending on a Hellenistic source, as with the examples of the charioteer and the helmsman. Though no appeal is made to the text of Genesis, the main point is consistent with Gen. 1:28, in which God gives humans "dominion over the fish of the sea, the fowl of the air, and every living creature that moves on the land." James, like Genesis, distinguishes humankind from the other kinds of creatures named and interprets the "dominion" of Genesis

Figure 6. *The Garden of Eden with the Fall of Man* (ca. 1615). This collaboration by two Flemish painters shows the wide variety of exotic animals known at this time. Jan Brueghel the Elder painted the landscape and the animals, and Peter Paul Rubens painted the human figures.

in terms of humans having power to tame and control every kind of beast and bird, reptile and sea creature. This conclusion is illustrated by examples already given. First, James shows human control of the horse, which Philo, probably drawing on a Hellenistic source, described as "the most spirited of animals," (*Opif.* 28 §86). Second, the control of a ship in the midst of the savage elements of wind and sea is used as evidence of human mastery.

3:8. **But the tongue no human is able to tame, [it is] an uncontrollable evil** [*akatastaton kakon*]**, full of deadly poison.** The tongue remains the subject of discussion and is mentioned at the beginning of the clause. It is of an altogether different "kind." No human can tame it. The opening "but" contrasts this failure to control the tongue with human mastery over every kind of creature (3:7). Overall mastery is mocked by the failure to control this small member, the tongue. This is but the first point.

James goes further than uncontrollable (cannot be bridled!). The tongue is uncontrollable evil, immoral evil. Or is it "an unstable evil"? The same word (*akatastatos*) is used in 1:8, "the double-minded person is unstable in every way." Perhaps the distinction is not great, since instability is not controlled, and the instability of the double-minded person is certainly not good but rather is an evil.

The final image, "full of deadly poison," has an illuminating resonance with Ps. 140:3 (139:4 LXX): "They have sharpened their tongues like a serpent;

adders' poison is under their lips." Probably the image of the poison tongue is drawn from an analogy with the forked tongue of the snake, and that might have been suggestive of the devil (Rev. 12:9). But James has refrained from making any specific reference to the devil, attributing temptation/testing neither to God nor to the devil. For James, temptation is rooted in desire (*epithymia*, 1:13–15).

Although James declares that no one can tame the tongue, he also asserts, "If anyone claims to be religious and does not bridle the tongue . . . , this person's religion is vain" (1:26). Note also the tension in the first two statements of 3:2. It may be that we need to allow James some rhetorical license when it comes to the uncontrollable evil power of the tongue. This emphasis makes clear the serious and deadly power of the tongue. Yet, the whole treatment of the tongue does not suggest that all effort to control the tongue is pointless. Rather, the whole point of the discourse is to exhort the readers to control the tongue in the face of evil and for the sake of good. This becomes clearer at the end of 3:10. Of course, for everyone, the tongue continues to threaten to destabilize and destroy. Mastery is never such as to justify complacency.

3:9. With it we bless the Lord and Father and with it we curse the humans, who have been made in the likeness of God. The unstable, unruly, and self-contradictory use of the tongue is here identified. It reflects badly on us because we are responsible for the use of the tongue, a point made in the examples highlighting that the horse has a rider and the ship a pilot who are responsible for their control. Similarly, we are responsible for the control of the tongue. Yet, with the tongue we bless and we curse. The absolute scandal of this is exposed when we curse those who are made in the likeness of God, whom we bless. The critique of such self-contradictory use of the tongue is common in Jewish sources (e.g., Ps. 62:4; Sir. 5:10–6:2).

Characteristic of Jewish sources is the notion and practice of blessing/praising God. James uses the LXX language of blessing God: "With [the tongue] we bless [*eulogoumen*] the Lord and Father." "Blessed art thou, O Lord, King of the Universe, who brings forth bread from the earth." The opening "Blessed art thou" in addressing God is common in the prayers known as the Eighteen Benedictions and finds a precedent in 1 Chron. 29:10: "Blessed are you, O Lord, the God of our ancestor Israel, forever and ever." While this is a partial parallel, the particular wording of James, "we bless the Lord and Father," has no exact parallel. Though lacking the opening blessing, "You, O Lord, are our father" (Isa. 63:16) comes close. Probably the lack of an exact parallel led to the change of "Lord" (*kyrios*) to "God" (*theos*) in some texts. Given the rich evidence of blessing the Lord and Father in the Jewish sources, there is no suspicion of anything inappropriate here.

The problem is that with the same tongue we curse humans, made in the likeness (*kath' homoiōsin*) of God. In the creation story of Gen. 1, God says, "Let us make humans in our image [*kat' eikona*] and in [our] likeness [*kath'*

123

homoiōsin]" (Gen. 1:26 LXX). With the reproduction of this precise Greek idiom, there can be little doubt that James is drawing directly on this creation tradition to emphasize the anomaly of blessing God and cursing humans. The basis of this critique provides a motive for joining the two great commandments as we find them in the Jesus tradition (Mark 12:28–31; on this, see the discussion on James 2:8). Does this not mean that all humans, made in the likeness of God, are in some significant sense children of God and thus brothers and sisters? This is implicit in the anomaly of blessing God and cursing humans, who are made in the likeness of God.

3:10. Blessing and curse proceed out of the same mouth. My brothers [and sisters], these things should not be so. The argument now turns to show that blessing and cursing from the same mouth (from the same tongue!) is totally inappropriate. Given that blessing is approved, this argument excludes all cursing. Such an exclusion of cursing apparently goes back to the teaching of Jesus: "Bless those who curse you" (Luke 6:28). And Paul writes, "Bless those who persecute you; bless and do not curse them" (Rom. 12:14 NRSV). Paul does not attribute the saying to Jesus, but his use appears to be both a quotation and explication. Blessing and cursing should not proceed out of the same mouth. Yet this does happen; we bless and we curse with the same double, unstable tongue. It is as if James here uses the duality of the tongue, in its instability, as an alternative image for the inclination (*yēṣer*) toward good or evil or for the duality of desire (*epithymia*; see the discussion on 1:14–15). While there is good and appropriate desire, in the treatment by Paul and James the emphasis has fallen on evil desire because of the inclination for this to be dominant. That is true also of the unrestrained/unbridled tongue.

3:11. Surely not [*mēti*] from the same spring gush out [*bryei*] fresh and salty water, do they? James turns to nature to provide two examples that by analogy show the incompatibility of blessing and cursing coming from the same mouth. The negative question introduced by *mēti* indicates that a negative response is expected: "No! They do not." Fresh (sweet) and salty (bitter) water do not gush from a single spring opening, and it should follow, from the example of nature, that blessing and cursing do not proceed from the same mouth. The mouth, rather than the tongue, fits this example because the analogy is with the mouth of the spring through which the water gushes. Logically, it could mean that there should be cursing mouths and blessing mouths. What is anomalous is a mouth that both blesses and curses. This is true of the logic of the following example as well. Yet that is clearly not what James means. The initial treatment in 3:9 properly excludes cursing, and the tradition of blessing is so firmly entrenched theologically and ethically that it is enough to show the incompatibility of blessing and cursing to reinforce the rejection of cursing.

3:12. It is not possible [*mē dynatai*], is it, my brothers [and sisters], for a fig tree to bear olives or a grapevine to bear figs? Neither can salt water make fresh. The discussion of the tongue opened with the address "my brothers [and sisters]," softening the initial directive "do not." The discussion now closes with an inclusio, a closing address to the readers, which also signals the use of Jesus tradition. James uses the tradition not so much as a source but rather as a resource for his own rhetorical purpose, to persuade the readers. In Matt. 7:15–20//Luke 6:43–44 Jesus teaches that a person is known by his or her works, because a good person produces good works. To make the point, he asks, "Surely grapes are not [*mē*] gathered from thorns or figs from thistles, are they?" Thus the bad (thorns and thistles) cannot produce good (grapes and figs; see also Matt. 12:33//Luke 6:43–44). James's example concerns only the singularity of the fruit from each tree or vine, excluding the fruit of both blessing and cursing from the same tree (mouth). The use of fig and olive trees with grapevine in this example leads Martin Dibelius (1976, 204–5) to see the influence of Stoic tradition, but in the eastern Mediterranean, these are the three common trees/vines, and this explains the Stoic use also.

The question in James 3:12, like the question of 3:11, has an implied answer. Each question is in negative form introduced by *mē*, which implies a negative answer: "No! A fig tree cannot bear olives, nor can a grapevine bear figs." Now the implied answer to the question of 3:11 is actually given: "Neither can salt water make fresh" (3:12b). In the normal course, far from producing fresh water, the presence of salt water contaminates the fresh. The final two metaphors remain mixed in a way that runs through much of the discussion of the tongue. On the one hand, it seems that blessing is good but cursing is evil, and on the other, it is just that they do not belong together. Figs, olives, and grapes are good; it is simply that they come from different plants. By contrast, the fresh water is good, and the salty water is bad and can contaminate the fresh. On the whole, the particular examples in the Jesus tradition seem more suitable than those used by James, because they make the point that the bad does not produce the good, nor does the good produce the bad. James has mixed a variety of good fruits, which are not produced by one tree, but one tree produces one kind of fruit. Though less clear, the use of the analogy makes its point.

Theological Issues

James gives significant attention to the need to develop speech ethics. Such is his view of the power of words that he would hardly agree with the sentiment "Sticks and stones may break my bones, but names will never hurt me." Today we have another saying: "Mud sticks." When something is said often enough, people begin to believe what is said, especially if it is something bad. Speech that misrepresents usually is self-serving and ultimately destructive. So we can speak of the power of words, whether the words are faithful and true or false

125

and deceiving. Words, spoken or written, are potentially powerful. Because the written word may be more carefully planned and expressed, there is another saying: "The pen is mightier than the sword." But written or spoken, when carefully planned, choosing words for their persuasive effect, we speak of rhetoric, the art of persuasion. It may seem surprising, but it is precisely because James lays such weight on the power of words that his first word about speech is "Be swift to hear, slow to speak" (1:19). The call to hold back speech has two sources. First, because speech has such power for good or evil, there is need for care to ensure that speech is faithful and true and not a misrepresentation to manipulate the hearer and that it is constructive and not destructive in its effect. Second, because of "desire" (*epithymia*), speech tends to be self-serving, and the tongue needs to be controlled/bridled (1:26). Speech needs to arise from the reception of the implanted word (1:21). Thus the call to be swift to hear turns the hearer from self-orientation to the other, to God and neighbor.

The critique of the tongue in 3:1–12 recognizes its destructive potential. The power of the tongue can be turned to good effect by God's gracious gift of the wisdom from above (1:5–8; 3:13–18). Rhetoric and wisdom from on high need one another if speech is to be ethical and constructive (see Painter 2005b, 235–73).

James 3:13–4:10

God and the World

Introductory Matters

In fifteen verses, James uses twelve words not found elsewhere in the NT:

> One is not found in the pre-Christian Greek corpus or in the Hebrew books translated in the LXX: "devilish" (*daimoniōdēs*, 3:15).
> Another is not found in the LXX: "sorrow" (*katēpheia*, 4:9).
> Two are not used in the Hebrew books translated in the LXX: "open to reason" (*eupeithēs*, 3:17) and "be turned to" (*metatrepō*, 4:9).
> Seven are found in the NT only in James: "understanding" (*epistēmōn*, 3:13), "bitter" (*pikros*, 3:14; cf. 3:11), "without prejudice" (*adiakritos*, 3:17), "friendship" (*philia*, 4:4), "vainly" (*kenōs*, 4:5), "to make to dwell" (*katoikizō*, 4:5), and "lament" (*talaipōreō*, 4:9; cf. *talaipōria* in 5:1; Rom. 3:16 [from Isa. 59:7], the only occurrences in the NT).

James also shares the use of "peaceful" (*eirēnikos*, 3:17) with Heb. 12:3. Of special interest is the use of *daimoniōdēs*, which is found only in the books composed in Greek in the LXX. This confirms the late appearance of this word, reflecting a changing worldview. James, though emerging from a Jewish tradition, was open to the Greek moral, rhetorical, and philosophical influences that are reflected in this language, especially in *eupeithēs*, *epistēmōn*, *adiakritos*, *philia*.

At first glance, there seems to be little connection between 3:13–18 and the earlier part of chapter 3. But the discussion of the role of teachers in

3:1 is closely connected to the wise and wisdom in 3:13–18. It is natural that the discussion of rhetoric (the tongue) should lead into wisdom, the proper substance of rhetoric. It is clear that, for a teacher in the church, sheer rhetoric is not enough because the uncontrolled tongue runs away into excess and needs to be controlled by the wise person in the interests of goodness and truth.

There are also significant connections between the two paragraphs of this section (3:13–18 and 4:1–10). Each one focuses on human relationships with God and with the world under two significant symbols, wisdom and friendship. Both of these motifs are central to the culture of the Hellenistic world. In James, it is a question of the wisdom of God versus earthly wisdom, friendship with God versus friendship with the world. The association of these two sections implies the understanding of earthly wisdom as the wisdom of the world. Earthly wisdom, in this sense, does not take God into account, and so the world is constituted as a godless system. Thus God's earth becomes the godless world.

Tracing the Train of Thought

Wisdom from Above and Wisdom of the Earth (3:13–18)

From the terrors of the unbridled tongue, James turns to the wisdom and understanding that underlie the control of the tongue. Each of the two verses of 3:13–14 follows a similar pattern. The first is a question followed by a command. The second is a conditional clause followed by a negative command. The first is an instruction to the person who is wise, expressed in a third-person singular exhortatory mode. The second is a negative command addressed to those who fulfill the conditional clause describing an antithesis to the meekness of wisdom.

3:13. Who is wise and understanding among you? The question is rhetorical. It is designed to draw the readers in, to involve them, especially those who consider themselves to be wise. The question may be aimed at those who are recognized as the wise, the teachers of the communities to which James's letter

---

Wisdom and Understanding

While *sophia* ("wisdom") is fairly common in the NT, being used over fifty times in twelve of its twenty-seven books, James 3:13 has the only use of *epistēmōn*, a word common in Greek from classical times. From this lexical group the English word *epistemology* is formed to denote the theory of knowledge. The use of *epistēmōn* to explicate the nature of wisdom may be based on the association of *sophos* and *epistēmōn* in the LXX to describe wise and understanding people (Deut. 1:13, 15; 4:6). For the use of *epistēmōn* in the LXX, see also Isa. 5:21; Dan. 1:4; 5:11; 6:4 (6:3 ET); 1 Esd. 8:43, 46 (8:44, 47 ET); Sir. prologue 4; 10:25; 21:15; 40:29; 47:12.

---

was sent. Having addressed them, James sets about establishing the nature of wisdom. First, wisdom and understanding are inseparably linked.

The usage suggests that understanding is a defining characteristic of wisdom and implies both theoretical and practical competence, the ability to do what is known. This is borne out by what follows. **Let that person show the works of his or her good manner of life in the meekness of wisdom.** James exhorts the person considered or claiming to be wise and understanding to show the evidence of good works by an appropriate (*kalos*) way of life. This gives a refreshingly new sense to "the good life." The manner of life is not merely morally correct but is also appealingly attractive in its transparent goodness.

Such is not the display of a braggart, referred to in 4:16. The *alazōn*, the arrogant boaster, makes inflated claims about status and achievement (see the sidebar "Boasting in James and Paul" in the discussion on 1:9–10). The wise person quietly and modestly allows a good way of life to speak for itself. This modesty or meekness is a feature of wisdom and a key virtue for James. It is foundational for his depiction of the wise and understanding person. At this point, James's conception of virtue and of wisdom and understanding is at odds with the values of the Greco-Roman world. Against this, in Israel, Moses was reputed to be "the meekest man in all the earth" (Num. 12:3). Jesus is likewise depicted as "meek and humble of heart" (Matt. 11:29; 21:5; 2 Cor. 10:1). The meek are also the subject of Jesus's blessing: "Blessed are the meek, for they shall inherit the earth" (Matt. 5:5). It is not surprising that meekness and humility are at the top of James's depiction of the virtues of wisdom and knowledge and are key marks of the wise person. In the construction "the meekness of wisdom," the genitive case of *sophias* ("of wisdom") could be objective or subjective, indicating either meekness's wisdom or wisdom's meekness. As the question is "Who is the wise person?" meekness is a characteristic of wisdom. But meekness does not exhaust what James means by "good manner of life." No doubt this includes works of compassion and

---

Kalos

This use of *kalos* is reminiscent of its use to translate *ṭôb* in the LXX of Gen. 1:4, 10, 12, 18, 21, 25, 31. As the narrator informs the reader, God saw that what God had created was "good." This language brings out an aesthetic perspective of goodness, which includes a sense of beauty and completeness, of what is fitting and appropriate. Note also Ps. 134:3 in the LXX (135:3 ET): "Praise the Lord, because the Lord is good [*agathos*, translating Heb. *ṭôb*]; sing to his name, for it is lovely/beautiful [*kalos*, translating Heb. *nāʿîm*]." The parallelism of the verse is clear, but the two Greek words—each of which sometimes translates *ṭôb*—here translate different words and bring out complementary shades of meaning.

---

mercy befitting the royal law according to the Scripture (2:8)—not only words but also actions, not only faith but also works (1:22–25; 2:14–26).

3:14. But if you have bitter jealousy and selfish rivalry in your heart . . . James returns to direct address in 3:14 ("But, if you . . ."). Here, as in 3:13, James sets out the evidence found in a way of life. In this case, the evidence falsifies the claim to be wise or displays an altogether different kind of wisdom (see 3:15). Bitter jealousy and rivalry (cf. the catalogs of vices in 2 Cor. 12:20; Gal. 5:20) expose the lie of those who claim to be wise. It is the antithesis of wisdom's meekness. Just as meekness is an attitude of the heart that is manifest in actions, so bitter jealousy and rivalry arise in the heart and can be hidden there. Thus the conditional clause addresses those who may recognize the presence of these traits in their hearts. This might identify leadership rivalry.

Those who harbor these aspirations are exhorted, **Do not boast and lie.** Two present imperative verbs are introduced by *mē* to express a negative double command: *mē katakauchasthe kai pseudesthe* ("Do not boast and [do not] lie"). The two verbs suggest two acts, but the single use of *mē* qualifying both verbs might imply the expression of one command in two forms, a case of hendiadys. The boast is actually a lie **suppressing the truth.** Self-assertive and divisive leadership that claimed to be wise could be impressive, demeaning wisdom characterized by meekness. Elsewhere James accuses, "Now you boast in your pride/arrogance [*alazoneia*]; all such boasting is evil" (4:16). Such arrogant boasting reveals heart attitudes that constitute the wisdom of the world in opposition to the wisdom of God. The wisdom of the world is the wisdom of self-interest. The world is constituted by the conflicting struggles between individual and sectional self-interests, overriding the well-being of the other and of others. The exposition of this situation continues through 3:15–16 and into 4:1–4. Note also the ungodly and worldly boasting criticized in 4:13–17. It constitutes practical atheism, living as if there is no God.

3:15. This is not the wisdom coming down from above [*anōthen*]. "This" bitter jealousy and selfish rivalry referred to in 3:14 are taken up again in 3:16. Although it is not explicitly called "wisdom," such is implied. The three adjectives used in 3:15b are feminine and can only qualify *sophia* from 3:15a. James emphatically denies that it is the wisdom coming down from above, though it can be seen as wisdom from a certain perspective and is commonly so called. Here the sense of *anōthen* is "from God," as it is in 1:17: "Every generous act of giving and every perfect gift is from above [*anōthen*], coming down [*katabainon*] from the Father of lights." Of the thirteen uses of *anōthen* in the NT, five are in John, three in James, and one in Matthew, Mark, Luke, Acts, and Galations. In the three references in James and four of those in John, *anōthen* is a metaphor for "from God." The description of the wisdom coming down from above (*hē sophia anōthen katerchomenē*) linguistically resonates with this description of the action of the generous gift-giving God. The wisdom coming down from above is an expression of God's generous giving and is a perfect gift, which, if lacked by anyone, is given generously by God to everyone who asks in genuine faith (1:5–6; see the discussion on 1:5, 17–18; on the divine wisdom from above, see Sir. 24:1–12; Wis. 9:4). Wisdom as a gift from God is a dominant motif of the wisdom tradition (Prov. 2:6; 8:22–31; Sir. 1:1–4; 24:1–12; Wis. 7:24–27; 9:4, 6, 9–18) and is associated with Solomon and his request for wisdom from God (1 Kings 3:5–12, 28; Wis. 8:21–9:18).

The stark contrast of the alien wisdom of 3:15b with the wisdom of God of 3:15a is signaled by the use of the strong adversative *alla* at the beginning of 3:15b: **but [*alla*] is earthly [*epigeios*], unspiritual [*psychikē*], demonic [*daimoniōdēs*] [wisdom].** This may appear to support an ascending order of seriousness or opposition to the wisdom of God in the three terms *epigeios*, *psychikē*, *daimoniōdēs* by which this other wisdom is characterized. The first term can be viewed as neutral, but there is no doubt about the negative evaluation of the third, and this might suggest that the middle term is ambiguous. However, this view does not give sufficient weight to the adversative *alla* ("but") that introduces all three. The negative weight of *alla* implies that the three following adjectives define the alien wisdom as opposed to the wisdom from above, from God.

Paradoxically, James first describes this false wisdom as "earthly." The earth, like the heavens, is the creation of God. But the heavens are also contrasted with the earth: "For as the heavens are higher than the earth, so are my ways higher than your ways" (Isa. 55:9 NRSV). In James 3:15 the wisdom of heaven/ above/God is contrasted with "earthly" wisdom. This wisdom is not from above but rather from below. Thus the first of three images contrasts the false earthly wisdom (from below) with the wisdom "from above." If "heavenly" is a circumlocution for "God," earthly is also a potential image of something else, as becomes clear with the use of the third defining adjective. But how does what is earthly, God's creation, become sinister?

Wisdom of God and Earthly Wisdom

James makes a stark contrast between the wisdom of God and earthly wisdom. This is necessary because of the collision of two value systems. One arises from creation theology rooted in Gen. 1 (Gen. 1:4, 10, 12, 18, 21, 25, 31) and the Psalms (Pss. 100:5; 106:1; 107:1; 118:1–4; 136:1) and finds expression in the teaching of Jesus (Matt. 6:25–34// Luke 12:22–31). The other is the dominant value system of the Roman Empire. James uses a rhetorical strategy to set off these two value systems against each other, claiming theological support for the wisdom of God. Paul uses a similar strategy in 1 Cor. 1:18–25, except that he sets the wisdom of God against the wisdom of the "world" (kosmos). First, Paul argues that even if the cross is an example of the foolishness of God, the foolishness of God is wiser than human (wisdom), and the weakness of God is stronger than human (strength). Second, using its wisdom (the wisdom of the world), the world failed to know God, and in fact, Christ is the wisdom of God and the power of God. From this argument, it becomes clear that Paul adopts the rhetoric of the world to the effect that the cross is an example of the foolishness and weakness of God, but he overturns the implied conclusion and instead states his own view: Christ is the wisdom of God and the power of God.

Although the earth remains the creation of God and is an expression of God's generous giving and perfect gifts, because of desire (epithymia, see 1:14–15), the earth can seduce humans into an obsession to control and possess it. Thus Jesus asks, "What will it profit a person to gain the whole world but lose his or her life [psychē]?" (Mark 8:36 par.). The wisdom that is earthly calculates strategies to bring about possession and control of the world for selfish ends. It is driven by desire. Paul links desire with the tenth commandment: "You shall not covet/desire" (Rom. 7:7–10). The comprehensive coverage of this commandment is expressed in terms of the neighbor's "household" and is summed up by the concluding clause, "or anything that is your neighbor's" (see Exod. 20:17). Paul takes this further, totally delimiting the commandment by using the language of the LXX (ouk epithymēseis, "You shall not covet"). This verb and the word used for "desire" (epithymia) are cognate terms. Covetousness, rooted in desire, is sinful desire. Because desire tends to be overreaching, it tends to be sinful desire. Both James and Paul know this, and for this reason, the earth tends to be the object of sinful desire. Earthly wisdom, or worldly wisdom, is wisdom in the service of selfish desire. James 4:1–10 shifts from the language of the earth to the language of the world, which is also common to Paul and John.

Selfish motives often masquerade as concern for the good of others, but this veneer is often thin, barely masking the will to power and possession.

Earthly wisdom is driven by and in the service of desire. As Rudolf Bultmann (1958, 39–43) has said, "By means of science men try to get possession of the world, but in fact the world gets possession of men." Such is a description of earthly wisdom.

This alien wisdom, or wisdom falsely so called, is "unspiritual" (*psychikē*). It is a puzzle that James uses a term known from its gnostic connotations (see Dibelius 1976, 211–12), where body and soul (*psychē*) belong to the material world and are incompatible with spirit. In the NT, the adjective *psychikos* is used elsewhere only in 1 Cor. 2:14; 15:44, 46; Jude 19. Of these, 1 Cor. 2:14 and Jude 19 are directly relevant. In the former text, Paul says that the "*psychikos* person is unable to receive the things of the Spirit of God; for they are foolishness to that person, and he or she is unable to understand [*gnōnai*], because they are spiritually [*pneumatikōs*] discerned." Jude reminds the reader of the apostolic warning of the coming messengers of ungodliness who would cause divisions and describes them as "*psychikoi*, not having spirit."

If we exclude the uses of *psychikos* in 1 Cor. 15 (which universalizes the order of first *psychikos* and then [if ever] the *pneumatikos*) from this small sample of references in the NT, the two other references (apart from James) denote an earthy person who cannot receive the spirit or does not have spirit. James 3:15 is somewhat different from all of these references. The adjective does not describe people but, like the other two adjectives in this verse, is feminine (*psychikē*) and describes the feminine noun *sophia* ("wisdom"). The contrast with the wisdom from above implies a derogatory meaning, but there

Demeaning and Devaluing the Earth

Naming false wisdom identifies it as earthly or worldly wisdom. This wisdom is directed toward possession, control, and exploitation of the world for selfish benefit. It is pervasive, and in this sense it is the wisdom of the world. But it is also deceptive because possession, control, and exploitation do not have the desired consequences. They do not guarantee happiness. Indeed, unbridled greed has led to a devaluation of the earth by Christians along with the rest of humanity down through the ages. This has helped to create conditions that have led to the ecological crisis of our time. Unbridled desire leads to obsession for the good things of the earth/world and unscrupulous determination to possess them, but this robs the world of its true meaning and value. The earth is not adequately viewed or valued when treated as a store of resources to be exploited by humans. Such exploitation results in the destruction of habitats that support life through land clearing and the pollution of land, air, sea, rivers, lakes, and even the rain. This demeaning (stripping the earth of its deeper and richer meaning) and devaluing (denying the intrinsic value of the earth and its constituent parts) now threaten all life as we know it.

is little in James to support the translation "unspiritual wisdom." That has a suitably derogatory sense, but James does not otherwise use "spiritual" language. The linking of wisdom with the spirit in the Wisdom literature (Job 32:7–8; Wis. 1:5–7; 7:7, 22–25; see also Gen. 41:38–39) opens up a possibility, but one that is not confirmed in James.

James uses "spirit" (*pneuma*) only twice (2:26; 4:5). In 2:26 "spirit" has the sense of "breath": "the body apart from spirit [*chōris pneumatos*] is dead." All living animals, including humans, have "the breath [*pneuma*] of life" ("everything that has the breath of life," Gen. 1:30). James makes no attempt to draw an analogy to the role of God' Spirit in life in the world. The reference in 4:5 is a little more promising. Referring to those who choose friendship with the world and enmity with God, James asks, "Do you suppose that Scripture speaks vainly, 'He [God] yearns jealously over the spirit he has made to dwell in/among us'?" Even here it is not clear that this is a reference to the Spirit of God rather than the *pneuma* referred to in 2:26. James provides little if any support for the view that the community is enlightened and empowered in its mission by the Spirit of God. Despite the failure to find corroborating evidence for the translation "unspiritual," it is the best we can do; this meaning may have been taken over with the choice of the word and been understood in this way by the readers.

The third adjective is unambiguously derogatory, describing wisdom as "demonic" (*daimoniōdēs*). Here we have one of three references in James to a power of evil opposed to the power of God, demonic wisdom opposed to the wisdom of God. According to 3:6, the destructive fire of the tongue is set on fire by hell (*geenna*). But this hellish source does not remove the responsibility to bridle the tongue. That is consistent with 4:7, where James exhorts, "Therefore submit to God; resist the devil, and he will flee from you." Far from making the devil a threat, this exhortation asserts the responsibility to resist and assures that the devil will flee from those who do so. Further, when dealing with temptation, James denies that God is the source of temptation and testing, and there is no suggestion that the devil is tempter or tester, as in Job 1–2, and in the narratives of the temptations of Jesus (Mark 1:12–13; Matt. 4:1–11; Luke 4:1–13). Rather, James 1:12–15 asserts that temptation is rooted in human desire (*epithymia*).

3:16. For where there is jealousy and selfish rivalry, there is chaos [*akatastasia*] and every vile practice. The three adjectives describing alien wisdom were laid out in 3:15. Now the evidence from 3:14 is repeated and expanded. The repetition of "jealousy" and "selfish rivalry" suggests that this wisdom is found among the leaders/teachers of the community. Whereas the wisdom from above produces unity and harmony (3:17; cf. Acts 1:12–14; 2:1), the alien wisdom produces jealousy and selfish rivalry (3:14, 16). Such a situation is unstable, chaotic. The term used here (*akatastasia*) is also used of the double-minded person (*dipsychos*), who is *akatastatos* in all ways (1:8). Such unruly disorder is encouraged by selfish rivalry, and, James adds for good measure, so is every other foul (*phaulos*) practice. The term *phaulos* expresses revulsion at such evil. This word is used only six times in the NT (John 3:20; 5:29; Rom. 9:11; 2 Cor. 5:10; Titus 2:8; James 3:16), much less than *kakos* and its cognates.

3:17. But the wisdom from above is first pure, then peaceful, considerate, open to reason, full of mercy and the fruits [*karpōn*] of goodness, without prejudice/favoritism, without hypocrisy. The characterization of the wisdom of God sounds very much like Paul's catalog of the fruit (*karpos*) of the Spirit (Gal. 5:22–23). James twice refers to the fruit associated with wisdom—first the fruits of goodness and then, in 3:18, the fruit of righteousness. We have already noted the association of wisdom with the spirit in the Wisdom literature, and there is an inclination to relate wisdom in James to the activity of the spirit. But what Paul attributes to the activity of the Spirit, James attributes to God's gracious gift of wisdom, which is first "pure" (*hagnē*). "Pure" is a ritual term, and James makes explicit that it is first. See also 1:27, which affirms that "pure [*kathara*] and undefiled [*amiantos*] religion" involves not only ethical commitments to the poor and needy but also remaining "unspotted [*aspilon*] by the world." After "pure," it is "peaceful" and so forth. This suggests that "pure" stands out from the rest, which might not be in any particular order of precedence. All these virtues are crucial for harmonious community relationships, nurturing and building up the various members without favoritism, and with concern for the weak and fragile, repudiating self-interest hiding under the false pretense of concern for others. Yet that "peaceful" comes immediately after "pure" and is strongly emphasized in 3:18 suggests that in the context of the competitive self-seeking leadership under critique, a way that makes for peace is a priority.

3:18. For the fruit of righteousness [*dikaiosynēs*] is sown in peace by those who make peace. The introduction of a new major category, "righteousness," suggests that this might have been a floating saying. If so, the references to fruit and peace connect 3:17 and 3:18, and peace links 3:18 to 4:1–2, with the problems of war, fighting, and murder building a bridge between these two related paragraphs (3:13–18 and 4:1–10). Given the imagery used, what is the fruit "of righteousness" (*dikaiosynēs*) that is sown? If *dikaiosynēs* is an objective genitive, then righteousness is the fruit that is sown in peace. That is to do justly, to act without favoritism but with fairness. A broader sense of righteousness, found in Deutero-Isaiah, also involves acting mercifully. This is characteristic of the wisdom from above (see also James 3:13). But it seems strange to speak of the fruit of righteousness being sown in peace when a more natural word picture would be to speak of the seed of righteousness being sown and bearing the fruit of peace. If a subjective genitive is read, it may be that peace is the fruit of righteousness that is sown in peace by those who make peace. I favor this reading, which is even more emphatic in its stress on peace. It makes excellent sense at the end of this paragraph, indeed at the end of this chapter, dealing with assertive and self-seeking leaders and the division and conflict that they bring to the community. It is also relevant to the subject of wars and fighting about to be introduced in the next verse (4:1). That righteousness bears the fruit of peace, and is in some way the source of peace, finds an echo in Paul: "Therefore, having been justified [in some sense "made righteous"] out of [*ek*] faith, we have [less likely, "let us have"] peace with God" (Rom. 5:1). Both Paul and James see peace as arising out of righteousness. In this sense, peace (Heb. *šālôm*) is not simply the cessation of fighting due to a victory or a truce; rather, it is the establishment of righteousness between those who are consequently at peace. Perhaps this is why genuine peace is so elusive in our world, where the common approach is to suppress opposition rather than deal with root causes of conflicts in what are often unjust and exploitative situations.

Friendship with the World Is Enmity with God (4:1–10)

The passions and the world (4:1–3). At first glance, 4:1 seems to introduce a totally new subject, wars and fighting. It soon becomes clear that these images are used to refer not to violent conflicts between nations but rather to community conflicts and the conflict of warring passions within individuals. The explicit reintroduction of the motif "desire/covet" (*epithymeō*) to elaborate "passion" (*hēdonē*) and as an alternative term for "covet" (*zēloō*) lays a basis for understanding "the world" not as creation but instead as a realm opposed to God, confirming the negative reading of "earthly" as an adjective describing the alien wisdom in 3:15.

The discussion of conflicts within the community—begun in 3:1 with reference to teachers and the failure to control the tongue and continued in 3:13 with reference to the divisive and destructive nature of earthly wisdom—now (4:1) turns explicitly to the cause of conflicts within the community.

4:1. From whence come wars and fighting among you? Chapter 4 opens with two questions (see the sidebar "Rhetorical Questions" in the discussion on 2:4), the second of which suggests an answer to the first. The first question is radically modified by the final two words, "among you" (*en hymin*). This is not a theory about the origin of war. It may well be relevant to this issue, but it makes no such claim. Rather, it is about the serious conflicts within the communities to which James is written. Without the second question, the first might express incredulity or despair. How can these things happen among those who are "brothers [and sisters]"? James has not used this form of address since 3:10, 12 and will not do so again until 4:11. But James has no illusions about those he addresses in such intimate terms. "Blessing and curse proceed out of the same mouth. My brothers [and sisters], these things should not be so" (3:10). But it is so! The shocking fact has a shocking cause. **"Is it not because of your passions?"** Athough the word translated "passions" is the genitive plural of *hēdonē*, which commonly means "pleasure," here it is used in the sense of passions, desires, the equivalent of covetousness (*epithymia*). In the tenth commandment, the LXX renders the Hebrew words underlying "You shall not covet" as *ouk epithymēseis*, using the second-person singular future as an imperative of the cognate verb *epithymeō* (cf. Paul's use of *ouk epithymēseis* in Rom. 7:7). This same verb is used in the second-person plural at the beginning of 4:2, which interprets *hēdonōn* by using *epithymeite*. Clearly, pleasure is not the root of evil, but desire is (see 1:14–15). James here links this use of *hēdonōn* with desire (4:2), to which James elsewhere (1:14–15) attributes a negative and destructive role. The effects that James attributes to *hēdonōn* are attributed to *epithymia* by Plato (*Phaed.* 66c), Cicero (*Fin.* 1.44), and Philo (*Decal.* 28 §§151–53; see Dibelius 1976, 215–16, including n41). In these sources, all ills, especially wars and murders, are attributed to *epithymia*. Given the evidence of this widely held view, James was well justified in expecting an affirmative answer to the question posed in response to the initial question "Is it not from your passions?" The question, introduced by the negative *ouk*, implies an affirmative answer (see the sidebar "Rhetorical Questions" in the discussion on 2:4).

The initial question concerns the origin of wars and fightings "among you." The second question asks, "Is it not from your passions, **which are at war among your members?**" The first question refers to external conflicts between people (*en hymin*), while the second one identifies an internal conflict within people (*en tois melesin hymōn*). The latter resonates with Paul in Romans: "But I see an alien law in my members making war with the law of my mind, taking me captive by the law of sin that is in my members [*en tois melesin mou*]" (Rom. 7:23). The parallel makes clear that the reference is to a conflict experienced within divided physical members of the human body. Disorder in the community is rooted in the conflicted physical reality of individuals in the community. What James calls "your passions," Paul names "the law of sin." There is sufficient overlap between Paul and James in this area to suppose that each draws from a common tradition, although, given the discussion in James 2:14–26, it is possible that James was aware of the Pauline treatment of the role of *epithymia* and here gives his own view on the subject. Because in both parts of James 4:1 "you" is plural ("among you . . . among your members"), the theme of the divided and conflicted self is clearer and more dramatically stated in Paul than in James, though James addresses his readers as *dipsychoi* in 4:8 (see also 1:8). That Paul speaks in the first person of this dilemma is also impressive, while James speaks critically of his readers in a way suggesting that he is included in this dilemma. James's use of the second-person plural in both parts of 4:1 raises the question whether verse 1b relates to conflicted individuals or conflicts between individuals as in verse 1a. The resonance with the language of Paul suggests that "among your members" refers to the different parts of the body (see the use of *melos* in 1 Cor. 12:12, 14–21). A symbolic interpretation of members as the diversity of leaders in the community has some support in 1 Cor. 12:27–31. On this reading, the wars and fighting are an expression of the conflicting passions, desires, and ambitions of the various leaders, continuing the discussion of 3:13–18. But reference to a collection of leaders who were individually torn by conflicting passions and desires makes better sense of the continuing plural address of "in your members" in 4:1b. This reading has a strong connection with Rom. 7, using the same language in the same way. Perhaps the ambiguity in James allows for both readings, given the internal conflicts of the *dipsychoi* and the internal community conflicts noted in 4:1a.

4:2. **You desire** [*epithymeite*], **and you do not have.** These words describe precisely what the tenth commandment prohibited. "You shall not covet [*ouk epithymēseis*] your neighbor's house . . . or anything that is your neighbor's" (Exod. 20:17). Desiring what you do not have is to desire what belongs to another, the neighbor. Here, as elsewhere, James sees violent action already present in desire. Thus, using second-person plural verbs—**you murder, and you covet** [*zēloute*], **and you are not able to obtain; you fight and wage war**—James has piled up a series of overlapping terms to amplify the meaning of this underlying cause of human misery: "your passions" (*hēdonai*, 4:1, 3), "you desire" (*epithymeite*, 4:2), "you covet" (*zēloute*, 4:2). The verb *zēloō* can also mean "to be zealous." Here the context shows that it has the meaning "to covet," since it amplifies "you desire" (*epithymeite*) used earlier in 4:2. In spite of this desire, they fail to obtain what they covet. This passion, if unbridled, has the power to overwhelm a person with destructive consequences all around. The following order of murder, then covet, then fail to obtain is puzzling. It would be more logical if "you murder" came at the end of that sequence. Frustrated desire can lead to murder (see the story of David and Bathsheba and the murder of her husband, Uriah the Hittite [2 Sam. 11]). Such desire is all-consuming and unscrupulous. The sequence ends by reversing the order of the initial question about the origin of wars and fightings (4:1), asserting of the readers, "You [pl.] fight and make war." All of this happens because people do not have what they desire. But the truth is, desire is unquenchable, inexhaustible. Desire does not recognize "enough." Desire has created the consumer society. Desire flourishes because it seems that there is always more, and more is never enough.

The final part of 4:2—**You do not have because you do not ask**—is part of a new phase in the discussion, looking back to 1:5–7 and continuing through 4:3. The nature of the composition of James in laying out various strands of tradition has led to some oversimplified transitions. The tradition of asking is critically important for James. Certainly, asking—presumably asking God—is preferable to seeking to acquire by force. At first glance, this correction suggests that desire can be satisfied by asking God. If you lack, ask God (1:5). But clearly this will not do.

4:3. James continues, **You ask, and you do not receive because you ask badly** [*kakōs*], **to spend it on your passions** [*hēdonais*]. Just as 1:5–7 recognized the faulty asking of the double-minded person (*anēr dipsychos*), so here James identifies the problem of asking badly, that is, asking wrongly, with a view to satisfying "your passions." Thus, this second use of the plural of *hēdonē* forms an inclusio with the first use in 4:1, indicating the close to a subsection dealing with "desire," "covetousness," "passions." Desire debases the earth and all that is in it and constitutes it as "the world," an entity opposed to God and the purpose of God.

Friendship with God or friendship with the world (4:4–6). What constitutes the creation as the world, at enmity with God, so that there is the wisdom of God and an alien wisdom of the world?

4:4. Unfaithful creatures [*moichalides*]! James addresses his readers literally as "adulteresses." Though this is almost certainly the original reading, there is a late and poorly attested reading (the probable original reading of minuscule 629; see UBS[3]) of the masculine "adulterers" (*moichoi*) and an earlier, better attested reading of "adulterers and adulteresses." Against the originality of the latter is the better textual support of the adopted reading and also, especially, the recognition that if the longer variant had been original, there would have been no variants. Further, in patriarchal "Palestine," adultery was more likely to be attributed to women than men. Of course, in the ancient world this reality was not restricted to "Palestine." An adulterous wife is made the image of Israel's relationship with God. In Hosea 1–3, the relationship of Hosea to his wife is made an allegory of the relationship of Yahweh to Israel (and concisely in Hosea 3:1; see also Isa. 1:21; Jer. 3:1–12; Ezek. 16:15–63; 23). The common analogy of the relationship of the people to God was that of a bride to her husband, and unfaithfulness was depicted as adultery. The patriarchal perspective is not the point of this term of address in James, which is best translated as "unfaithful creatures." This connects those addressed to the creation, the earth.

Nevertheless, because of desire, the earth is ambiguous, and as an object of desire, the earth becomes the world. Here James asks the first of two questions in 4:4–5: **Do you not [*ouk*] know, friendship [*philia*] with the world is enmity [*echthra*] with God? Therefore, whoever chooses to be a friend [*philos*] of the world is proved to be an enemy [*echthros*] of God.** The word *philia* occurs only here in the NT but was discussed by Greek and Roman writers, including Plato, Aristotle, and Cicero. In the books translated from Hebrew in the LXX, the word occurs only eight or nine times in Proverbs. It occurs more frequently in the Greek writings of the LXX, confirming that the discussion of friendship was not native to Judaism, though the theme is explored without using that language in the depiction of the relationship between David and Jonathan.

The negative question, introduced by *ouk*, implies an affirmative answer: "Yes! We know this." The rhetoric is designed to carry the readers with the argument. By addressing the readers as "faithless creatures," James implies the widespread temptation of worldly values, as well as the seductive power of

139

the world, among those who know that these are incompatible with friendship with God. The address is a shock tactic, accentuated by the implied consequence. Friendship with the world brings alienation from God. James uses two antithetical pairs of cognate nouns: *philia/echthra* ("friendship/enmity") and *philos/echthros* ("friend/enemy"). The antithetical pairs make clear that God and the world are opposed and that to choose the one is to reject the other. Having expressed the matter in a question, James reasserts the point in a conclusive statement.

On this matter, James resonates with the exhortation in 1 John 2:15–17:

> Do not love the world or the things in the world. The love of the Father is not in those who love the world; because everything that is in the world—the desire [*epithymia*] of the flesh and the desire [*epithymia*] of the eyes and the ostentatious boastfulness of the possessions of life [*hē alazoneia tou biou*]—is not of the Father but is of the world. And the world is passing away, but the person who does the will of God abides forever.

While there is resonant agreement with James in substance, 1 John gives a negative command (*mē* with the present imperative *agapate*), "Do not love the world or the things in the world," which requires explanation, while James asks a rhetorical question with an implied affirmative answer and then states the self-evident conclusion. In 1 John it is apparent that it is the desire (*epithymia*) of the flesh and of the eyes that constitutes the world, which is not creation in itself. Love of the world and the things of the world is the desire to possess it. Here human love of the things of the world is covetous desire to possess and is opposed to the gracious and giving love of God for the world, which constitutes creation. To love the world with possessive desire is to become a slave to those desires and to lose one's self/life. Thus Jesus asked, "What will it profit a person to gain the whole world but lose his or her life?" (Mark 8:36 par.; see the discussion on 3:15). James implies that the readers know that friendship with the world brings enmity with God but nevertheless act as if they can sustain both friendships. James concludes with a definitive statement of what is implicitly obvious: "Therefore, whoever chooses to be a friend of the world is proved to be an enemy of God."

4:5. Or do you suppose Scripture speaks vainly [*kenōs*]? The second question may be asked tentatively to explore why those who seek to maintain both friendships think they can do so, given that they acknowledge that a friend of the world is an enemy of God. But is it really so? That is, do they know this proposition but contest its truth? Is a particular Scripture alluded to in the following words? **The spirit that [God] has made to dwell in/among us yearns jealously [*pros phthonon epipothei*].** The first problem is to identify the Scripture quoted or alluded to here. No convincing identification has been made, so we are faced with accepting an unknown reference indicated by "Scripture says/speaks." Without a known text, construing the quotation is difficult, because the subjects of the verbs are not specified. That God is the subject of "has made to dwell" (*katōkisen*) is likely because this is the widely attested role of God with humans. Here "the spirit" may refer to the Spirit of God, but James otherwise makes no reference to the Holy Spirit/Spirit of God. It is more likely that the reference in 4:5 is to the human spirit, the breath (*pneuma*) of life in humans, breathed by God, making a living *nepeš* (Heb.) or *psychē* (Gk.; Gen. 2:7). This expresses not a body/soul dualism but rather a psychosomatic unity, portrayed in the only other use of "spirit," in James 2:26. There the analogy is made between the body without the spirit and faith without works. As the body without the spirit is dead, so too is faith without works, clearly implying that "the spirit" is the breath of life.

If God makes the life-giving spirit to dwell in us, what does it mean that this spirit "yearns jealously"? This jealous yearning is covetousness, desire (*epithymei*) for the world and the things of the world. Although the Jewish teaching concerning the two inclinations, the good and the evil *yēṣer*, implies that desire may be healthy/good or evil, the dominant use of *epithymia* in Paul and James relates to the evil inclination, perhaps because it is through *epithymia* that the world gains obsessive control of men and women. By all means men and women strive to gain control of and to possess the world, but it is the world that enslaves humans by their passions, and even the whole world does not satisfy desire. Desire is insatiable.

4:6. Although jealous desire threatens to overpower and enslave humans to their passions, grasping for the world, there is another perspective: **but [God] gives more grace [*charin*]**. This is James's only use of "grace" (*charis*) apart from the quotation that follows. It could be said that this use occurs because it is dependent on that quotation. Alternatively, the quotation follows precisely because of this reference to grace: **therefore it [Scripture] says, "God resists the proud [*hyperēphanois*] but gives grace [*charin*] to the humble [*tapeinois*]."** There is no problem with the identification of this quotation, which is from the LXX of Prov. 3:34, except that James uses "God" (*theos*) instead of "Lord" (*kyrios*), which translates the Hebrew Tetragrammaton, "YHWH." Had James been alone in this, we might have supposed that James modified the text to suit the context of the lead-in "but *God* gives more grace." But this is not explicit. God is implied, not mentioned, in this clause, though the discussion of enmity and friendship with "God" in 4:4 is probably contextually close enough to justify the identification of God as the subject in the translation of 4:6a. If James had used *kyrios* in quoting Prov. 3:34 LXX, this might have been ambiguous, because James twice uses *kyrios* in relation to Jesus (1:1; 2:1). Given that 4:6a is not explicit, James might have replaced *kyrios* in the LXX quotation with *theos* to make clear that the subject of *didōsin* ("who gives [*didōsin*] more grace") is God. But James is not alone in modifying the text of Prov. 3:34 in this way. It is quoted in the same way in 1 Pet. 5:5–6 and *1 Clem.* 30.2.

What intertextual relationships are implied here? This is but one strand of evidence, and it has to be assessed in the context of the uncertainty of the relative dating of the three writings. Further, by the late second or early third century CE, Christian copies of the Greek OT translated the Tetragrammaton either by *kyrios* or *theos* (see Howard 1992, 392–93). It is likely that this flexibility in translation was early enough to influence this agreement between James, 1 Peter, and *1 Clement*. But the points of contact go beyond this, especially between James and 1 Peter. The relationship between James 4:6–10 and 1 Pet. 5:5–6 is intriguing. Not only do they share this quotation with the same modification, but also each addresses defense against the devil, and each also has "be subject" (*hypotagēte*), "be humble" (*tapeinōthēte*), and the verb "to exalt" (*hypsoō*), which James uses in the future tense and indicative mood to assert that God "will exalt [*hypsōsei*] you," and 1 Peter uses an aorist tense in the subjunctive mood with *hina* ("that [*hina*] God may exalt [*hypsōsē*] you"). As striking as these similarities are, it is unlikely that James or 1 Peter is dependent on the other. The theme of God putting down the mighty and exalting the humble is characteristic and widely known (e.g., 1 Sam. 2:4–8; Luke 1:52–53), and differences in the way each treats this theme undermine the case for direct literary dependence. Given that there is precedent for translating the divine name YHWH as "God," it is more likely that an indirect relationship of some sort explains the common quotation of Prov. 3:34 in 1 Peter and *1 Clement*.

The reference to "the humble" linguistically connects this quotation with James 1:9–10, which contrasts the humble poor (*tapeinos*) with the rich (*plousios*). Just as James associated *tapeinos* with the poor in 1:9, so too it is likely that in 4:6 the proud (*hyperēphanois*) are identified with the rich. The warning against boasting in 4:13–16 picks up the theme of boasting in 1:9–11. The boasting recommended to the rich in 1:9–11 is in their humbling, but the boasting criticized in 4:13–16 is the arrogant boasting of the rich and powerful. The warning to the rich concerning the judgment that is coming upon them follows (5:1–6). This resonates with the end of the rich spoken of in 1:11: "so also the rich in their pursuit of wealth will whither away." In this way, James gives some clues as to the way God resists the proud. In what ways does God give grace to the humble? First of all, those who endure are promised the crown of life (1:12). But the reference to God giving more grace occurs in the context of the alluring power of the world to seduce people into obsessive desire to acquire and possess. In the face of this reality, God gives more grace to the humble, who rely on the goodness of God, who is the source of all generous giving and good gifts (1:17). Grace here has the sense of the generosity of God in relation to those who trust God. In particular, God gives the gift of wisdom to those who ask in faith (1:5–8). The gift of wisdom is an enabling power from God. Reference to the humble provides a link to the following exhortations.

Exhortations (4:7–10). The following exhortations initially appear to be a random collection. Upon reflection, they seem to be addressed first to the humble (4:7–8a), then to the proud (4:8b–10). Yet each of these two orientations is made up of smaller parts. This small section is dominated by ten imperatives, nine in the second-person plural direct command and one in the third-person singular of exhortation: "submit," "resist," "draw near," "cleanse," "purify," "lament," "mourn," "weep," "let it be turned," "be humbled." The opening and closing exhortations form an inclusio of mutually inclusive terms that connect 4:7–10 with 4:6.

4:7–8a. Therefore submit to God is the first and foundational exhortation from which all else flows. To submit to God is to acknowledge God as God and to recognize that humans are the work of God's hands. This is implied in the first commandment, which recognizes the oneness of God and is elaborated in the Shema: "Hear, O Israel, the Lord our God, the Lord is one, and you shall love the Lord your God with all your heart . . . self . . . strength" (Deut. 6:4–5; cf. 10:12). Recognition of the one God implies the exclusive service of the one God (cf. Matt. 22:37; Mark 12:33; Luke 10:27). The complement to "submit to God" is **but resist the devil, and he will flee from you** (on resisting the devil and on the devil's flight, see also 1 Pet. 5:8–9; Eph. 6:13; *T. Iss.* 7.7; *T. Dan* 5.1; *T. Naph.* 8.4; *T. Ash.* 3.2). This is the first of two exhortations followed by a promise in 4:7b–8a: "Resist, . . . and the devil will flee. . . . Draw near to God, and God will draw near to you." The two may be related. In James it is the human action that is stressed because it is uncertain and in doubt, because "No one can serve two masters. . . . You cannot serve God and mammon" (Matt. 6:24//Luke 16:13; cf. Luke 16:9, 11; 1QS 6.2; CD 14.20). The opposition between God and mammon (wealth) is surprising in the same way that the opposition between God and earth/world is. Through human *epithymia*, wealth and the world compete with God and stand on the side of the devil. This is the third reference related to the devil; note 3:6: "The tongue is a fire, . . . set on fire by Gehenna," which seems to imply a devilish source of the fire; and in 3:15 the alien wisdom is described as demonic (*daimoniōdēs*). The devil is portrayed not as an almighty power but rather as one that can be repelled with help from God. What is essential is that the one who submits to God should also resist the devil. That such resistance should be guided by the wisdom of God may well be implied. Certainly this involves single-minded devotion to God expressed in good works, and it is quite the reverse of the "double-minded," wavering person of 1:8. Although James does not ignore the aggressive onslaught of the devil in persecution (see 1:2–4; cf. 1 Pet. 5:8–11), the dominant threat seems to be the lure of the world, temptation via desire (*epithymia*). In this context, single-minded devotion to God becomes the critical call. Contrast 1 Peter, where the devil roams about like a roaring lion seeking someone to devour; for James, the devil can be resisted, and when dealing with temptation, James makes no mention of the devil. Rather, the source of temptation is desire (*epithymia*; 1:13–15).

Resisting the devil is a corollary of the reciprocal relation to God, which is promised to those who draw near: **Draw near to God, and God will draw near to you** (4:8a). Fundamental devotion to God is crucial for resisting the devil and controlling desire. This means that desire, when transformed and redirected toward God and neighbor, does not have acquisitive and possessive intent but instead is devoted to serving God and neighbor (2:8; 4:6–8).

4:8b–9. Cleanse [*katharisate*] your hands, you sinners, and purify [*hagnisate*] your hearts, you double-minded [*dipsychoi*] (4:8b). Reference to "you sinners" apparently indicates those who have willfully sinned and thus have soiled their hands. But how are sinners to cleanse their hands? This does not fit the call to deal with bad actions by means of ritual that would allow bad actions to continue. Rather, it is a call to repentance, to act justly (see Mic. 6:8). Thus it is likely that reference to clean hands in this context relates to ethical actions rather than ritual purity. It concerns purity of outward action as well as inward thought and intention. Note Ps. 23:3–4 LXX (24:3–4 ET): "Who shall ascend the mountain of the Lord, and who shall stand in his holy place? Even the person with innocent hands and a pure [*katharos*] heart." In this combination, it is not ritually clean hands but rather hands that have committed no wrong that are linked to purity of motive, thought, and commitment. Given that these words are addressed to the sinners, it is a call to repentance, to a change of outward action and inward orientation and commitment.

The call to purify hearts is addressed to the double-*minded* and resonates with Jesus's words "Blessed are the pure [*ho katharoi*] in heart, for they shall see God" (Matt. 5:8). In James 1:6–8 the double-minded person is described as unstable, uncertain, uncommitted, and dissembling in a time of crisis. Interestingly, here the double-minded are called on to cleanse their hearts. We often say to such a person, "Make up your mind!" The mixed metaphors of mind and heart are best clarified if purity of heart is identified with "single-minded" commitment, as the opposition to the double-minded confirms. The double-minded are vacillating in their commitment. To some extent, these mixed metaphors reflect the Greek and Hebrew insight into what is the core of a human being. For the Greeks, it was the intellect, the mind; for the Hebrews, it was the heart, understood as a metaphor of the emotional and moral core of being. While this may be an oversimplification, because the metaphors overlap in meaning, there is a different balance that is caught by the contrast. But the linking of them in this exhortation suggests that the intellectual and the aesthetic are closely connected, while the emotional and the moral find expression in the double command to love God wholeheartedly (single-mindedly) and to love the neighbor as oneself. Here the heart is a more appropriate image. Service of God has a rational basis, "the LORD our God is one," but that is not enough. It is the character of God revealed that leads to the commands to love God completely, wholeheartedly, single-mindedly and the neighbor as oneself. The service of God and neighbor is not simply the consequence of a rational decision; it is a decision of the heart, in response to the love of God, to love God and neighbor.

Though the explicit vocabulary of repentance (*metanoeō* and *metanoia*) is not used in James, the call to repentance is at the heart of 4:8b–10 and becomes increasingly clear in the complex response demanded in **Lament** [*talaipōrēsate*] **and mourn** [*penthēsate*] **and weep** [*klausate*]. **Let your laughter be turned** [*metatrapētō*] **to mourning** [*penthos*] **and your joy** [*chara*] **to gloom/depression** [*katēpheian*] (4:9). This language foreshadows the opening pronouncement of judgment to come upon the rich in 5:1: "Come now, you rich people, weep [*klausate*] and wail [*ololyzontes*] at the calamities [*talaipōriais*] that are coming upon you." Given that the rich are characterized as the proud and arrogant, it may be that they are the object of this tirade in 4:8b–10 also. The story of the rich man and Lazarus, told by Jesus in Luke 16:19–31, provides a basis for understanding this call for repentance, arising out of a sense of having done wrong, which in the OT was expressed with appropriate signs of sorrow, remorse, and the determination to turn from evil ways and turn to God and God's ways. The stress in 4:9–10a is on the appropriate evidence of sorrow and remorse with an acknowledgment of sin (see, e.g., Jon. 3:6–9). In the face of such awareness of sin, laughter and joy are inappropriate and should be replaced by lamentation, mourning, weeping, and deep depression. There is no sense here that a quick "Sorry!" is good enough, with acceptance a foregone conclusion. Nothing less than genuine remorse for sin and determined commitment to a changed life pleasing to God will do. Even then, the assumption of automatic acceptance by God is presumptuous (cf. Jon. 3:9).

4:10. Be humbled before the Lord, and he will exalt you. The call is for the proud/rich to be humbled before God (see 1:9–11). Now there is a promise for those who humble themselves before the Lord: "He will exalt [*hypsōsei*] you." Given that in 1:1 and 2:1 the Lord (*kyrios*) is Jesus (contrast *ho theos* in 4:6, 7, 8), it may seem that here the one who exalts the humble is Jesus, and the exaltation may presuppose an act of eschatological judgment. But the command of 4:10, "Humble yourselves before the Lord," looks like a variation on 4:7, "Submit yourselves to God." Just as the call is to submit now, the call to "humble yourself" is in the present time even if the exaltation, "he will exalt you," awaits the future judgment. It is God who exalts both Jesus and those who humble themselves.

Theological Issues

The two passages considered in this section draw attention to the relationship between God and the world. While the dominant perspective of 3:13–4:10 is of a conflictual relationship, this builds on the affirmation of the goodness of God's creation (see the discussion on 1:17). The subtitle of Eberhard Jüngel's

Kyrios and Theos

Kyrios is used fourteen times in James alongside sixteen uses of theos. In the LXX, the name of God ("YHWH") is usually translated as kyrios ("Lord"), while kyrios and theos are commonly used to refer to God. It is not surprising that James does likewise. This is complicated by the use of kyrios to refer to Jesus in James 1:1, where James refers to himself as "servant of God and Lord Jesus Christ," setting the expectation of a distinction between the use of theos and kyrios. James 2:1 also uses kyrios in an unmistakable reference to "our Lord Jesus Christ." A strong case can also be made for taking two references to the imminent coming (parousia) of the Lord (5:7–8) in judgment (5:9) as references to Jesus, given the traditional use of this language (see Matt. 24:3, 27, 37, 39; 1 Cor.15:23; 1 Thess. 2:19; 3:13; 4:15; 5:23; 2 Thess. 2:1, 8; 2 Pet. 3:4; 1 John 2:28) to refer to the coming of Jesus as judge at the end of history.

On the other side, two uses of kyrios refer to God: "we bless the Lord and Father" (3:9); and in 5:4 the cries of the poor exploited by the rich landowners have "come to the ears of Lord Sabaoth," a common scriptural reference to God (Isa. 5:9 LXX, and another sixty uses in Isaiah).

Some other texts in James favor reference to God when taken in context. For example, those who lack wisdom are exhorted to ask God (1:5), and those who do not ask in faith are told not to suppose that they will receive anything from the Lord (1:7). In 5:10, that "the prophets spoke in the name of the Lord" is fairly clearly a reference to God, as is the confession that "the Lord is compassionate and merciful" (5:11), which echoes Exod. 34:6 (see also Pss. 103:8 [102:8 LXX]; 112:4 [111:4 LXX]; Sir. 2:11). Similarly, following 4:7–8 ("be subject to God . . . draw near to God"), the reference in 4:10 ("humble yourselves before the Lord") is a reference to God. Probably, "if the Lord wills" (4:15) is also a reference to God. In the context of the story of Job, "the purpose of the Lord" is also a reference to God (5:11), confirmed by the second use of "Lord" in that verse. Reference to prayer "in the name of the Lord" (5:14) is ambiguous, given the practice of prayer in the name of Jesus, though this is not otherwise attested in James. Reference to "the Lord will raise him up" (5:15) is a reference to God, because prayer in the name of Jesus is addressed to God.

book *God as the Mystery of the World* is *On the Foundation of the Theology of the Crucified One in the Dispute between Theism and Atheism.* This title, illuminated by its subtitle, has some relevance to James, but the subtitle would require adjustment to read something like "On the Foundation of the Theology of the Renewer of Creation in the Dispute between Theism and Atheism." This is illustrated by James 1:17–18: "Every generous act of giving and every perfect gift is from above, coming down from the Father of lights, with whom there is no variation or shadow caused by change. By the [Father's] will the [Father] begot us by the word of truth that we should be a kind of firstfruit of the [Father's] creatures."

For James's theism, creation is not so much a theory about the origin of the universe as it is a belief in its intrinsic character and purpose. The Father of lights, who begets humans by the word of truth, renews the creation. Consequently, those so begotten know that the generosity of goodness is at the heart of the universe and that there is an obligation and energy to live out of the experience of generosity and goodness in relation to others. This generosity comes into conflict with desire (*hēdonē* and *epithymeō*, 4:1–2). Unbridled desire is an expression of practical atheism. It is to live in the world in the absence of God, corrupting the generosity of God and God's creation so that the world becomes turned in on itself in desire to possess the other. At the same time, the other becomes a competitor, leading to conflict, fighting, and wars (4:1–6). The wisdom of the world is the wisdom of acquisition and consumption in competition with other consumers, because in a world of limited resources, what others have, I cannot have (3:13–18).

But in a creation where all is gratuitously given, there is the possibility of an ethic of generosity to the other and others rather than a philosophy of selfishness in competition. The question is, what is the character of reality? Is generosity at the heart of the universe, or is life a struggle for survival, the survival of the fittest, where each competes for the limited good? Does generosity make even the weak fit for survival, or should the weak perish because might is right? Unrestrained desire is practical atheism, and it is at the heart of the conflicts between individuals, groups, and nations (3:13–15; 4:1–4). To live selfishly, as if one were in control of one's destiny, is to live in denial of God's generosity (4:13–17). This is the dispute between the theism of James—the belief in the generous, gift-giving God—and the practical atheism of those who affirm the power of the strong to achieve and possess all that is desired. Such practical atheism fails to recognize that unbridled desire not only destroys the other but also is ultimately self-destructive, and perhaps this is the judgment of God. Here again, James and Paul meet on firm ground: "For the whole law is fulfilled in one word, in this: 'You shall love your neighbor as yourself.' But if you bite and devour one another [*allēlous*], beware lest you destroy one another" (Gal. 5:14–15; cf. James 2:8; 4:1–6).

For James, peace is the fruit of righteousness. Without righteousness, there is no peace but only oppression. The period since the end of the so-called Second World War has certainly not been a time of peace, though many people speak of it in this way. Not only have there been violent conflicts in Korea, Vietnam, Israel, Palestine, Afghanistan, Iraq, Ireland, Spain, Thailand, and many other places, but also the great powers continue to organize the world for their own benefit, and one aspect of the rise of terrorism is widespread dissatisfaction with the disparity between rich and poor nations and between rich and poor within nations. So-called development is driven by desire to possess and control, not by justice or compassion. In such a world there can be no peace.

James 4:11–5:6

Admonitions and Warnings

Introductory Matters

Ten words in this section are not found elsewhere in the NT, and another four are found elsewhere only in Paul. Another word is found only in James, Paul, and 1 John 2:16. Of those found only in James in the NT, one ("moth-eaten," *sētobrōtos*, 5:2) is not found in the pre-Christian Greek corpus, and another ("to rust," *katioomai*, 5:3) is not found in the Hebrew books translated in the LXX. The other eight are as follows: "lawgiver" (*nomothetēs*, 4:12), "come" (*age*, 4:13; 5:1), "wail" (*ololyzōm*, 5:1), "rot" (*sēpō*, 5:2), "mow" (*amaō*, 5:4), "withhold" (*aphystereō*, 5:4), "shout" (*boē*, 5:4), and "to live in luxury" (*tryphaō*, 5:5). Of the four words that James shares only with Paul, two occur together in 4:16, along with another related word that appears, in addition to Paul and James, in 1 John 2:16. The two in Paul and James are cognate terms: the verb *kauchaomai* ("to boast"; see the discussion on James 1:9–10 and the sidebar there "Boasting in James and Paul") and the noun *kauchēsis* ("boasting"). The word appearing also in 1 John 2:16, *alazoneia* ("arrogant pride"), is related to the public persona projected falsely by a social climber. The third word found only in James and Paul is *talaipōria* ("calamity"; see the use of the verb *talaipōreō* in 4:9), and the fourth, *spatalaō* ("to live in self-indulgent luxury"), has an overlapping meaning with *tryphaō* (both in 5:5), a word used only by James (see above). The linguistic evidence continues to build a picture of the distinctive character of James alongside a distinctive overlap with Paul and shared perspective with 1 John.

Tracing the Train of Thought

This section contains a series of specific warnings, which extend the exhortations of 4:7–10. But whereas the exhortations deal positively with the relationship of the reader to God, advocating how to establish and maintain the relationship, these warnings (4:11–5:6) concern specific unacceptable patterns of behavior: judging, boasting, trusting in riches.

Warning about Judging a Brother/Sister (4:11–12)

4:11. Do not speak against one another [*allēlōn*], brothers [and sisters]. The first of these warnings is a negative command introduced by *mē* with the present imperative *katalaleite*. It sets the tone of this series of warnings. The verb *katalaleō* has the basic meaning "to speak against" and covers slander as well as negative criticism. It might even cover giving evidence against a brother or sister in a court of law. Paul expresses disapproval of such a situation in 1 Cor. 6:1. James says of the rich in 2:6, "Is it not the rich who . . . drag you into the lawcourts?" Speaking against one another in the courts would certainly have drawn sharp criticism from James. But a legal context is not indicated in 4:11.

Any form of speaking that is destructive of the other person qualifies. This is especially true of slander, which implies that the negative criticism is not based on reality and misrepresents the other person. The use of the reciprocal "one another" suggests that a situation of leadership rivalry again surfaces here. Addressing the readers as "brothers [and sisters]" forcefully emphasizes the inappropriateness of this bitter rivalry. Indeed, it now becomes apparent that such behavior is an attack on the law. **The person speaking against a brother [or sister] or judging a brother [or sister] speaks against the law and judges the law.** The reciprocal pronoun *allēlōn*, which is the object of *katalaleō*, is explicated by reference to speaking against a brother (or sister). James shares this linguistic variation with the Johannine literature, where it is chiefly associated with the love command (see Painter 2002a, 100–102, 181–83). Obviously, *katalalia* is inconsistent with sibling relationships in a group characterized as a community of brothers and sisters.

The overlap between "one another" and "the brother" in the love command of 1 John is relevant to the overlapping use of James 4:11–12, especially because

---

James 4:11–5:6 in the Rhetorical Flow

Address/salutation (1:1)

Epitome of the exhortation of James (1:2–27)

Warning against partiality (2:1–13)

Faith and works (2:14–26)

The tongue (3:1–12)

God and the world (3:13–4:10)

▶ Admonitions and warnings (4:11–5:6)

Warning about judging a brother/sister (4:11–12)

Warning against boasting (4:13–17)

Warning to the rich (5:1–6)

Brothers (and Sisters) and "One Another" in John

The love command takes the form of "love one another" in John 13:34 (2x), 35; 15:12, 17. This form of the command also occurs in 1 John 3:11, 23; 4:7, 11, 12; 2 John 5. But 1 John also characteristically speaks of the commandment to love the brother (and sister) (1 John 2:10; 3:10, 14; 4:20–21). This idiom emerges first in a context that polarizes light and darkness, love and hate (2:7–11), and then focuses on the role of Cain, who failed to love and instead hated his brother and murdered him (3:11–15). This pivotal example gives added force to the idiom, so that it is a major alternative to the love command "love one another." The identification of the brother makes the failure to love, that is, to hate, more scandalous. This is true also in James 4:11, where speaking against one another (*allēlōn*) is explicated as speaking against a brother (or sister)—an act of hatred in Johannine terms.

the overlapping use of "the neighbor" (*plēsion*) in 4:12 and 2:8 suggests the love command in the form used by James: "the royal law according to the Scripture [Lev. 19:18], you shall love your neighbor [*plēsion*] as yourself." If that is the case, speaking against one another / a brother (or sister) in 4:11 implies breaking this form of the love command. That it does so is suggested by the way James first refers to speaking against / judging "one another" and then the "brother" before asking "Who are you, who judges the neighbor?" (4:12).

If the variation of language noted indicates some relationship to the love command, James nowhere uses the Johannine forms of the love command, "to love one another" and "to love the brother [or sister]," though he does use "one another" and "brother [sister]" in a context that refers back to the royal law according to the Scripture (of Lev. 19:18), "You shall love your neighbor as yourself" (2:8). This introduces a third form of the love command, which is widely quoted in the NT, including by Jesus in the Synoptics (Matt. 19:19; 22:39; Mark 12:31; Luke 10:27), by Paul (Rom. 13:8–10; Gal. 5:14), and in James 2:8, but not in the Johannine writings. Certainly, speaking against one another and judging a brother or sister is a breach of the command "You shall love your neighbor as yourself"; it is to speak against the law and to be critical/judgmental of it.

It follows, **but if you judge the law, you are not a doer [*poiētēs*] of the law but a judge [*kritēs*].** This is a nicely balanced summary statement: "not a doer but a judge." But they are to "be doers of the word [law]," not judges of it or hearers only. Of anyone who is a "doer of the work," James says that such a person "will be blessed in his or her doing" (1:22, 25). The "word/law" is referred to as "the perfect law of liberty" (1:25).

4:12. There is one lawgiver and judge who is able to save and to destroy; but who are you who judges the neighbor [*plēsion*]? The deeply inappropriate spitefuliling reading:

nature of such human action now becomes apparent. There is only one law-giver and judge, and that is God (see Gen. 18:25; Deut. 32:35, 39; Ps. 9:19–20; Matt. 10:28; John 5:17–30; Rom. 12:19; 14:4; Heb. 10:30). Humans who usurp this role not only sin against the neighbor, thus infringing the command to love the neighbor, but also brazenly challenge God, the lawgiver, creator, and redeemer, who is both judge of all and savior. By the end of 4:12, James has used three terms to describe the members of the communities to which he writes: "one another," "brother/sister," "neighbor." The last of these confirms that the royal law according to the Scripture—"You shall love your neighbor as yourself"—is here recalled (from 2:8) to expose spiteful competition where rival leaders speak ill of one another (*allēlōn*). Such behavior is outrageous in the shadow of God's judgment. Words of Jesus, "Do not judge lest you be judged" (Matt. 7:1), resonate here in James's treatment of judging one another, the brother/sister, the neighbor.

Warning against Boasting (4:13–17)

Although neither this nor the following warning (5:1–6) is introduced by a negative command as in 4:11, both are correctional warnings that make their negative point by describing the behavior in strongly disparaging terms. Like the first warning, they focus on what is wrong, but they do so with repetition of the imperative singular "come now" (*age nyn*). This imperative is conventionally used to address a plural audience in both 4:13 and 5:1. Thus *age nyn* functions as a rhetorical linking device, connecting the three warnings. It is found in the NT only in these two verses. This passage builds on 1:9–11.

4:13. Come [sg.] now [*age nyn*], you [pl.] who say, "Today or tomorrow we will go into such and such a city and live for a year and we will trade and make a profit" is addressed to any of the recipients who think and speak about the future as if they were in control of it. This group is identified not by a name (contrast 5:1) but rather by description. They boast glibly about matters over which they have little or no control. Specifically, the description seems to fit the activities of merchant traders. This group constitutes not the truly rich but perhaps those on the way up, on the way to making a fortune before settling down at ease in luxurious circumstances. The problem of their self-confident thinking becomes apparent in the following words.

4:14. You who do not know what tomorrow brings, for what is your life? For you are a vapor/mist, which appears for a little while and then vanishes. The presumption that they could speak certainly about the future offends James (cf. the parable of the rich fool in Luke 12:16–20). They do not know what tomorrow brings. James asks, "What is your life?" It is a rhetorical question, which he answers in terms reminiscent of Ecclesiastes (see also Job 7:7, 9, 16; Prov. 27:1; Sir. 11:18–19; Luke 12:16–20; James 1:9–11). The uncertainty and the transience of all life dominate this perspective. In the light of this, a more circumspect and humble attitude is appropriate.

4:15. Instead you should say, "If the Lord wills, we will live and we will do this or that." Jewish, Christian, and Roman writers recognize the very limited control that humans have over their lives. James advises humility before God. This need not exclude planning for the future, but it does mark all such plans as provisional. This perspective implies the wisdom of humble submission to the will of God (see 4:7, 10; cf. 1:5; 3:13–18).

4:16. But now you [pl.] boast in your arrogance [*kauchasthe en tais alazoneiais hymōn*]; all such boasting [*kauchēsis*] is evil. The initial proposition in 4:13 is now characterized as boastful arrogance. The boasting is identified as manifestly going beyond what anyone could credibly claim. There is a profusion of boasting vocabulary here. The use of *alazoneia* makes clear that this boasting is manifestly "a lot of hot air," the foolish boasting of a braggart, and identifies the speaker as a "buffoon," to be taken seriously by no one. However, it is wrong to think of such foolishness as harmless. It is also arrogant, and "all such boasting is evil," that is, morally evil (*ponēros*) and destructive of God's good creation (for a related use of *alazoneia*, see 1 John 2:16; for reference to the *alazōn* ["braggart"], see Rom. 1:30; 2 Tim. 3:2; see also the discussion on James 1:9 and the sidebar there, "Boasting in James and Paul").

4:17. Therefore, for the one who knows to do good and does not do it, for this person it is sin [*hamartia*]. The idiom changes from that of address, using the second-person plural, to the impersonal third-person singular. There is also a change of categories. This suggests that 4:17 might not have originated with 4:13–16, but it nevertheless forms a useful transitional conclusion between 4:13–16 and 5:1–6. If such boasting is evil (*ponēros*, 4:16), knowing the good (*kalos*) but failing to do it is sin (*hamartia*). Evil is evil, whether recognized or not, but here the identification of sin is apparently dependent upon knowing the good but failing to do it. Such knowledge makes the person culpable, whereas ignorance is a mitigating factor. Sinning knowingly might be willful, high-handed, and intentional or a sin of weakness. This difference was also important for Judaism. David's sin with Bathsheba would be seen as a sin of weakness, though it was compounded in the events that flowed from it based on coolly calculated actions. Judaism also recognized sins of ignorance (cf. Acts 17:30; 1 Tim. 1:13). Both weakness and ignorance were mitigating factors, but not excuses. In 1 Tim. 1:13, a saying attributed to Paul acknowledges, "Though formerly being a blasphemer and persecutor and man of violence, I received mercy because, being ignorant, I acted in unbelief" (see a comparable statement in 1 Cor. 15:8–10 that implies ignorance). Ignorance does not remove guilt, but it does keep open the opportunity for forgiveness. The person who sins knowingly and intentionally is in a more serious situation, being hardened against what is good.

Warning to the Rich (5:1–6)

After warning the merchant traders, who aspired to riches, concerning their brash overconfidence, James turns to those whom he describes as rich (cf. 1:10).

The address to those who aspire to riches (4:13–17) and the following address to the rich (5:1–6) are connected by their common beginning, "Come now."

5:1. Come now [*age nyn*], you rich people. It may be that those who are becoming rich (the merchant traders), or at least desire to do so, are more crudely brash and inclined to brag, as if they have already arrived where they actually aspire to be. This is the common caricature of the newly rich and those aspiring to be rich. The sins of those who actually are rich are more seriously unscrupulous and exploitative, and James's criticisms are correspondingly stronger, using graphic terms to describe the end of the rich: **Weep [*klausate*] and wail [*ololyzontes*] at the calamities [*talaipōriais*] that are coming upon you.** This language overlaps the call made to the sinners and double-minded in 4:8–9 (for the use of comparable language in a similar rhetorical context, see Isa. 10:10; 13:6; 14:31 in the LXX). It is a prophetic announcement of what is coming upon the rich, calling upon them to respond with a wailing lament in light of the coming calamities. There is a piling up of language rarely used in the NT (*talaipōria*, only in Rom. 3:16; James 5:1; cf. *talaipōreō* in James 4:9, the lone occurrence) or not found elsewhere in the NT (*ololyzō*, only in James 5:1). This multiplication of the language of despair and disaster communicates an overwhelming sense of distress and anguish.

It is true that here James issues no explicit call for repentance. This need not mean that the rhetorical purpose of this passage is simply to gloat over the fate about to befall the rich and is not aimed at repentance. Note the complaint of Jonah to God in Jon. 4:1–2. Jonah was sent to proclaim judgment on Nineveh because of its wickedness, which after some delay, Jonah did. There was no call for repentance but only a proclamation of impending judgment (Jon. 3:4). Yet when the people repented, God had mercy on them. Jonah then complains that he knew God would respond in this way, and this was the reason for his reluctance to go and proclaim judgment. Whether James intended to provoke repentance or not is perhaps debatable. Repentance is always a possible outcome of such an announcement of imminent judgment, and it is unlikely that James was unaware of this or that the literary form was not produced to have that effect. This need not mean that James has high hopes that the rich will become compassionate carers for those in need. This tirade may also function to dissuade any who are tempted by the attraction of the way of the rich. Wealth has its place, but if it is hoarded for selfish satisfaction, it will not only fail to do the good that might be achieved but will also fail to satisfy the hoarders.

5:2–3c. **Your wealth has rotted [*sesēpen*], and your clothing is moth-eaten [*sētobrōtos*]** (5:2). This is just the beginning of the description of the stripping away of all that is valued from the rich. Some of the details follow: **Your gold and your silver have rusted [*katiōtai*], and their rust will be evidence [*martyrion*] against you and will eat your flesh like fire** (5:3a–c). The transience of material wealth is stressed in 5:2–3a by using three verbs in the perfect tense

153

that stress the completion of the destructive process: "your wealth has rotted," "your clothing is moth-eaten," and "your gold and silver have rusted." Of course, gold and silver are not ferrous metals and do not rust, but this is not a case of James showing ignorance. In the cultures of James's time, the rusting of precious metals was a proverbial image for the waste of precious resources, which were meant to be used, not hoarded: "Lose your silver for the sake of a brother or a friend, and do not let it rust under a stone and be lost" (Sir. 29:10). But that is not all. The rusted, unused, wasted resources are evidence against the rich of their heartless disregard for the poor, of their unwillingness to come to the aid of the poor, to provide alms (see Sir. 29:9–12). Matthew 6:19–21 and Luke 12:33–34 (Q material) provide sayings about storing up treasures on earth, where moth and rust consume, and a number of parables add their critique, such as the parable of the rich fool, who built bigger barns to store up an excessive harvest (Luke 12:13–21), and the parable of the rich man and Lazarus (Luke 16:19–31). The first shows the folly of hoarding wealth and not using it for a good purpose ("You fool! This night your life will be taken from you!" Luke 12:20). Note also "Every work decays and ceases to exist, and the one who made it will pass away with it" (Sir. 14:19). The second parable condemns the rich man for willful disregard of the plight of the poor man, narrating their reversal of fortunes in the "afterlife" beyond death. The fate of the rich man is described in Luke 16:22–28. He is in torment, in agony in the flames, his tongue hot and dry, while Lazarus is in paradise, in Abraham's bosom. This image of torment in the flames seems to be a variant on the notion of the rust of wasted resources eating into the flesh like fire. For James, hoarded wealth is wasted; it is evidence of the heartlessness of the rich, and the dissolution (rust) will fuel the fire of their torment.

5:3d. You stored up treasure in the last days. Such treasures are the result of exploitation and greed without concern for those in desperate need. These treasures are evidence against the rich, who continued to accumulate them, disregarding the time. For James, the dawning of "the last day" is the signal that judgment is about to begin (5:7–9). Despite this, the rich continue to accumulate as if this life will go on unchanged forever. The statement in 5:3c suggests that although the evidence of their accumulated wealth will eat up their flesh like fire, such is their obsessive disorder that they continue to accumulate what will become more evidence as the last day dawns. In what follows (5:4–6), James describes their unscrupulous behavior from a variety of perspectives.

5:4. See, the wages of the workers who mowed your fields, which you withheld from them, cry out, and the cries of the harvesters have come to the ears of the Lord of hosts [sabaōth]. As one example of this exploitation, James rhetorically calls on them to "see" the wages withheld from the mowers and harvesters, together with the cries of the harvesters, which have come "to the ears of the Lord of sabaōth," an expression found in Isa. 5:9 LXX.

Fifty-three of the sixty-four uses of *sabaōth* in the LXX occur in Isaiah, but the expression is found only twice in the NT—here in James 5:4 and in Rom. 9:29, which is a quotation of Isa. 1:9. This Greek form is the translation of the Hebrew *yhwh ṣĕbā'ôt*, which occurs 259 times in the Hebrew Bible and is usually translated in the LXX as *kyrios pantokratōr*, variations of which appear ten times in the NT (1x in 2 Cor. 6:18; 9x in Revelation). In Revelation, the name occurs almost exclusively in liturgical passages of praise as God's eschatological reign is manifest. Both the Hebrew and the Greek forms express the transcendent and universal power of God, often in contexts of eschatological judgment.

Here the rich are depicted as exploiting their workers, withholding their wages. For the rich to do this was heartless and unscrupulous, creating great hardship for the poor. The law explicitly forbade this practice: "The wages of the workers shall not remain with you until morning" (Lev. 19:13). Vividly, James depicts these withheld wages as crying out, along with the cries of the unpaid workers rising to the ears of the Lord of hosts. The presence of what should have been paid to the workers, retained unjustifiably by the rich land-owners, was damning evidence and, with the cries of the workers, called for justice. This is a stark warning, but the cynical rich owners could disregard it. For James, however, the judge already stands at the door. The day of reckoning is impending as doom to the exploiters of the poor.

5:5. You have lived in self-indulgence and luxury on the earth, and you have fed/fattened your hearts in a day of slaughter. The accusations begun in 5:3d continue in 5:4, which is an indirect accusation of withholding wages, but set in the form of a complaint arising to the ears of the Lord of hosts. The terms that begin and end the opening clause in Greek, translated as "you have lived in self-indulgence [*etryphēsate*]" and "you have lived in luxury [*espatalēsate*]," overlap in meaning, and their translations are interchangeable. The first is used only by James, and the second only by James and Paul in the NT. This piling up of language is supposed to communicate a level of luxury that is obscene, especially when seen in relation to the poverty of those whose exploitation made that luxury possible. What makes it obscene is the wasteful squandering of rich resources while the poor struggle to survive from day to day. By emphasizing that this luxury is enjoyed "on earth," James sounds the warning of what is about to come upon the rich in 5:1. Meanwhile, the ruthless rich grow fatter as the poor are slaughtered through their exploitation (see Sir. 34:22–26; *1 En.* 100.7). This reading makes good sense, but the meaning of "a day of slaughter" may have some reference to the day of judgment, as in 5:3. The latter is supported by *1 En.* 94.9, which speaks of the judgment of the rich, who "have become ready for the day of slaughter, and the day of darkness, and the day of great judgment." An alternative reference from Qumran is also relevant: "But the wicked you created for the Day of Massacre" (1QH 7.20; see also 1QS 10; CD 19.15, 19). On the way this combines perspectives, see the discussion on 5:3. A main point seems to be that the rich live in the light of impending judgment as if their luxury will last forever.

5:6. You have condemned [*katedikasate*], you have murdered [*ephoneusate*] the righteous one. This final accusation against the rich, using a combination of two aorist verbs (*katedikasate* and *ephoneusate*), makes clear that they are charged with judicial murder. Could this be the outcome of the charge against the rich in 2:6: "Is it not [*ouch*] the rich who oppress you and drag you into courts?" This negative question implies the answer, "Yes! It is the rich who do this." A death penalty might be the outcome of such action. It would not, however, be the rich who pronounced and carried out the death penalty. That is the function of the court and judge, before whom the trial took place. But 5:6 attributes the actions of condemning and murdering the righteous person directly to the rich. And if a specific case is in view, who is this righteous person?

The Gospel writers portray Jesus as innocent and yet condemned to death. In John 18:38 Pilate, after interviewing Jesus, reports his conclusion to the Jews: "I find in him no basis for a criminal charge [*aitia*]." In Luke 23:47 the centurion standing by the cross exclaimed when Jesus died, "Truly, this was a righteous [innocent] man." Other specific references to Jesus as the righteous one occur in Acts 3:14; 7:52; 22:14. In these three texts Jesus is referred to by the title "the righteous one"—first by Peter, then by Stephen, and finally by Paul. For other references designating Jesus as righteous, see 1 Pet. 3:18; 1 John 2:1, 29; 3:7.

Alternatively, Eusebius gathers a large number of texts concerning James, known as the brother of the Lord (Jesus) in the NT, and commonly known as James the Just/Righteous in postapostolic texts (for a full treatment, see Painter 1997a; 2004, chap. 5). According to Eusebius, James was known as the Just "for his excellence of virtue" and was the first to be elected to the episcopal throne of the Jerusalem church. In support of this view, he quotes Clement of Alexandria (Eusebius, *Hist. eccl.* 2.1.2–5). Later, Eusebius draws on Hegesippus to explain that this James was the one "everyone from the Lord's time till our own has named the 'Just,' for there were many Jameses, but this one was holy from birth; he drank no wine or intoxicating liquor and ate no animal flesh; no razor came near his head; he did not smear himself with oil, and he took no baths" (*Hist. eccl.* 2.23.4–6). He is described as wearing linen clothes in the sanctuary, kneeling and making extended prayers to God for the forgiveness of the people and in prolonged worship of God so that his knees became calloused like those of a camel. "Because of this unsurpassed righteousness he was called the Just and Oblias—in Greek, 'Bulwark of the people and Righteousness'" (*Hist. eccl.* 2.23.7).

In *Hist. eccl.* 2.23 Eusebius focuses attention on the death of James, emphasizing his innocence/righteousness, and asserts that even the wise among the Jews thought that the siege of Jerusalem, which followed "immediately after his martyrdom," happened "for no other reason than the crime they committed against him" (*Hist. eccl.* 2.23.19). In support, he appeals to Josephus: "And these things happened to the Jews to avenge James the Just, who was the brother of Jesus the so-called Christ, for the Jews killed him despite his great righteousness" (*Hist. eccl.* 2.23.20). Although this text is not found in extant copies of Josephus, it is used some seventy years earlier (between 244 and 249 CE) by Origen on three occasions (*Cels.* 1.47; 2.13; *Comm. Matt.* 10.17, on Matt. 13:53–58). Through these passages, Origen develops the point that Josephus asserts that the destruction of Jerusalem was a consequence of what the Jews did to James the Just. For Origen, this was remarkable because Josephus was not a Christian, and yet he almost got it right: Josephus should have said that Jerusalem was destroyed because of what was done to Jesus. Eusebius appears to build on this in the awareness that a considerable gap separated the death of Jesus and the destruction of Jerusalem. He says, "After the passion of the Savior, . . . disaster befell the entire nation, . . . but it was held back by the presence of James and the apostles in Jerusalem" (*Hist. eccl.* 3.7.7–8). "After the martyrdom of James, . . . the capture of Jerusalem . . . instantly followed" (*Hist. eccl.* 3.11.1). Thus Eusebius makes a remarkable connection between these two deaths. The intermingling of the traditions of the righteous Jesus and the righteous James makes both of them candidates to be identified with the righteous person condemned and murdered in James 5:6. Against identifying either of them as this righteous martyr is that Jesus was executed by the Romans, and according to Josephus, James was executed on the orders of the high priest Ananus in dubious legal circumstances (*Ant.* 20.9.1 §§197–203). It may be that the involvement of the rich high-priestly faction in both deaths sufficiently accounts for James 5:6, especially if one or both of them was perceived to threaten the stability of the status quo that safeguarded the wealth of the rich. According to John 11:45–53, Caiphas took this view of Jesus, which led to the decision to put Jesus to death.

It may be, however, that reference to "the righteous person" is general rather than specific. The accusation would then be of the kind that relates to the rich down through the ages, including the time of James. It then can be seen as an expression of the tradition of the righteous sufferer known in the Psalms and the Wisdom literature, especially Wis. 2:10–3:6 (see Painter 1997a; 2004, 254–59).

Nevertheless, it is difficult to suppose that these pregnant words would fail to be understood with reference to the judicial "murders" of Jesus and James. It is possible to see in both situations a clash with the interests of the rich Jerusalem priestly/high-priestly families. Thus the conflict may be socioeconomic (between rich and poor) as well as religious, between the followers of Jesus and "establishment Judaism." Certainly this critique of the rich seems to locate them uneasily inside (2:1–4), and as a hostile presence outside, the community of brothers and sisters.

Surprisingly, following two aorist verbs in the first part of 5:6, the final clause, **he does not resist you,** contains a verb in the present tense. This places the acts against the righteous one in the past but puts his continuing action in the present. It may be that the nonresistance of the righteous is described characteristically (see Isa. 53:7–8, 11). The righteous servant is submissive and not resistant to the evil that befalls him, implicitly trusting in God's future. This reading seems to be preferable to taking the last clause as a question: "Does he not resist you?" In Greek, the opening *ouk* of *ouk antitassetai hymin* could be read as introducing a negative question that implies a positive answer: "Yes, he does!" It is suggestive that, following 5:6, James calls on the readers to be patient "until the coming of the Lord" (5:7); "because the coming of the Lord has drawn near" (5:8); "behold, the judge is standing at the doors" (5:9). Reference to "the coming of the Lord" (*hē parousia tou kyriou*) can only indicate the return of the risen and exalted Jesus. It may be that, in light of what follows, the final clause of 5:6 is ambiguous. It announces the patient endurance of the righteous in the face of unjust violence, but it raises the question of whether the righteous one will remain passive forever. But patient endurance is the present lot of the righteous. An alternative is to read this last clause as a question and to understand the righteous person typically and the resistance passively. It is not Maccabean-style resistance that is described but rather unswerving commitment to the path of righteousness that will not be swayed by force, not even the threat of death. While both Jesus and James opposed exploitation, they did so nonviolently, and they resisted nonviolently.

Theological Issues

James has placed this discussion of community relationships under the searching light of impending judgment: "Behold, the judge is standing at the doors" (5:9; cf. 2:12–13; 5:1–6). The pervasive presence of this motif throughout James confirms that it was a significant structural element in his theology. It also gives the impression that James thought some would not modify their selfish and ruthless exploitation of those weaker than themselves unless under threat. Those who act judgmentally in relation to others will be judged (4:11–12). Those who show no mercy will receive no mercy (2:12–13). Misery was about to befall those who had exploited the poor (5:1–6). The judge was at the doors (5:9).

The sense of ultimate accountability before God is bound to this notion of judgment. Associated with this is the awareness that humans are not in control of their own destiny even in this present life. That does not rule out prudent planning, but it does mean that the wise are humble and cautious in planning the future. Here again James exposes human weakness expressed in boastful behavior. Such behavior is designed to impress others, is self-assertive and self-interested. It finds a home in the ethics of self-promotion so common in the Roman Empire and also present in our contemporary culture. There is a saying "Self-praise is no recommendation," but in the culture of the early twenty-first century, self-promotion has become the norm. In the workplace of today, promotion often depends on people's ability to "sell themselves" rather than on evidence of skill and achievements attested by others. This does not seem to lead to the most-qualified person getting the job. But that is only one side of the problem. A culture of self-promotion (boasting) promotes selfishness and a failure to show concern for others. Of this, James says, "All such boasting is evil."

Two other matters call for comment. The first is James's running critique of the rich and the obscenity of their wasteful self-indulgence in the face of the poverty of the suffering poor. The world of the twenty-first century will need to face the injustice of the dichotomy of rich and poor because a small minority of the world's population consumes the vast majority of the world's resources. The gap between rich and poor nations is broadening, as is the gap between rich and poor within nations. As James would say, "My brothers and sisters, these things ought not to be so!" (3:10).

Second, the world of the strong asserts its will by the use of force, deadly force. Too often, deadly force seems to be used unjustifiably. There were no weapons of mass destruction in Iraq, but their supposed presence was given as the justifying reason for the use of deadly force against Iraq. Altogether at odds with this is the fate of the righteous one in James 5:6. James accuses the rich and powerful of his judicial murder. Concerning the righteous one, James says, "He does not resist you." This present tense may appeal to the characteristic response of the righteous one in the face of violence. Is this the righteous servant of Isa. 53, or Jesus, or Stephen, or James the Just/Righteous, or does it encompass them all? None of these figures offered violent resistance. And should we add modern figures such as Martin Luther King and Nelson Mandela? The tradition of the righteous sufferer is long and impressive (see Painter discussion in 1997a; 2004, 254–60). Certainly these figures challenge us in the twenty-first century to find a better way to cope with violence than by responding to deadly force with greater deadly force or even striking preemptively where we fear there might be trouble, thus escalating death and destruction. Again, as James would say, "My brothers and sisters, these things ought not to be so!" (3:10). In the end, James would say that "the coming of the Lord is near," that "the judge is at the doors" (5:8–9).

James 5:7–20

Concluding Pastoral Advice

Introductory Matters

Four words in this section are found in the NT only in James. One of these, *polysplanchnos* ("compassionate," 5:11), is first known to us in James. The other three words are *proïmos* and *opsimos* ("early" and "late," 5:7) and *kakopathia* ("suffering," 5:10; cf. *kakopatheō* in 5:13). James also uses two words found otherwise only in Paul: *kakopatheō* ("to suffer," 5:13; 2 Tim. 2:9; 4:5) and *psallō* ("to sing," 5:13; Rom. 15:9; 1 Cor. 14:15; Eph. 5:19). Another four words in James are used elsewhere only by either Luke-Acts or Hebrews: *oiktirmōn* ("merciful," 5:11; Luke 6:36), *euthymeō* ("to be happy," 5:13; Acts 27:22, 25), *kamnō* ("to be sick," 5:15; Heb. 12:3), and *homoiopathēs* ("like passion," 5:17; Acts 14:15).

James uses fourteen imperatives in 5:7–20, which is the next highest concentration in the epistle after the ten imperatives in 4:7–10. This is consistent with the highly directive character of James, and an increased concentration is to be expected in the closing words. Because this is a circular letter, the closing words are not sharply focused but instead bring together responses to some common problems that emerge in the light of the previous section (5:1–6).

Tracing the Train of Thought

The preceding paragraph (5:1–6) was aimed at the rich, whether inside or outside the circle of communities, though the hostility of the paragraph implies that the rich are largely outsiders. There is a marked change from the strident polemical tone of 5:1–6 to a nurturing pastoral tone suitable for the closing words to the communities addressed in 5:7–20. While 5:7–11 sustains a fairly coherent theme of patient endurance, it is separated from 5:13–20 by 5:12, which is not related to either part. Prayer roughly binds 5:13–16 and 5:17–18 together. But 5:13–16 also deals with anointing and confession. For 5:17–18, Elijah is an exemplar of effective prayer. James concludes with encouragement to turn back to the truth those who err (5:19–20). Overall, the pastoral focus and tone provide a reasonable epistolary conclusion.

Patience and the Compassion of God (5:7–11)

5:7. Be patient, therefore, brothers [and sisters]. James explicitly turns back to encourage the members of the communities, addressing them in his customary fashion as brothers (and sisters). In the face of the assault by the rich on the poor, James announced imminent harsh judgment coming on the rich. The complementary word to the poor is "Be patient, therefore," the first of five imperatives in 5:7–11. The tirade threatening judgment on the rich is now replaced by instruction. Given that it is the rich who oppress the poor, the announcement of judgment about to befall the rich is matched by a call to the oppressed to be patient. What becomes explicit only at the end of this passage is that the call for patience is rooted in God's long-suffering compassion. The imperative *makrothymēsate* ("be patient") opens 5:7 and is repeated at the beginning of 5:8. In between, the participle of the same verb is used to describe the patient waiting of the farmer as an analogy of the patience here called for by James. The cognate noun *makrothymia* is used of the patience of the prophets in 5:10. Patience is not only a human virtue, a fruit of the Spirit (Gal. 5:22; cf. 1 Cor. 13:4); it is also characteristic of God in dealing with fragile humans (Rom. 2:4; 9:22; 1 Pet. 3:20; 2 Pet. 3:15). Patience is necessary in the present **until the coming [*parousias*] of the Lord.** The present regime continues until then. Now is the time of opportunity to turn to God. "The coming of the Lord" is almost certainly a reference to Jesus's coming in judgment as the exalted Lord (see Matt. 24:3, 27; 1 Cor. 15:23; 1 Thess. 2:19; 4:15; 5:23; 2 Thess. 2:1; 2 Pet. 1:16; 3:4; 1 John 2:28), though the coming of God (see James 3:9; 5:4) has some support. But the widely spread evidence in

---

James 5:7–20 in the Rhetorical Flow

Address/salutation (1:1)

Epitome of the exhortation of James (1:2–27)

Warning against partiality (2:1–13)

Faith and works (2:14–26)

The tongue (3:1–12)

God and the world (3:13–4:10)

Admonitions and warnings (4:11–5:6)

► Concluding pastoral advice (5:7–20)

    Patience and the compassion of God (5:7–11)

    Above all, no oaths (5:12)

    Prayer and other advice (5:13–16)

    Elijah as prayer exemplar (5:17–18)

    Restoring a sinner from the way of error (5:19–20)

support of the reference to the coming of the exalted Lord is persuasive. An analogy for the fruitfulness of patient waiting follows. **See, the farmer awaits the precious fruit of the earth, being patient with it until it receives the early and the late rains.** The reader/hearer is called on to observe the practice of the farmer, not a hired laborer (5:4). Before the harvest, the crop needs both "the early and the late rain" (see the LXX of Deut. 11:14; Jer. 5:24; Hosea 6:3; Joel 2:23) to bring it to mature development. Whether this expression reveals awareness of agricultural practice in Israel is debatable. It could be based on a literary reference. Regardless, the reference illustrates the need for patient waiting, and the balance of the phrase is appealing.

5:8. **You also be patient; make firm the resolve of your hearts** [*stērizate tas kardias hymōn*], **because the coming of the Lord has drawn near** [*hē parousia tou kyriou ēngiken*]. On the basis of the example of the farmer, the previous call for patience is repeated: "You also be patient." But this is not simply repetition. The nature of the patience required is clarified by a third imperative. Because it is patience in the face of aggressive oppressive behavior, the call is to reinforce commitment and determination, "to establish your hearts." But how does a person go about establishing or strengthening the resolve of the heart? Whereas James calls on the recipients of this letter to do this, Paul prays to God "to establish your hearts blameless in holiness before our God and Father at the coming of our Lord Jesus Christ with all his saints" (1 Thess. 3:13). The parallel is the more interesting because it goes beyond the common language "to establish your hearts" by linking this with "the coming of the Lord," as James does also. Both James and Paul (in 1 Thessalonians) portray that coming as near. In 5:7 James calls his readers to be patient until the coming of the Lord, but now in 5:8 he asserts that "the coming of the Lord has drawn near [*ēngiken*]" (on this expression, note Mark 1:15: "the kingdom of God has drawn near"). We might ask, "In what way, if any, are the two related?" But *engizō* is also used in relation to the end-time coming of the Lord (Rom. 13:12; Heb. 10:25; 1 Pet. 4:7). Perhaps James thinks that keeping in mind the nearness of the Lord's coming will provide an incentive for strengthening the resolve of the heart.

5:9. **Do not grumble/complain about one another** [*mē stenazate . . . kat' allēlōn*], **brothers [and sisters], lest you be judged.** The renewed address of the readers as "brothers [and sisters]," in conjunction with an apparent change of subject, suggests that we have moved to a new topic, but the motif of patience and endurance returns in 5:10–11. Could it be that such grumbling is a form of complaining against each other, an undermining of resolve and commitment? The directive (negative command) not to complain about one another echoes the earlier directive (negative command) in 4:11–12: "Do not speak against one another [*mē katalaleite allēlōn*]." But whereas "speaking against" was equated with "judging" a brother (or sister), the one who complains or grumbles is threatened with judgment and warned, **Behold, the judge is standing at the**

doors. This is both an assurance to those who have strengthened the resolve of their hearts and a threat to those who grumble and complain about their brothers (and sisters) and to those who exploit the righteous poor. This sense of imminent judgment undergirds the forceful warning in 5:1–6. Very likely the Jesus tradition underlying this development is found in Matt. 7:1–5, which begins, "Do not judge lest you be judged." This warning is especially pressing because the judge has drawn near and stands at the door (see Mark 13:29).

5:10. Take the example [*hypodeigma*], brothers [and sisters], of the sufferings and patience [*makrothymia*] of the prophets who spoke in the name of the Lord. The final two verses of this section return to the call for patience in the face of suffering and oppression and are introduced by a renewed use of the address "brothers [and sisters]." Now James directs with the fifth imperative: "Take the example of the prophets." The word *hypodeigma* is used only six times in the NT (John 13:15; Heb. 4:11; 8:5; 9:23; James 5:10; 2 Pet. 2:6), and it occurs five times in the LXX (Ezek. 42:15; Sir. 44:16; 2 Macc. 6:28, 31; 4 Macc. 17:23). It indicates something like a normative model or example. The choice of the prophets is far from random. They fit the current situation admirably. Here and in 5:11, "the Lord" represents the name of God ("YHWH") and is not a reference to Jesus. The prophets spoke in the name of the Lord, and they suffered. Nevertheless, they showed patience. Such patience in suffering is an expression of trust in God and of waiting for God's time. The word for "suffering" (*kakopatheia*) is used only here in the NT, though the cognate verb (*kakopatheō*) is used in James 5:13; 2 Tim. 2:9; 4:5. The noun and verb imply the evil of such suffering, though it is borne and endured in the service of God (cf. Heb. 11:32–38). There is already in this reference a hint of a characteristic of patience that is about to be unfolded.

5:11. Behold, we consider blessed those who were steadfast [*tous hypomeinantas*]. In the first instance, this is a reference back to 1:12: "Blessed is the person who endures [*hypomenei*] testing." The steadfast are those who endure the testing that confronts the faithful in a hostile world. The blessing that James pronounces on the steadfast is an expression of the Jesus tradition found in Matt. 5:10: "Blessed are those who are persecuted for the sake of righteousness, for theirs is the kingdom of heaven." The general reference to the prophets is followed by a reference to the proverbial righteous sufferer, Job: You have heard of the steadfastness [*tēn hypomonēn*] of Job, and you know the end/purpose [*telos*] of the Lord, because the Lord is compassionate and merciful [*polysplanchnos kai oiktirmōn*]. The use of *polysplanchnos* is a biblical hapax legomenon, but from the late second century CE it enters the wider Christian vocabulary (e.g., *Shepherd of Hermas*, Clement of Alexandria, *Acts of Thomas*). The clause "the Lord is compassionate and merciful" (*polysplanchnos estin ho kyrios kai oiktirmōn*) echoes the words of a foundational revelation and confession of the name of God in Exod. 34:6, which re-echoes in Ps. 103:8 (102:8 LXX) and Sir. 2:11 (*oiktirmōn kai eleēmōn ho kyrios*; cf.

Ps. 112:4 [111:4 LXX]). In James, *polysplanchnos* has replaced *eleēmōn*. This might be a change similar to the move from translating *ḥesed we'ĕmet* as *eleos kai alētheia* to the translation *charis kai alētheia* in the later books of the LXX and later Hellenistic Judaism (note John 1:14; see Dodd 1953a, 175).

What started as a call for patience (*makrothymēsate*) in 5:7 quickly takes on the sense of endurance (*hypomonē*), because it is not simply a matter of waiting for time to pass. Rather, patience is confronted by aggressive and destructive forces that challenge faithfulness to God and love of neighbor. Such challenges call for active resistance and determined commitment to faithfulness to God and active concern for the well-being of the neighbor. In a hostile environment, endurance is not for the fainthearted. The example of Job confirms the serious trials to be faced by those who determine to be faithful to God and neighbor. Job's story is a history of trials and tribulations. Yet James reminds us of the end: "you know the end [*telos*]." The simplest reading is "you know the end of the story." In the end it turned out all right. Job was restored to health and wealth. But what of the destruction and loss of life along the way? Does none of that matter, as long as Job is all right? But it is not simply "you know the end." Rather, the text reads, "you know the end of the Lord," and the word translated as "end" can mean "goal" or "purpose." What would "you know the purpose of the Lord" mean? Although the role of Satan in Job is not easily reconciled with James, the motif of the testing of faithfulness is prominent (see James 1:2–4, 12–15). In Job, Satan more or less acts as God's agent in the testing of Job, but James categorically rejects the notion that God is in any way responsible for testing and instead outlines an alternative view in 1:13–15. We could say that it is God's purpose to bring good out of evil, to bring a good outcome out of the testing caused by suffering (*kakopathia*), which is in itself evil. The good outcome is the perfecting of those who endure faithfully. This good outcome is the purpose because "the Lord is compassionate and merciful," a confession at the very heart of the revelation of God (see Exod. 34:6).

Above All, No Oaths (5:12)

5:12. Above all, my brothers [and sisters], do not swear, whether by heaven, or by earth, or any other oath; but let your yes be yes and no be no, lest you fall under judgment. The renewed address of the readers as "brothers [and sisters]" suggests a new topic and may signal use of Jesus tradition. "Above all" suggests the prioritizing of this subject, but it does not seem to be related to the preceding verses or lead into what follows. Perhaps the discussion was suggested by the use of oaths in conclusions. A fairly close parallel to the prohibition in James is found in Matt. 5:34–37 (cf. Matt. 23:16–22). The parallel agrees generally in its prohibition: "Do not swear, neither by heaven . . . nor by earth. . . . Let your yes be yes and your no be no." It seems that the sayings of Matthew and James are variants of the same saying. Yet the situation is complicated by the recognition of Jewish and Greek traditions that critique the common use of oaths, such as Sir. 23:9–11, which criticizes the use of many oaths, or Epictetus (*Ench*. 33.5), who counseled the avoidance of oaths, if possible. Nevertheless, the prohibition of oaths is distinctive enough in principle, and in the particulars of Matthew and James, to identify their common use of Jesus tradition, perhaps James's use of the tradition known in Matthew. While this prohibition of oaths does not specifically make the point, it seems to follow that truthfulness is guaranteed by a simple yes or no. Again James concludes this discussion with the threat of judgment for those who will not abide by the simple binding yes or no. This comes close to the verdict in Matt. 5:37, that anything more is of the evil one, presumably the devil. With such speech, truthfulness becomes normative. The recurring theme of judgment loosely connects James 5:12 to 5:7, 9 in the previous section.

Prayer and Other Advice (5:13–16)

The following advice, including 5:17–18, is concentrated on prayer, though other related topics are drawn into the discussion as occasions calling for prayer.

5:13. Is anyone among you suffering [*kakopathei*]? Let him or her pray. Is anyone happy? Let him or her sing. In 5:13–14 James proceeds with a series of leading questions where a series of conditional sentences would have served a similar purpose. "If anyone among you is suffering" has much the same function as the question "Is anyone among you suffering?" Neither is a statement concerning what is the case, and each allows a response to be made to a hypothetical situation. James has written a series of three short questions, each of them followed by a third-person singular imperative in response to the situation. The third-person form functions as an exhortation: "Let that person . . ."

The UBS editors have vacillated over whether 5:13–14 contains three questions or three statements. The second edition printed three questions, but UBS[3] and UBS[4] have made these into three statements, in agreement with NA[26] and NA[27]. The RSV, NRSV, NEB, and REB print three questions. The original Greek texts, which lack punctuation, allow either questions or statements. Thus, the change is not a matter of new textual evidence but instead reflects changes in editorial personnel for the later UBS text. If the three sentences are taken as statements, the assumption of the writer is that someone is suffering, someone is happy, someone is sick. This is rather artificial, especially because this circular letter is addressed widely (see 1:1). It might be argued that the states described are so general that invariably someone would fit them, but the text does not read naturally as three statements, and James makes frequent use of rhetorical questions. No good case has been made against taking what is written as three short and succinct questions.

The first question concerns someone suffering. The verb used here (*kakopatheō*) is cognate to the noun (*kakopathia*) used of the suffering of

165

the prophets in 5:10. The use of this particular root here and in 5:10 draws attention to the evil of suffering. Consequently, though bravely bearing suffering may be "character building" in the sense of strengthening one's faith and commitment to God, suffering is not good in itself, and the person suffering is directed to pray. While no content for such prayer is indicated, it would be strange if the prayer did not include a petition for deliverance from suffering, though the prayer for patience and endurance is also relevant. Given that the prayer of Jesus includes the petition "but deliver us from the evil one" (Matt. 6:13), it seems reasonable to suppose that the petition "deliver us from the evil of suffering" is also appropriate. The direction to anyone who is happy is more straightforward, "let him or her sing [*psalletō*]," with the verb *psallō* indicating the singing of praise, a psalm of praise, or a hymn (cf. Rom. 15:9; 1 Cor. 14:15; Eph. 5:19; see also Phil. 4:4–5). For James, joy and rejoicing are underrated values that should be normative in daily life (see 1:1–2).

5:14. Is anyone among you sick [*asthenei*]? Let him or her call the elders of the church [*ekklēsias*]. The word translated as "sick" covers any sort of debilitating weakness and is commonly used of a sick person. That this is the sense here is confirmed by the use of *kamnonta* to describe the sick person in 5:15. Given the common understanding of sickness in the ancient world—either as a punishment by God or as an affliction caused by evil powers—the solution is to call not a physician but rather the elders of the church. James directs this course of action with two third-person imperatives. Because it is a hypothetical sick person, who cannot be addressed by a direct command, the directive can only be indirect: "let him or her call" (*proskalesasthō*). That the elders are summoned implies a serious, perhaps life-threatening illness. Reference to the elders of the "church" coming to the sick person stands in contrast to the reference to a rich man coming into the addressees' "synagogue" in 2:2. The difference in language may reflect the fact that the Hebrew *qāhāl* is translated in the LXX as either *synagōgē* or *ekklēsia*. The use of *synagōgē* in 2:2 is appropriate because the rich man came into a gathering of the community; the use of *ekklēsia* in 5:14 is a reference to the community but not to its gathering or coming together. Though the Letter of James is addressed to "the twelve tribes of the Diaspora" without restriction to the followers of Jesus, the sender(s) may have assumed that the likelihood of a broader reception was small. Whether *synagōgē* or *ekklēsia* is used, it is possible that the elders are believing Jews in a Jewish synagogue/church of followers of Jesus. The language used by James does not require this, given the interchangeable use of *synagōgē* or *ekklēsia*.

The second directive is addressed to the elders. It is a double third-person plural construction, the first part of which is expressed with an imperative, **let them pray over him**, and the second part with a participle functioning as an imperative, **anointing him or her with oil in the name of the Lord**, which has the sense "let them anoint." The use of the participle links the second act with the first, so that anointing is part of the action of prayer they are instructed to make (for anointing with oil in healing, see Mark 6:13). This does not appear to be a medicinal use of oil, as in Luke 10:34. Rather, in James it is done as a symbolic action in conjunction with the pronouncement of the name of the Lord, identifying the power at work in the prayer for the sick person. Determining whether the "name of the Lord" is the name of God ("YHWH"; see 3:9; 4:10, 15; 5:4, 11) or the name of Jesus (see 5:7, 8, 10) is problematic. This is borne out by the confused textual evidence at this point. Codex Vaticanus (fourth century) omits *tou kyriou* ("of the Lord") altogether. Such a reading could account for all other readings. Codex Sinaiticus (fourth century) has the adopted reading, which also has important early patristic support, including that of Origen and a mass of minuscules dating from the ninth to the fifteenth centuries. The latter confirms that it became the adopted reading. Some other manuscripts broadly support this reading but omit the definite article (*tou*). There is late, weak support for the readings "in the name of the Lord Jesus," and "in the name of Jesus Christ." All of these readings are explicable as attempted clarifications of an original text that read "anointing him with oil in the name." The adopted reading could explain the addition of some form of the name of Jesus but does not explain the reading of Vaticanus, which omits "of the Lord."

Given a reading of "in the name" or "in the name of the Lord," should this be understood as a reference to God or to Jesus? Baptism was performed in the name of Jesus Christ or of the Lord Jesus (Acts 2:38; 8:16; 10:48; 19:5), and there is reference to exorcisms in the name of Jesus (Mark 9:38; Luke 10:17; Acts 3:6, 16; 4:7, 10; 9:34). But the reference to the Lord in James 5:15 likely indicates the name of God, whose power is effective in healing and raising up the sick person.

The role of the elders appears to be an identifiable responsibility corporately undertaken on behalf of the church, the local community of followers. At the same time, because James has to detail the process, it may not have been a well-established practice in every place. The sick needed to be instructed concerning this resource, and the elders needed to be instructed in the fulfillment of their responsibility to the sick.

5:15. And the prayer of faith will save/heal [*sōsei*] the sick person [*ton kamnonta*], and the Lord will raise [*egerei*] him or her; even if he or she has committed sins, they will be forgiven him or her. Reference to "the prayer of faith" echoes the petition for wisdom (1:5–6), where the need to ask in faith is strongly emphasized. Consequently, it seems that the gracious God, who gives to all who ask in faith, is willing to provide more than wisdom, because God is the source of every generous act of giving and every perfect gift (1:17). The sick person has expressed faith by calling the elders, but the prayer of faith is the prayer of the elders of the church for the sick person, and it will save that person. Here, employing the verb *sōzō*, James uses the imagery of "saving" to express "healing," an idiom known from the accounts of the ministry of Jesus in the Gospels (Matt. 9:21–22; Mark 5:23, 28, 34; 6:56; 10:52). The opening statement gives the impression that the prayer of faith directly achieves the healing. That impression is now corrected: it is the Lord who will raise the sick person to health. Here another image of healing is employed with the verb in the future tense: "the Lord will raise." The imagery is suggestive of the resurrection, in terms of both the verb used and its future tense (*egerei*), which suggest the resurrection on the last day. In this way, healing becomes an image and token of resurrection, in which the fullness of healing becomes reality.

While James associates sin and sickness, this is not an inseparable connection, since 5:15c identifies only the possibility of sins committed: "and even if he or she has committed sins." The process of healing includes the forgiveness of sins; if they have been committed, "they will be forgiven." No mention has been made of penitence or of confession, though in the light of 5:16, this might be assumed. From prayer for the sick, the topic turns to confession of sins, but without leaving the discussion of prayer behind.

5:16. Therefore, confess [your] sins to one another [*allēlōn*] and pray for one another [*allēlōn*], that you may be healed. The connection with 5:15 is signaled by "therefore" (*oun*). The second-person plural imperative "confess" (*exomologeisthe*) makes clear to the community that confessing sins is essential for them all and for the good of the community. This is a matter of confessing sins not to God but rather to one another, which probably means confessing to the person or persons sinned against. Whether this occurs at a community gathering or in some other way is not specified. They are also to pray for one another. The repeated use of *allēlōn* is important. This pronoun expresses the reciprocity of community relationships, a reality that exposes speaking against one another (4:11–12) and grumbling/complaining against one another (5:9) as self-destructive and destructive to the community. Instead of their engaging in such destructive behavior, James urges, "Confess [*exomologeisthe*] your sins to one another and pray [*euchesthe*] for one another." Both of these second-person plural imperatives make a strong directive to the community about what is good for them. Fulfilling these directives is a condition of healing, or to keep to the idiom of James, it is the means by which they may be healed (*hopōs iathēte*). Failing to follow these directives strengthens the grip that sin has on them. For James, spiritual health is dependent on following these directives, as is perhaps physical health as well.

The directive to pray for one another turns the discussion back to prayer. James, having talked about the prayer of faith (5:15), now identifies effective prayer. The effective [*energoumenē*] prayer of a righteous person [*dikaiou*] has great power. No satisfactory understanding of the participle *energoumenē*, describing prayer, is evident. There is nothing so far to suggest that James thinks that enthusiasm, fervor, energy, or the like makes prayer effective. The power of prayer is God, and faithful prayer taps into the power of God via the righteous person who engages in faithful prayer. What follows seems to be an example of such prayer.

Elijah as Prayer Exemplar (5:17–18)

5:17–18. Elijah was a human like us, and he prayed fervently [*proseuchē proseuxato*] that it might not rain, and it did not rain on the earth for three years and six months; and again he prayed [*proseuxato*], and the heaven gave rain, and the earth yielded its fruit. In the illustration, Elijah is a human like us, but is he a righteous human? James does not say so, but we may assume that this is to be taken as given in the light of 5:16. The features of the story used in the illustration (the prayer of Elijah and the three-and-a-half-year drought) are drawn not from 1 Kings 17–18 but rather from Jewish tradition (see 2 Esd. 7:109 [*4 Ezra* 7:39]). The linguistic construction used to express Elijah's act of praying seems to be a Hebraism used in the LXX to translate the Hebrew infinitive absolute. The noun in the dative case, *proseuchē*, is used with the cognate verb *proseuxato* to mean literally "he prayed with prayer," and this is taken to convey an intensity of action. But is it the intensity of Elijah's prayer that stopped up the heavens and then opened them again for the life-giving rains? Given that Elijah here is depicted not as a prophetic giant but simply as a human like us, might this not turn attention back to God, who does these things? But why then choose Elijah, if the point is that he is simply another human like any of us? The implied answer to that question seems to turn the attention back to the power and passion of Elijah's prayer. And if so, we might need to reconsider the nature of the prayer of the righteous person that has great power. Does the *energoumenē* prayer of the righteous person in 5:16 mean the "fervent prayer" (*proseuchē proseuxato*)? That expression seems to link 5:16 to Elijah the exemplar. Or does the intensification of the construction in 5:17 imply Elijah's absolute belief in God and God's purpose? Does the example show what is possible when an ordinary person unites with the will and purpose of God? And that may be the point. The righteous person is an ordinary person aligned with the will and purpose of God.

Restoring a Sinner from the Way of Error (5:19–20)

5:19. My brothers [and sisters], . . . The first words of the final sentence, "My brothers [and sisters]," address the readers/hearers fondly for the last time in these familiar, familial terms. The body of the letter is enclosed between the opening address with these words in 1:2 and the closing address of 5:19. In this letter, the endearing words of address often follow a directive given by a verb in the imperative mood (see 1:2, 16, 19; 2:5; 3:12; 4:11; 5:7, 9, 10). In this sentence, the imperative comes in the middle, at the beginning of 5:20, and is more informative than directive. The first half of the sentence constitutes a double condition: **If anyone [*ean tis*] among you is led astray [*planēthē*] from**

the truth and [if] someone [*tis*] brings him back . . . This is a hypothetical situation. Because the verb (*planēthē*) is passive, the agent doing the leading astray is not identified. It is unclear whether straying from the truth has an internal or external cause. Desire (*epithymia*) may lead a person astray (1:12–15). Alternatively, false teachers may lead others astray, but James makes no criticism of false teachers troubling the community (contrast 1 John 2:18–19; 4:1–6). Like 1 John, James critiques the world as a sphere that has the power to attract and corrupt the community (James 3:13–18; 4:1–5; 1 John 2:15–17). Such attraction has its hold only through "desire" (*epithymia*), and desire unchecked causes chaos (4:1–2). Despite a somewhat dualistic worldview that sets the world in opposition to God, there is no mention of the devil when James deals with the problem of "desire." When the devil is mentioned in 4:7, the devil's significance is minimized: "Therefore submit to God; resist the devil, and he will flee from you." Elsewhere, related references are few: "even the demons believe and tremble" (2:19); "the tongue is a fire set alight by Gehenna [hell]" (3:6). This is a meager haul with which to support the notion that our being in error and going astray are the work of the devil. Rather, James stresses human responsibility for these things and identifies unbridled desire as the root cause. But if someone is led astray, it is also possible that someone else will bring that person back again.

The motifs of straying from the truth and being brought back from "the way of error" (*planēs hodou*, 5:20) to the way of truth are widespread, not only in the Jewish and Christian writings. Deuteronomy develops the language of the two ways between which Israel must choose. This framework is reinforced by the prophetic literature that calls Israel to turn back to the way from which they have strayed, the way they have forsaken. The language of turning back and "repenting" became foundational in the early Christian writings, building on the message of John the Baptist and the preaching of Jesus (Mark 1:4, 15). See the teaching about the two ways by Jesus (Matt. 7:13–14//Luke 13:23–24) and in the *Didache* (*Did*. 1–7). This language was also shared by the Jewish sect that left their literary remains in the caves of Qumran as a gift for posterity. In these writings, the sectarians claim to be the people of the way, identifying this image with Isa. 40:3 ("A voice cries out, 'In the wilderness prepare the way of the LORD' "), a text also used by the John the Baptist (Mark 1:3). Both John and the Qumran community "withdrew" to the desert, perhaps in response to this text. John called for the repentance of all who came to him. The Qumran sect withdrew to the desert to study the law, away from Israel as a whole, because the sectarians believed that the nation had strayed from the way (see 1QS 8.8–12). Members of the sect might also stray. They developed strict rules and conditions for those who would return from the error of their way.

In James, no complex conditions are evident for those brought back from the error of their way. Nevertheless, James leaves no room for doubt that to return an errant brother or sister from the way of error to the truth is a matter of life and death. Thus, although James does not use the technical vocabulary of repentance (*metanoia* and *metanoeō*), the substance of repentance is described. Here James is not concerned about conditions to be fulfilled by the penitent person; rather, attention is turned to the one who brings back an erring brother or sister.

5:20. The beginning of the second half of this final sentence, **let him or her know [*ginōsketō*] that**, is textually unclear.

1. With Vaticanus (fourth century), the Syriac[h] and Ethiopic versions, and a couple of later minuscules from the twelfth century in support, UBS[2] and the NRSV read "you [pl.] should know that" (*ginōskete hoti* [second-person plural imperative]). The editors of UBS[2] did not rate the adopted reading highly, giving it only a D rating. The readers/hearers are informed of the significance of this action, performed presumably by one of them.
2. With Sinaiticus (fourth century), Alexandrinus (fifth century), K and P (ninth century), a mass of later manuscripts, and the Old Latin, Vulgate, Syriac[b], Coptic[bo], and Armenian versions and the Byzantine Lectionary[m] in support, UBS[3], UBS[4], and the RSV adopt the reading "let him or her know that" (*ginōsketō hoti* [third-person singular imperative]). UBS[4] gives this reading a B rating, though UBS[3] gives it only a C rating. While not addressed directly to the person who brought back the sinner from error to the truth (James is addressed to Diaspora communities), it indirectly addresses that person by using the third-person singular imperative so that the person will know the significance of his or her action.

The textual evidence has not changed, so this change of ratings is perplexing. The D rating for the first reading (*ginōskete hoti*) is the weakest level of support for a chosen reading and indicates that it is an uncertain choice. Using the same evidence, later editions of the UBS text adopt the second reading (*ginōsketō hoti*). Neither edition gives it a minimal D rating, and UBS[4] rates this strongly as a B. The textual support is clearly wider and stronger for the second reading than the evidence for the first reading. The style of the third-person singular imperative is Jamesian, though a continued second-person plural address of the readers/hearers might be deemed more natural, and that might account for the variant. James has been addressing his readers as a whole as "brothers [and sisters]," and it would follow very naturally if he exhorted them "you [pl.] should know that" the person who restores the sinner "will save his or her life." Probably the expectation that the reading/hearing community is addressed accounts for a copying error, which involves only the incorrect copying of one letter, a final epsilon (*e*) instead of an original final omega (*ō*). The earlier and more Jamesian text, "let him or her know," alerts the one who brought the errant sinner back "from the error of his or her way" of two consequences. This form of exhortation is characteristic of James, but it is a little unexpected in the context of this final sentence, which might be expected to address the community.

The first of two consequences is that **the person who returns a sinner from the error [*planēs*] of his or her way will save his or her life [*psychē*] from death.** The language of being led astray (*planēthē*) in 5:19 and error (*planēs*) in 5:20 is drawn from a culture different from the theological and ethical context of Judaism and the law. Yet James has integrated this language with the more traditional vocabulary of sin and sinners. While the language of error is characteristic of gnosticism, Judaism in the Hellenistic world experienced challenges from different worldviews and values and from those who advocated them in a way that led others astray. A struggle of this sort is evident at Qumran between the Righteous Teacher and "the man of lies." Similar struggles are evident in the early Christian writings (See 1 John 2:26; 3:7; cf. 2:18–25; 4:1–6). The language used in James reflects such a situation but does so without identifying the misleading source. For James, involvement in such error is sin and places the sinner in deadly peril.

While possibly the meaning is that the one who returns the sinner from the way of error may save his or her own life from death, this reading is unlikely. We would expect a clearer indication of the reflexive "his or her *own* life." Further, such a reading does not follow the sequence of thought. It follows naturally that the sinner who has been returned from the way of error has been saved from death. There is nothing to suggest that the one who restores that sinner is in deadly peril. The idiom "save one's *psychē* from death" builds on the Hebraic use of *nepeš*/*psychē*, which refers to the whole person. To bring the person back to the way of truth is to save the person from death. There may be a sense of saving the person from physical death, because of the possible relationship between sin and sickness in 5:14–16, but 5:15c does not assert a necessary connection between sin and sickness. The idea of saving the person from final death on the day of judgment, a day that James perceives as imminent (5:9), is also in view.

A second consequence seems to follow. Restoration from the way of error saves the sinner's life from death **and will cover a multitude of sins.** According to Prov. 10:12, "Hatred stirs up strife, but love covers all offenses" (NRSV). This idea underlies both James 5:20c and 1 Pet. 4:8: "love covers a multitude of sins." The language of James and 1 Peter is almost identical, the only difference between their common words being that James uses the future tense (*kalypsei*) and 1 Peter the present tense (*kalyptei*) of the verb "to cover." James introduces the clause with "and" (*kai*), and 1 Peter uses a causal *hoti* ("because"). The linguistic differences from Proverbs and the agreement between James and 1 Peter suggest the use of an underlying Christian paraenetic tradition. Given that both Proverbs and 1 Peter state that what causes the covering is "love" (though Proverbs uses *philia*, and 1 Peter uses *agapē*), it is likely that James perceives the act of restoring someone who has strayed from the way of truth as an act of love for the straying brother or sister.

But whose sins are covered by this act of love? And what does the image of covering a multitude of sins depict? It seems to be an image of atonement or forgiveness (Ps. 32:1–2 [31:1–2 LXX]; Rom. 4:6–8). The means of covering sins is crucial. Here it is achieved by leading back to the way of truth someone who has been led astray. The drift of the argument suggests that the benefit may apply to the person who brought back the sinner. The emphasis on the multitude of sins covered probably emphasizes the abundant value of such a compassionate act of mercy, which itself generates mercy (cf. James 2:13). Ezekiel 3:18–21 and 33:9 teach the necessity of warning the righteous who have gone astray. Whether or not the warning is heeded, it exonerates the one who makes the warning. It may be that something like this is close to the meaning of James. It is an act of mercy, which opens mercy to the merciful (Matt. 5:7; James 2:13).

Theological Issues

James introduces the notion of "endurance" (*hypomonē*) early (1:3–4) and develops the theme of enduring (*hypomenō*) testing/temptation in 1:12–14. Such endurance has a rather more active sense than is expressed in the call to be patient (*makrothymeō*) toward the end (5:7–10), but even here patience (*makrothymia*) in suffering becomes endurance/steadfastness (*hypomonē*) in 5:11. Initially, the patience is in waiting for the coming of the Lord, like a farmer who has done all the planting and now waits for the growth before the harvest. The notion of the harvest is implicit here and is frequently used as an image of judgment. Here the sense of patient waiting is appropriate..When the theme turns to the suffering of the prophets and of Job, James returns to the language of endurance/steadfastness (*hypomonē*). We may conclude that patience and endurance are closely related, and the nuance of difference between the two perhaps depends on the absence or presence of dire circumstances. James teaches that sometimes circumstances arise that we cannot change, and then all we can do is patiently endure whatever is thrown at us. But James says nothing to imply that circumstances should not be changed when that is possible. When they cannot be changed, all we can do is patiently endure and trust in God for whatever may come. James taught that God's outcome was near: "The judge is standing at the doors."

After dealing with arduous testing, James turns to the issue of sickness, which is no less pressing in our day, when medical science brings healing to many. Mortality is inevitable and by any count continues to strike many far too soon. Although James has not excluded a relationship between sin and

173

sickness, he certainly does not assert a simple causal relationship (see 5:15). But where sin is involved, confession of sin, especially made to the person wronged, is called for. The initiative of the sick person is fundamental in calling the elders of the church. James lays down a procedure to be followed by the elders. This involves prayer and anointing with oil. The anointing is a religious ritual rather than a medicinal application and symbolizes God's healing activity. The prayer offered is described in 5:15 as "the prayer of faith" (cf. 1:5–6). Asking God in faith is exactly the meaning of "the prayer of faith." In 1:5–6, what is asked for is wisdom, which the asker is assured God will give to those who ask in faith. In 5:15, the prayer of faith is assured of fulfillment: "the Lord will raise up" the sick person, whose sins will be forgiven. Although confession is mentioned at the end of this process (5:16), it is presumed at the beginning, before prayer and anointing. This passage in James has influenced the development of the ministry of healing in the church from earliest times.

Jude

David A. deSilva

Preface to Jude

If Bible publishers stopped printing Jude, it might take years for some people to notice. And even then, not everyone would mind. Jude's short letter is almost wholly concerned with proclaiming divine judgment and declaring certain rival teachers to stand condemned under that judgment. His rant is not in keeping with a culture that values "dialogue" and that promotes pluralism and tolerance. He relies perhaps too much on obscure "scriptures" such as *1 Enoch*, which few modern people have ever heard of, let alone read. Nevertheless, underneath the polemic is a timeless conviction: God's favor toward us is meant to accomplish a transformation in our lives, not leave us the way we were before we knew God. Failing to allow God's gift to have its full effect amounts to denying Christ's lordship. This word is all the more precious as it may, in fact, be the only surviving testimony of one of Jesus's own half brothers.

I am grateful to the series editors, Mikeal Parsons and Charles Talbert, for allowing me to contribute to their excellent Paideia series with this short commentary. It is an honor for me to share the company of so many distinguished scholars, including the coauthor of this volume. As always, James Ernest and the production staff at Baker Academic have been a pleasure to work with.

The title of this series—"Paideia," the Greek word used to speak of the formative process of education—moves me to use this opportunity to express my appreciation for a long-time friend and colleague, Noah Clayton Croy of Trinity Lutheran Seminary. I know no scholar who is so devoted to students, so inventive in the classroom, so invested in critical reflection upon pedagogy as he. Clayton is for me a model of dedication to *paideia*, and it is with deep respect that I dedicate this work to him.

David A. deSilva
Easter Triduum, 2012

Introduction to Jude

Authorship

The author presents himself as Jude (Judas), the brother of James (v. 1). Of all the people bearing the names "Judas" and "James" in the early church, only the half brothers of Jesus seem to fit the bill here (Matt. 13:55; Mark 6:3). It was not customary to identify oneself by one's brother, unless he was a person of great prominence. James the half brother of Jesus rose to such prominence within the early church, becoming the leader of the church in Jerusalem after Peter's departure (Acts 15; 21). Leadership in the Jewish Christian churches remains largely "in the family" throughout the first century, for at the conclusion of the same we find Jesus's grandnephews, the grandsons of Jude, exercising leadership among the churches in Palestine (Bauckham 1990, 105; Eusebius, *Hist. eccl.* 3.19.1–3.20.8). This letter presents an example of the pastoral oversight provided by a lesser-known member of Jesus's family.

But did Jude the brother of James really compose this letter, or is the ascription of authorship a literary fiction? The debate hinges on several questions. First, does the letter show signs typical of the postapostolic period, which often include a fading expectation of Jesus's imminent return, an increased interest in church offices and hierarchy, and an emphasis on "the faith" as a body of doctrine to be carefully preserved rather than on "faith" as a vital trust in Jesus's death and resurrection? Second, was the historical Jude likely to have acquired the proficiency in Greek exhibited by this letter? Third, does the author look back on the deaths of the apostles in verses 17–18?

Jude does not fit the characteristics associated with postapostolic writings. The author has a lively expectation of the return of Christ and the judgment of God, on which he hangs the rhetorical force of his argument (vv. 14–15, 21, 24; Webb 1996). He appeals to no church authorities to correct, silence, or expel the intruding teachers and so gives no evidence of a developed church

The Name "Jude/Judas" in the New Testament

A surprising number of persons with varying forms of the name "Jude/Judas" (*Ioudas*) are mentioned in the NT.

Judas the brother of James and Joseph and Simon (Matt. 13:55; Mark 6:3)
Judas the son of James (Luke 6:16; Acts 1:13), who may be the same person as "Judas, not Iscariot" in John 14:22
Judas Iscariot (e.g., Matt. 10:4; 26:14, 25)
Judas the Galilean, a revolutionary (Acts 5:37; see Josephus, *J.W.* 2.17.8 §433; *Ant.* 18.1.1 §§1–10)
Judas of Damascus (Acts 9:11)
Judas Barsabbas (Acts 15:22, 27, 32)

"order." When Jude urges his readers to contend for "the faith that had been handed down once for all to the saints" (v. 3), he does use "faith" to describe a pattern of belief and way of life (all that constitutes "being a Christian"). This sense differs from Paul's typical use of "faith" to denote a more dynamic faithfulness and trust between disciples and Jesus. It does not follow, however, that Jude's use of the term reflects a later development, a use appropriate only to the second-century disputes against gnostic Christians or other heretics (as in Lohse 1981, 216; Kelly 1969, 233–34). Paul himself remembers Judean Christians speaking just a few short years after his conversion about how Paul now preached "the faith that he once attacked" (Gal. 1:23). Here, already, "faith" denotes the convictions and way of life that flow from accepting the gospel, and it is an undeniably early use. Jude's use of "faith" would have been at home in Judea in the period before Paul's missionary journeys. Paul will also use "faith" with this meaning (Phil. 1:27), again in the context of opposition and defense (as in Gal. 1:23; Jude 3).

The second question is more difficult. Widely divergent positions have been taken on the general level of knowledge of Greek in Galilee. On one side, J. Daryl Charles (1991b, 118) observes that Galilee produced "Josephus the historian, Theodorus the rhetorician, Meleager the poet, and Philodemus the philosopher," whom he puts forward as evidence against "the myth of 'Galilean illiteracy.'" Galilee contained Greek cities such as Sepphoris and Scythopolis and was neighbor to significant Greek coastal cities. Martin Hengel (1989, 8) considers Judea, Samaria, and Galilee to be "bilingual or trilingual areas," claiming that Jesus would have spoken Greek when he conversed with a centurion, the Syrophoenician woman, and Pilate (1989, 17; see also Witherington 2007, 565). On the other side, Richard Horsley (1996, 154–75) has argued that Greek literacy in Galilee was restricted to the political and social elite. One could expect at most a kind of "Pidgin Greek" to be spoken broadly among the Jewish population, just adequate for doing business with non-Jewish neighbors.

Scholars further debate what exposure to Greek Jude in particular might have had, and thus whether it is plausible that a junior son in a Galilean artisan family could have written such a letter, which some scholars flatly deny (e.g., Kelly 1969, 233; Neyrey 1993, 31). While we should be careful not to assume too fluid a grasp of Greek on the part of artisans from Nazareth, Jude may well have had a sufficiently solid foundation upon which to build in his postconversion work as a Christian missionary and leader.

Jesus's family and disciples were located in Jerusalem after the resurrection. Jerusalem was a center for Hellenistic Jews, as it was the epicenter for Hellenization in Judea several centuries earlier (2 Macc. 4:7–17). Greek-speaking Jews were present in number within the city and within the Christian movement taking shape there (Acts 6–7). Many of Gamaliel's own students were said to have been "trained in the wisdom of the Greeks" (Daube 1949). In Jerusalem, Jude would also have come into close contact with Jewish pilgrims from all over the Diaspora, for whom Greek would have been the primary means of communicating even with their coreligionists in Jerusalem. As a member of the inner circle of Christian leaders, Jude would likely have been thrust into the work of teaching, converting, and conversing with fellow Jews in both Aramaic and Greek from Pentecost onward.

It is also possible that Jude was an itinerant preacher for at least part of his life. Julius Africanus knows of a tradition that located the relatives of Jesus in Galilee as missionaries (according to Eusebius, *Hist. eccl.* 1.7.14), but they might have traveled further. In 1 Cor. 9:5 Paul speaks of "the other apostles and the brothers of the Lord" (which would not have included James, who was resident in Jerusalem for the duration of Paul's ministry) exercising an itinerant ministry while taking along their wives, for whom the churches provided support alongside the preacher, expecting the Corinthian Christians to be familiar with this practice (perhaps through firsthand observation). If Jude was a missionary to Diaspora Jews, he had even more opportunity to grow in facility in Greek. The fact that a cousin of Jesus, rather than a younger brother, succeeded James as head of the Jerusalem church suggests that these brothers were involved in missionary work outside of Jerusalem, perhaps outside of Judea (Schnabel 2004, 1:749–50; Witherington 2007, 562).

Jude exhibits a wide Greek vocabulary but unremarkable style, the former being easier to acquire with exposure to Greek over time (Bauckham 1983, 6–7, 15–16). The author, like several other authors of early Christian letters, may have had the assistance of an unnamed secretary (Richards 2004; Green 2008, 8). We know precious little of Jude's life or experiences either before or after his conversion, but the clues that we do possess suggest that it would have been quite possible for him to acquire sufficient proficiency in Greek while in Galilee or Judea, and all the more so if his missionary travels extended farther.

181

Jude 17–18 has sometimes been read to reflect a situation after the deaths of the apostles, and hence a period after 70 or 80 CE, in all probability beyond the lifetime of Jude himself (see, e.g., Neyrey 1993, 33–34). The author, however, does not ask the hearers to remember the apostles, as though remembering a deceased generation (so, rightly, Bauckham 1990, 170–71), but rather he exhorts the audience to "remember the *words* spoken in advance by the apostles of our Lord Jesus Christ" (v. 17). Such words would have been uttered by the particular apostles who founded and nurtured this congregation (or these congregations) at some time in the past. The author presumes that his audience heard these words from the apostles' own lips ("because they used to say to you," v. 18). Jude's audience is more likely not a later generation of believers who know the apostles only by memory but rather are the converts of these very apostles, who may have simply moved on to further mission fields (Bauckham 1983, 13).

This short letter's rootedness in Jewish traditions, particularly those most at home in Palestine, adds weight to the view that it is an authentic document. First, the author knows the Jewish Scriptures in a form closer to the Hebrew text than to the Septuagint (LXX), the Greek translation widely used in the Greek-speaking Jewish Diaspora. In verse 12, Jude speaks of the intruders as "waterless clouds being driven on by winds." This image echoes the Hebrew text of Prov. 25:14, where the boastful person is compared to "clouds and wind without rain." The LXX translation compared the boastful person instead to "winds and clouds and rains," clearly missing the main point of the image: a blustery storm that yields nothing useful. In the subsequent verse, Jude compares the intruders to "wild waves of the sea, dredging up their degradation like sea foam." This image recalls the Hebrew text of Isa. 57:20, where wicked people are compared to "the tossing sea" whose "waters toss up mire and mud." The powerful image of a churning sea dredging up the muck on the bottom is absent from the LXX, which says that the wicked "will be tossed to and fro by waves and shall not be able to rest" (Bauckham 1983, 7).

The author is familiar with *1 Enoch*, a text that originated in Palestine and was authoritative among Judean sects such as the Qumran community. Jude's worldview is consonant with the apocalyptic worldview articulated by that text. He seems to be familiar also with extrabiblical traditions about Cain, Balaam, and Moses that are otherwise mainly attested in Palestine—for example, in the targumim (the Aramaic paraphrases of the Hebrew Bible).

This brief letter may very well, then, provide us with a window into the thought and activity of Jude, a leader within Jewish Christianity and within the circle of Jesus's blood relations, and thus to an oft-neglected stream of tradition within the early church. It is difficult to discern the letter's date. The author's silence about the death of James and the destruction of the temple is probably not a reliable indicator of date in so short a document (contra Witherington 2007, 564, 577). The letter may have been written as early as the earliest letters of Paul or come from a period as late as 80–85 CE, the approximate outer limit for the life span of Jesus's younger half brother.

Occasion and Setting

Jude falls within that part of the NT traditionally known as the General, or Catholic, Epistles. The title suggests that these letters (including 1–2 Peter, James, and Jude) were written to Christians in many locations and facing a broad variety of challenges. Whereas James explicitly addresses Christians scattered throughout the "Diaspora" (1:1) and presents a collection of good advice for churches in any locale, Jude addresses a particular problem posed by the emergence of particular teachers who have insinuated themselves into a particular congregation. Indeed, Jude appears to have turned aside from writing a more general letter concerning "the salvation we share" to address this new exigency (vv. 3–4).

Several clues suggest that those whom Jude opposes come from outside the congregation and are acting as teachers or authority figures. First, Jude's charge that these persons are "shepherding" or "feeding" themselves employs a popular image for religious leaders (shepherds) and a traditional critique of the same (they look after their own needs at the expense of the flock for which they ought to care; see Ezek. 34:1–16; John 10:1–18). Second, Jude's assertion that these persons go astray through their "dreaming" suggests that they claim authority for their message and practice on the basis of visionary experiences. Itinerant teachers claiming revelations from God were familiar enough in the early church, using their gifts sometimes to enrich the experience of congregations, sometimes to enrich themselves. Third, the image of "sneaking in" and threatening to change the character of the community accords best with a view of these individuals as people from outside who are actively trying to reshape the community after their own image. That they presented themselves as Christians is evident because the congregation admitted them to the communal meal, the "love feast" (v. 12; Green 2008, 19).

Little can be known about the teachers' "doctrine." Some scholars formerly identified them as gnostics (as in Kelly 1969, 231), though the telltale indications of gnostic thought are not mirrored in this letter. There is no hint of the gnostic denigration of physical matter or of gnostic creation myths involving an inferior deity's fashioning of the physical world, including the body (Bauckham 1990, 164–64; Green 2008, 9, 17). Nor are there signs of the kind of early dispute over the nature and person of Christ reflected in 1 John. Rather, Jude takes issue primarily with the intruders' ethical practice, accusing them of "transforming the favor of our God into [an excuse for] animalistic self-indulgence" (v. 4). Jude accuses them of posing as Christian teachers for the sake of indulging their own greed and lust, claiming to be Spirit-led visionaries, when in fact they rebel against God's moral authority (Davids 2006, 21). They are no better than other self-serving peddlers of philosophies in the marketplace, using flattery to gain their ends (v. 16), eager to make a profit from religion (vv. 11–12a), indulging the belly and the loins (vv. 4, 12, 16, 18).

Granted that Jude seeks to present these teachers in the most negative light possible, there is probably a great deal of substance in his charges and innuendos. Paul taught that Christ followers were no longer under the Torah, the Jewish law, and were free to follow the guidance of the Spirit (Gal. 3:23–4:7; 5:4–5, 16–26). While Paul himself taught that the Spirit-led life entailed a rigorous ethic of mastery of the passions and giving oneself to virtue and Christlike service, others took his proclamation of Christian freedom to signal an opportunity to set aside conventional morality and make room for greater self-indulgence. Some of Paul's own disciples in Corinth took "grace" in this direction, as is seen in their sexual indiscretions and indifference to participating in idolatry to some degree (see 1 Cor. 5–6; 8). Later in the first century, some Christian teachers in Asia Minor promoted similar practices (see Rev. 2:14–16, 20–25). Paul himself had been accused of turning God's grace into an excuse to sin (Rom. 3:8; 6:1), and he defended himself by showing how God's gift of the Spirit was meant to empower a self-controlled, moral life that remained in alignment with the ethical standards of God's law (Rom. 6:1–8:11).

The intruders may well have claimed prophetic authority on the basis of visions and revelations received in a state of religious ecstasy (which Jude disparagingly refers to as "dreaming," v. 8), encouraging their fellow Christians to cast off the shackles of irrelevant moral restrictions that apply to ordinary people but not to the "spiritual" person (see Kelly 1969, 230). The fact that Jude compares them with figures known to have taught a more libertine practice (Cain and Balaam, v. 11) suggests that moral laxity was part of their message, not merely their practice. It remains possible, however, that their message was not so thoroughly thought through. Perhaps the intruders were merely posturing, charismatic sponges, people who claimed spiritual power and pretended to exercise it, making themselves look powerful by speaking disdainfully of spirit beings (see vv. 8–10a), all the while exploiting Christian hospitality and intimacy (vv. 10b, 12–13, 16).

There is no compelling reason to believe that the intruders have challenged Jude's honor and authority, making the letter a riposte to such attack (contra Neyrey 1993, 51–52; Brosend 2004, 184–85). The opening verses of Jude do not offer such "a strong defense of the author's honor, i.e., his role and status" (Neyrey 1993, 51) as to suggest that these have come under fire. Rather, these verses assert no more than what was suitable to establish a speaker's credibility at the outset of an address. When compared to Gal. 1:1–10, where another Christian leader actually is responding to attacks on his authority, the remarkable restraint in Jude's opening indicates the absence of personal challenges to Jude's honor and authority from the intruders (so also Perkins

Testing Prophets in the Early Church

The early church experienced a revival of the gift of God's prophetic spirit. Paul expects that those gathered for worship would experience and share prophetic words, revelations, ecstatic speech ("tongues"), and the translation of such speech (1 Cor. 12:1–11, 27–31; 14:26–33). Such experiences provided encouragement and guidance, empowering the Christian movement and its mission, but they could also be counterfeited or abused, serving the interests of self-seeking teachers, introducing unorthodox innovations, or perverting the practice of disciples.

It became important from the outset to distinguish genuine words spoken in the Spirit from false ones (1 Cor. 14:29; 1 Thess. 5:20–21), whether uttered by members of the congregation or by teachers and prophets coming from outside. Matthew preserves a Jesus saying that warns against "false prophets" who speak like genuine disciples but really seek to take advantage of the church (Matt. 7:15–20). The disciples are to examine the results of these prophets' work in their midst, to determine if they are genuine. Paul warns the Christians in Colossae that visions of angels and the practice of austere lifestyles are not sufficient guarantees against fraud: real authority flows from connection with Christ. John the elder framed doctrinal tests alongside ethical ones: prophets failing to acknowledge that Jesus was the Christ come in the flesh do not speak from God's Spirit (1 John 4:1–6).

The *Didache*, or *Teaching of the Twelve Apostles*, is a manual on Christian ethics, church order, liturgy, and eschatology dating from the late first century or early second century. It contains the most extensive treatment of how to welcome, and how to test, itinerant prophets. Such prophets enjoyed great liberty and authority, but they were not above suspicion. If they used prophetic speech to solicit money or other material assistance for their own use, or if they lingered more than three days at the community's expense, they were to be shown the communal door. Charismatic endowments were not meal tickets.

There were no simple, universal tests: a prophet's theology, behavior, motives, and fruits could attest either to genuineness or fraud. Prophets were subject to the apostolic faith and the ethics taught and approved within the church, which remained the authoritative norm. Jude provides a window into this process of discernment at work.

1995, 150; Witherington 2007, 610n97). If anything, Jude strikes the first blow with his demolition of the intruders' credibility in verses 5–19.

Jude does not specify his readers' location, as Paul does in his letters. He assumes that they will be familiar with Jewish extrabiblical traditions about Cain, the fallen angels, and Moses, as well as with texts such as *1 Enoch* that had their home in Palestinian Jewish circles. It is likely that Jewish Christians, who would have greater exposure to these traditions, made up a significant portion of the audience, though the presence of gentile converts (people like Cornelius and his household; see Acts 10) may also have been substantial.

Most scholars believe that the letter was sent to congregations somewhere in Palestine (Kelly 1969, 234; Grundmann 1974, 19–20; Bauckham 1990, 131–33, 177–78; Charles 1993, 65–81; Green 2008, 12–13), where the relatives of Jesus practiced the closest oversight of the Christian movement. The intruders' ethically looser practice (and possibly message) would not have been welcomed in the more rural villages of Palestine, but it would have resonated well with the lifestyle of Greeks and other non-Jews living in the Hellenized cities of Palestine, such as the cities in the coastal plains or the Decapolis. Gene Green (2008, 15) has plausibly suggested that one facet of their program involved introducing the culture of Greek symposia (involving a freer indulgence of eating, drinking, and "companionship") into the Christian agape meal. In these areas, Jewish Christians might well have had a greater degree of acculturation to non-Jewish practices and mores and thus have been more at risk of succumbing to the intruders' vision. An urban destination within Palestine would also explain why the letter was written in Greek rather than Aramaic (Green 2008, 13–14).

Genre and Purpose

The primary genre of Jude is that of a letter. A letter typically opened by naming the sender and the recipient(s), followed by a word of greeting and/or a wish on behalf of the recipient(s). Jude 1–2 follows this pattern, developing it in ways appropriate for an assembly of Christian recipients. Jude names the exigency that elicits this letter (vv. 3–4), which is also typical of occasional letters, and transitions to the letter body using a customary formula of desiring to make something known or remind the recipients of something (v. 5; Watson 1988, 50; White 1972, 32–36, 38, 41).

Jude combines two recognized types of letter in antiquity: the "advisory" type, in which the author exhorts the recipients to (or dissuades them from) some action, and the "vituperative" type, in which the author lays bare "the badness of someone's character or the offensiveness of (his) action against someone" (Pseudo-Demetrius, *Epistolary Types*, quoted in Malherbe 1988, 37). Jude concludes, however, not with the elements typical of letter closings (parting greetings, travel plans) but rather with a doxology (vv. 24–25), a particularly appropriate substitute if Jude envisioned his letter being read aloud when the congregation assembled for worship as a kind of "epistolary sermon" (Bauckham 1983, 3). The following outline highlights this structure:

Letter opening (vv. 1–2)
Statement of presenting problem (vv. 3–4)
Letter body (vv. 5–23)
Liturgical closing in the form of a doxology (vv. 24–25)

Granted that Jude is a letter and thus should be analyzed as such as far as possible, rhetorical analysis has also proved fruitful for going beyond what epistolary analysis alone can achieve. The cursory nature of ancient handbooks on letter writing suggests that the development of the content of a letter would be left to other disciplines, with the result that an author's awareness of rhetoric would supplement the composition of a letter. The author of an "advisory" type of letter would certainly draw upon the strategies of deliberative rhetoric in trying to achieve effective persuasion or dissuasion. Similarly, the author of a "vituperative" type of letter would not refrain from drawing upon the rhetorical resources available for finding damning things to say about an opponent or other figure in a vituperative speech (a species of epideictic rhetoric). Rhetorical critics often go astray in trying to force a NT letter into the mold of a classical oration (Davids 2006, 24; Neyrey 1993, 26–27), but a knowledge of classical rhetoric, judiciously applied, can aid our analysis of the kinds of strategies and arguments that any author within the Greco-Roman world might put forward to achieve the goals for the letter.

Jude interprets the congregation's immediate situation in light of the certainty of God's judgment. Jude's immediate goal for this letter, insofar as it is "advisory," is to persuade the congregation not to be influenced by the intruders' practice and, likely, teaching (vv. 3–4). He urges them instead to engage in practices that will continue to nurture the whole community in alignment with the apostles' teaching and vision for discipleship (vv. 20–23), with the result that they will stand before God "blameless" (v. 24). To support this goal, Jude engages in extensive vituperation of the intruders (vv. 5–19), naming practices that are out of alignment with the vision for God's people communicated in the sacred tradition and the apostolic preaching, and demonstrating what the outcome of the intruders' way of life will be from historical examples of God's judgment in the sacred tradition. Because the intruders stand under God's impending condemnation, continued association with them and continued toleration of their influence will prove detrimental to the congregation, since their influence will lead others into condemnation as well.

Influence and Canonicity

The most immediate indication of Jude's influence is its relationship to 2 Peter. Like Jude, 2 Peter was written in response to an intrusive message disrupting the church's faith and practice, though the teachers opposed by this author are of a very different sort. Rather than relying on access to divine revelation, as did the intruders in Jude, these teachers ground their position in rational, philosophical critique of religion (Bauckham 1983, 154–57; Neyrey 1993, 122–28). These teachers show the influence of Epicurus, who taught that the gods did not trouble themselves with human affairs, being free from anger and the desire

187

for vengeance, a proof of which is the slowness with which justice overtakes a criminal or a wicked person—if indeed it ever catches up with them at all (see Diogenes Laertius, *Vit.* 10.139; Cicero, *Nat. d.* 1.117; Lucretius, *Rer. nat.* 5.1194–97; see also Neyrey 1980, 407–22). The new intruders seek to "liberate" Christians from fear of God's judgment, pointing to the unexpected delay of Jesus's second coming as a reason for sensible Christians to abandon their unenlightened apocalyptic hope (2 Pet. 3:3–7). An unfortunate side effect of such freedom is a tendency toward self-gratification and license (see 2 Pet. 2:18).

The author of 2 Peter uses Jude's polemic as a resource in his own attempt to counter the influence of these teachers, adapting the material to a new audience, as even a casual reading of 2 Pet. 2:1–3:4 alongside Jude 4–18 shows. Most notably, the author removes Jude's direct references to the more obscure texts and traditions—*1 Enoch* and the noncanonical story of the dispute over Moses's body—either generalizing the material or replacing it with more accessible texts (such as Proverbs and sayings of Jesus). The author of 2 Peter clearly valued Jude's letter.

Christian leaders from the late second through the fourth century continued to use Jude, finding its polemic useful in their own controversies with contemporary heresies (see Bray 2000, 245–59; Jones 2001). Clement of Alexandria (*Strom.* 3.2.11), for example, read Jude as a prophetic denouncement of the Carpocratians, a gnostic group making progress among Egyptian churches during Clement's lifetime (see Green 2008, 12).

Jude fell into neglect after the Reformation. Martin Luther considered it to be a pseudonymous "extract or copy of St. Peter's second epistle" and hence not an apostolic writing (or rather, a redundant extract from an apostolic writing). Relying on the tradition that Jude evangelized in Persia, Luther surmised that he would not have written Greek and therefore could not be the author of this epistle. John Calvin, however, graced Jude with a commentary and affirmed its authenticity. Nevertheless, strong prejudices arose in the nineteenth century against Jude as an alleged example of postapostolic "early catholicism" coming from the period after, and inferior to, Paul's vigorous and creative formulation of the gospel. In the twentieth century, prejudice against Jude's intolerance toward diversity of voice and practice has worked against its recovering ground as a canonical voice.

Early Christians were divided concerning the canonical authority of Jude. Already in the third century, Origen shows awareness of debates on this topic (*Comm. Jo.* 19.6). Jude was omitted from the Peshitta, the early Syriac version of the NT, though it was included in the sixth-century revision of the same. Positively, Jude was listed as Scripture in the Muratorian Canon (second or fourth century CE) and by Athanasius in his thirty-ninth Paschal Letter of 367 CE (for evidence of acceptance, see Cantinat 1973, 276–82).

A key factor in these debates is Jude's citation of *1 Enoch* as an authoritative text, even attributing the material he quotes to the "historical" Enoch who spoke in the seventh generation from Adam (cf. Gen. 5:3–18). The early church, however, knew this material only from the pseudepigraphic *1 Enoch*, a work whose authorship could never be verified, and hence a book that would not be canonical in either Jewish or most Christian circles. This did not cast doubts upon Jude among his earliest readers, from the time of the author of 2 Peter through Clement of Alexandria. By the fourth century, however, Jerome is aware that many excluded Jude from their canon on this basis, though Jerome himself did not: "By age and use it has gained authority and is reckoned among the Holy Scriptures" (*Vir. ill.* 4). In England, Jude also had difficulty gaining acceptance on account of its use of *1 Enoch*, a book of dubious origins that contained "incredible things about giants, who had angels instead of men as fathers, and which are clearly lies" (Bede, *On Jude*, PL 93:129; Bray 2000, 255; see also Augustine, *Civ.* 15.23; 18.38). But Bede (*On Jude*, PL 93:129; Bray 2000, 255) argued that Jude's citation of a verse from the noncanonical *1 Enoch* should not disqualify Jude from the Christian canon, since the verse that he recites (*1 En.* 1.9) is thoroughly consonant with Christian teaching.

From another point of view, Jude testifies to the influence of *1 Enoch* within the early Christian movement, first and foremost on Jude itself. Jude's use of *1 Enoch* became an argument in some Christian circles that *1 Enoch* should also be accorded canonical authority, most famously by Tertullian, who attributes its noncanonical status among Jewish communities to its clear witness to Christ and the apocalyptic hope (*Cult. fem.* 3.3). The book of *1 Enoch* remains canonical for the Ethiopic Christian Church, which may be another fruit of Jude's influence as an "apostolic" voice attesting to *1 Enoch*'s value and authority.

An Outline of Jude

Letter opening (1–4)

Opening greeting (1–2)

Occasion for writing (3–4)

Intruders' behavior illumined from history (5–10)

Three historical examples and their relevance (5–8)

A fourth example and its relevance (9–10)

Intruders' behavior illumined from history, nature, and prophecy (11–15)

Three brief, applied historical examples (11)

Amplification of intruders' viciousness (12–13)

Indictment from *1 Enoch* (14–15)

Exhortations and conclusion (16–25)

First contrast and exhortation (16–18)

Second contrast and exhortation (19–23)

Liturgical conclusion (24–25)

Jude 1–4

Letter Opening

Introductory Matters

Jude writes a public letter to be read aloud to the assembled congregation, and he writes explicitly to counter the influence of other, local teachers. Although Jude writes a letter, the rhetorical setting requires him to be attentive to the challenges of public address about contested topics. In the opening verses, one can find substantial overlap in rhetorical effect between Jude's letter and the typical speech. This is especially true in regard to appeals to *ethos*, attempts made by the one addressing the assembly to establish credibility—to give evidence of being a person of "good sense, virtue, and goodwill" (Aristotle, *Rhet.* 2.1.5)—and, when the situation calls for it, to undermine the credibility of opposing speakers. Classical rhetoricians regarded appeals of this kind to be the foundation of rhetorical success (Aristotle, *Rhet.* 1.2.4; Quintilian, *Inst.* 3.8.13). Establishing credibility and arousing prejudice against rival speakers were particularly important in the opening and closing sections of a discourse (Aristotle, *Rhet.* 3.14.6–7; 3.19.1; Anaximenes, *Rhet. Alex.* 1436a.33–37).

Letter openings, like the introduction to a classical speech (the *exordium*), also tended to announce the key topics, giving some indication of the subject that would be developed. Jude gives a clear statement of this in verses 3b–4, but he also introduces a number of keywords that will recur and give thematic consistency to the whole. Jude describes the addressees as people who are "kept in Jesus Christ" (v. 1), and he will later urge the hearers to "keep" themselves in the love of God (v. 21) in contrast with the intruders,

190

for whom the dark gloom of the underworld is "kept" (v. 13) because they have ranged themselves alongside the fallen angels who did not "keep to their realm" and so are now "kept in eternal chains" in that same gloom (v. 6). Similarly, the introduction of these intruders as "ungodly" (v. 4) links them with the targets of God's judgment in the predictions of *1 Enoch* and of the apostles (vv. 15, 18). (Compare also the recurrences of "mercy" in vv. 2, 21, 22–23

> **Jude 1–4 in the Rhetorical Flow**
>
> ▶ **Letter opening (1–4)**
> Opening greeting (1–2)
> Occasion for writing (3–4)

and forms of "love, beloved" in vv. 1, 2, 12, 17, 20, 21.) The opening of Jude, therefore, accomplishes the essential rhetorical goals of the opening of a classical speech.

Tracing the Train of Thought

Opening Greeting (1–2)

1a. The author makes two opening claims to authority: he is a **slave of Jesus Christ** and **the brother of James**, who was the leader of the Jerusalem church and half brother of the Lord himself. Though slavery generally signaled dishonor, "slave" became an honorific title for those who served God in a special capacity. Being a "slave of God" gave Moses (Neh. 9:14), Joshua (Josh. 24:29; Judg. 2:8), David (2 Sam. 7:25–29), and the prophets in general (Rev. 11:18; 22:6) a special claim to authority as those enacting God's will on earth. It is the proper self-understanding for the person addressed and called by God, as in the case of Samuel (1 Sam. 3:9–10). Paul (Rom. 1:1; Gal. 1:10; Phil. 1:1), James (James 1:1), the author of 2 Peter (2 Pet. 1:1), and John the Seer (Rev. 1:1) use the title to the same effect. Jude's second claim to honor and authority is grounded in kinship with honorable people (Neyrey 1993, 45; see Pseudo-Oecumenius, *Commentary on Jude*, PG 119:705; Bray 2000, 246). James enjoyed exceptionally high status within the Christian group (see Gal. 2:9, 11–12; Acts 15:13–21; 21:18; *Gos. Thom.* 12). He appears to have been respected even by non-Christian Jews on account of his Torah observance and personal piety (Eusebius, *Hist. eccl.* 2.23.4–7). By identifying himself as the Judas who was James's brother, the author of Jude also locates himself among the half brothers of Jesus himself. Although Jesus's blood relations may have opposed him during his life (Mark 3:31–35; John 7:2–10), they were among his followers after the resurrection (Acts 1:14), exercising an itinerant ministry (1 Cor. 9:5), apart from James, who remained head of the church in Jerusalem.

1b–2. Establishing authority or prestige is only one facet of establishing *ethos*. It was also important for Jude to demonstrate goodwill toward the audience. He affirms that the hearers are **called, beloved in Father God and**

Triplets in Jude's Letter

The opening salutation of the letter includes the phrase "mercy and peace and love," one of the first of many triplets in Jude. This is considered to be a distinctive feature of Jude's style, though not a feature woodenly followed by him (there are also several instances of paired phrases and fourfold images). The triplets, like the other accumulations, increase the rhetorical weight of what is said through the multiplication of related terms and images. Other examples include:

"Egypt ... angels ... Sodom and Gomorrah" (vv. 5–7)
"defile flesh, reject lordship, and defame glorious beings" (v. 8)
"Cain ... Balaam ... Korah" (v. 11)
"ones causing divisions, worldly-minded, not having the Spirit" (v. 19)
"show mercy ... save ... show mercy" (vv. 22–23)
"before this whole age ... now ... unto all ages" (v. 25)

---

kept for Jesus Christ (v. 1b), expressing the esteem in which he holds them as he addresses them. As was common in the early church (see Phil. 3:3; 1 Pet. 2:9–10), Jude describes the early Christians by using terms applied to historic Israel in the Hebrew Bible (see, e.g., Isa. 41:8–9; 43:1–4; 48:12–15). He expands the typical "greeting" to a fulsome wish for God's continued pouring out of God's gifts upon them: **May mercy and peace and love be multiplied for you** (v. 2). Wishing good is, by definition, the essence of goodwill.

Occasion for Writing (3–4)

3–4a. Jude addresses the audience directly as **Beloved** (v. 3a), using a term of endearment evocative of friendly feelings, which in turn will render the hearers a little more receptive to his address. Jude repeats this term in verses 17, 20, further stimulating identification between author and congregation, over against the intruders who are upsetting the applecart (vv. 16, 19). Jude further demonstrates goodwill by speaking of his diligent investment of himself in the hearers' edification, first in **making every effort to compose something for you about our shared experience of deliverance** (v. 3a), then in responding to a more pressing need to write to them, **exhorting [them] to contend for the faith that had been handed down once for all to the saints** (v. 3b). Jude presents himself honorably as a defender of the faith, a role in which he invites the congregation to participate, drawing them in to take their stand alongside him (Watson 1988, 35). He adds a rationale (signaled by *gar*, "for"), explaining the cause for urgency: **For some people have sneakily slipped in** (v. 4a). The presence and activity of these intruders threatens the integrity of the religious knowledge and the way of life—the "faith"—that are the shared and precious possessions of Jude and the hearers. That Jude would interrupt another composition to write the present letter about the intruders serves to amplify the importance of the threat they pose and thus to prioritize the hearers' formulation of a timely and effective response (Watson 1988, 37–38). (Itinerant teachers or prophets were a frequent source of potential problems in the early church [see Matt. 7:15–20; 24:4–5; Acts 19:11–16; Gal. 1:6–9; 2 Cor. 10–11; 1 John 4:1; *Did.* 11–13; Rev. 2:2, 6, 14–15].)

The language of verse 4 tersely and economically puts the intruders in the worst possible light, calling their motives, message, and practice into question all at once. Jude is still attending to establishing *ethos*, this time by undermining the credibility and goodwill ascribed to these teachers. These others have "sneakily slipped in," just as Paul says in Gal. 2:4 of certain "false brothers" who intruded upon Paul's meeting with the Jerusalem apostles and whose influence in that meeting Paul vigorously (and successfully) opposed. Such language does not seek to present an accurate description of the intruders' conscious modus operandi (contra Reese 2007, 38) but rather to alert the hearers that these teachers are not what they appear to be and have a hidden agenda toward which they are working beneath their appearances. English idioms such as "weaseled their way in" (Green 2008, 52) or "wormed their way in" capture the negative connotations quite well.

4b. The intruders were **long ago marked out for this condemnation.** This is admittedly difficult to untangle (for a fuller discussion of possibilities, see Bauckham 1983, 35–37), particularly where the passage is read as a claim that the activity of the intruders and their consequent judgment have been predicted in some specific text (apart from the apostolic warnings, vv. 17–18). The verb *prographō*, however, used to denote predictive writing, can also simply indicate public announcement or display, as in Gal. 3:1 (see Green 2008, 58). The proofs that follow in verses 5–16 do not in fact establish that these intruders' actions and destiny were predicted and thus in some sense determined; rather, they confirm that God's judgment for the kinds of actions that the intruders exhibit is a matter of historical record, and thus the future judgment of the intruders and all who persist in their way of life is certain. The condemnation of the intruders was made known in the actions and condemnation of figures such as Cain, Balaam, and Korah (v. 11). The "ancient" declarations of God's judgment against all ungodly persons for their ungodly speech and deeds (*1 En.* 1.9, quoted in Jude 14–15) announced long ago the condemnation of these particular **ungodly people** (v. 4b) as well.

It is difficult to escape the notion, however, that Jude considers these intruders also to have been predestined to play the role of "false teacher" and to face the consequences thereof, as Judas was predestined to play his role and come to a bad end (see Andreas, *Catena*, in Bray 2000, 249–50), or as Pharaoh in the exodus story (see Rom. 9:14–18). If the appearance of false teachers was foretold by the apostles (vv. 17–18), these intruders are playing out a part that was foreseen for them, a script that had been written for them before they stepped onto the stage, a plot that will have a predictable ending (unless the audience intervenes, vv. 22–23). The intruders stand in stark contrast to the audience, who are "called" (v. 1), selected by God to be part of God's people and to come to a favorable end (v. 24). Jude's descriptions distance the audience from the intruders and from their influence, since at the present time God has so sharply distinguished their destinies.

4c. These intruders err, Jude asserts, by **transforming the favor of our God into indecent self-indulgence and denying our only master and Lord, Jesus Christ.** The new manifestation of God's favor, or "grace" (*charis*), was a central topic of "the faith" (v. 3) particularly emphasized in Pauline Christianity. The language of "grace" taps into the important social practices of patronage and benefaction and also into the social ethos of reciprocity, according to which accepting a gift meant also accepting an obligation to show appropriate gratitude toward the giver. This always included honoring the giver. In personal patronage, it also included remaining loyal to the giver and looking for opportunities to return favor, even if only in the form of service when called upon (see further deSilva 2000, 95–156). Using a gift contrary to the purposes of the giver, thus showing contempt for the giver and gift, was a gross violation of the code of reciprocity and the ancient conception of justice (deSilva 2000, 104–19). Jude accuses the intruders of doing this very thing. Instead of using the favor that God has shed abroad in Christ as an opportunity to flee from all vice and slavery to baser cravings, the intruders use it as an excuse to engage in and promote the sinful self-indulgence that affronts the giver.

The early church was a target for charlatans seeking to sponge off a religious group known for its generosity and commitment to sharing (see the story of Lucian's *Peregrinus*). The intruders use what knowledge they have of Christianity and their ability to act the part of the Christian prophet to make a cozy living for themselves at the expense of this congregation. But they apparently also claim to be above conventional morality on the basis of their "spiritual" status and on the authority of their visionary experiences (their "dreaming," v. 8; Bauckham 1990, 167). Jude develops this as he gives their self-gratifying practices further attention (see vv. 8a, 10b, 12–13).

These intruders deny Jesus as "master and Lord," not by verbally opposing the church's claims about Jesus, but by failing to submit to the authority of Jesus's teachings about ethical behavior and accept their own accountability to these ethical standards. They serve not Jesus as their Lord and master but instead their own cravings (Bauckham 1990, 167, 303; 1983, 40). (Calling Jesus "our only sovereign and lord" within the dominion of the Roman emperor is a confession that also had significant political ramifications [see Davids 2006, 30].) Jesus himself taught that confession of his status without living according to his teachings meant nothing: "Why do you call me 'Lord, Lord,' and not do the things that I say?" (Luke 6:46). The intruders' failure to acknowledge proper authority—and accountability before God and the Lord Jesus at the judgment—is also developed in the body of the letter (vv. 8–10, 14–15). Their functional repudiation of the lordship of Jesus Christ is another point of incompatibility between them and the audience, whom Jude described as "kept for Jesus Christ" (v. 1).

"Contending for the faith" will mean, in part, resisting the influence of these intruders (and no longer wasting resources supporting them). But Jude will also invite the congregation to reverse the direction of influence, showing the intruders what spiritual power truly looks like and calling them to a genuine engagement with the Lord, with whom they feign acquaintance (vv. 20–23).

Theological Issues

Christian historians and theologians have tended to focus on the great missionary apostles Peter and Paul, connected to the great "gentile" centers of Christianity such as Rome, Ephesus, and Corinth, overlooking the important role played in Palestine and beyond by the family of Jesus except as foils to Paul's broader theological vision. Despite its brevity, the Letter of Jude raises many important theological, ethical, and ecclesiological issues and brings a distinctive voice to bear on these issues.

One issue involves discerning the center and the boundaries of Christian faith and practice. When Jude speaks of "the faith that had been handed down once for all to the saints" (v. 3), he may seem to have a fossilized, dogmatic conception of the Christian revelation. But Jude's expression is shaped by the polemical situation in which he finds himself, just as Paul's was when he pronounced a curse upon anyone who preached a gospel different from the one that his converts had previously heard from him (Gal. 1:6–9). Paul was well aware of the breadth of the "gray area" between the core of the gospel and the boundaries of Christian faith and practice, and he sought to protect this gray area of conscience's dominion from the tyranny of external rulings (see, e.g., Rom. 14:1–15:2; 1 Cor. 8:1–13; 10:23–32; 13:8–12). But when something central to the gospel was at risk of being undermined, Paul invoked the congregation's earlier instruction in the faith as a fixed standard against which to assess the message introduced by new teachers.

This is precisely what Jude does in his letter. He might indeed acknowledge many gray areas (though he does not give space to such matters in his brief letter), but he understands the intruders to be calling several core beliefs into question by their practice and interests. It is, however, a mark of Jude's anti-authoritarianism that he combats their influence as he does. He appeals not to his authority but rather to the authority of the knowledge about God's actions in the world and God's desired responses from humankind (the "faith") that both he and the hearers have shared and to which they had both committed themselves. God's favor is intended to motivate and empower ethical transformation; calling Jesus "Lord" (and enjoying the alliance that such an acknowledgment creates) entails acting as an obedient follower of this Lord; God will hold all persons accountable to God's standards. Such core affirmations of the "faith" are not rhetorical propaganda to be manipulated; they are a shared body of authoritative knowledge to which Jude, his hearers, and his opponents are accountable, on the basis of which it becomes possible reliably to discern the boundaries.

Perhaps the major theological issue raised in Jude concerns the question of what God's grace is really for, what it can and is meant to accomplish. For Jude, God's favor sets and sustains disciples on a trajectory toward standing blameless in the presence of God's glory (v. 24), such that they can encounter God without regret when God comes to hold the world accountable for all ungodly speech and action. Paul, the apostle most explicitly associated with the gospel of "grace," understood that the self-giving love and favor of God revealed in Christ's death and resurrection indebted the recipients of such favor to live a new kind of life—no longer for themselves, but for the one who died and was raised on their behalf (2 Cor. 5:15). He asserted that the freedom of the Christian is not freedom for self-indulgence but rather freedom to live responsively under the guidance and with the empowerment of the Spirit (Gal. 5:1, 13–26). God's gift of the Holy Spirit brought also the obligation to use that gift, and the freedom from Torah that the gift signaled, for God's purposes rather than the purposes of one's own cravings and self-gratification. Disciples are even to restrict their legitimate freedom where the spiritual health of another Christian requires it (1 Cor. 8:13; 10:23–31). Paul would later be accused of promoting self-indulgence (Rom. 3:8), but he would answer that the freedom of grace meant, instead, freedom to submit to God from the heart (Rom. 6:1–2, 15–23).

Jude depicts the intruders as people who have dramatically misunderstood God's grace as license to indulge their own cravings rather than to receive God's empowerment to live definitively beyond the power of those cravings. He stands alongside Paul in his insistence that such a lifestyle within the church represents a perversion of God's grace, calling his hearers to "contend for the faith," in part, by contending against every such rationalization that would allow them to make room for indulging their passions rather than allowing grace to have its full effect—their sanctification. Jude leaves the hearers with confidence in God's ability to bring about the goal of God's grace, as long as they direct their own hearts toward being kept (v. 21) by the one who is able to keep them (v. 24).

Jude 5–10

Intruders' Behavior Illumined from History

Introductory Matters

The first challenge in interpreting any text is to establish its actual wording. Our knowledge of the exact wording of the NT comes not from the original manuscripts written by Jude, Paul, Luke, and others but rather from manuscripts dating to the fourth century and later. Because scribes did not always copy a manuscript exactly (sometimes because of simple errors on their part, sometimes because they sought to iron out what they perceived to be problems in the manuscript from which they were copying), there are many variations among these NT manuscripts. The discipline of trying to determine the most likely original wording—the wording that would have given rise to the other variants—is called "textual criticism."

There are two important text-critical issues in Jude 5. First, who is credited with leading the Hebrews out of Egypt? Second, is the author affirming that the audience has received a decisively complete education in the faith, or is he affirming that the Lord decisively saved the Hebrews from Egypt (though later all but two of these Hebrews perished in the desert)?

"Jesus" has the broadest and earliest support among manuscripts, early translations (Latin, Coptic, and Ethiopic), and quotations of the verse in the church fathers (Cyril and Jerome; see Metzger 1994, 657–58; Wikgren 1967). It is also the more difficult reading, which is a weighty consideration for textual critics because scribes tended to smooth over rather than create difficulties in their intentional changes to the text. "Jesus" is an unusual way to refer to the preincarnate Son ("Christ" would be more typical), and the

---

Different Readings of Jude 5

The verse begins as follows: "Now I want to remind you, . . ."

Codex Sinaiticus (fourth century) and the original hand in Codex Ephraemi Rescriptus (fifth century) continue the sentence in this way: "who have come to know all things, that the Lord, after delivering a people out of the land of Egypt once for all [*hapax*], . . ."

Codex Vaticanus (fourth century) and Codex Alexandrinus (fifth century) continue the sentence in this way: "who have come to know all things once for all [*hapax*], that Jesus, after delivering a people out of the land of Egypt, . . ."

$\mathfrak{P}^{72}$ (late third / early fourth century) continues the sentence in this way: "who have come to know all things once for all [*hapax*], that God Christ, after delivering a people out of the land of Egypt, . . ."

The sentence is then completed as follows: "the second time around destroyed those who did not exhibit trust."

---

other readings could also be explained as attempts to resolve the perceived difficulty of attributing the exodus events to the man Jesus (Bauckham 1990, 308–9).

Jude, however, does not otherwise refer to Jesus without adding "Christ" (vv. 1 [2x], 17, 21, 25). This presents strong internal evidence against reading "Jesus" as the original text (Bauckham 1990, 308–9). If "Lord" was the original, all other variants ("Jesus," "God," even "God Christ") could still be explained as attempts to resolve the ambiguity concerning whom Jude meant by "Lord"— God the Father or God the Son. Most modern translations follow the reading "Lord," though the ESV reads "Jesus." The practical import of these observations is that we can say more about how scribes were thinking about this verse than about the original wording itself. We need to be very tentative, therefore, in regard to theological claims that we might make concerning Jude's view of the larger scope of Jesus's activity based on reading the ESV (for example). Some early manuscripts bear witness to such a belief, and this coheres with other NT passages that attribute to the agency of Christ events narrated in Genesis (see Heb. 1:1–3) or Exodus (see 1 Cor. 10:4). It also remains quite possible that Jude himself understood "Lord" in this way. But uncertainty about the text requires a particular humility in regard to its theological interpretation.

The second textual question—the relationship of the adverb *hapax* ("once," "one time," "once for all")—to the rest of the sentence—is also somewhat difficult. There is broad, early support for connecting this with the audience's

Figure 7. 𝔓⁷⁸ (P.Oxy. 2684). This papyrus fragment from the Ashmolean Museum, at the University of Oxford, dates to the third or fourth century and shows Jude 4–5 on the front and 7–8 on the back.

experience of being instructed: "you, who have understood once for all [*hapax*]." This coheres with Jude's earlier description of "the faith" (as a way of life and body of beliefs) as something "handed down once for all [*hapax*] to the saints" (v. 3), with the result that the addressees already know all they need to know to discern the intruders' error and to persevere in the path of genuine discipleship (Neyrey 1993, 61; cf. NASB, RSV, ESV). A similar use of *hapax* occurs in Heb. 6:4, whose author describes the addressees as having been "enlightened once for all," thus "decisively enlightened," in the course of their conversion and training, such that they should know how to respond to their present challenges reliably.

The alternative reading, in which *hapax* ("once, one time," perhaps "once for all") describes the divine act of deliverance in the exodus, shows signs of being a stylistic correction. The reading in Codex Sinaiticus provides a more pleasing parallelism in the two phrases describing the Lord's antithetical actions, with *hapax* ("once, one time") now providing a counterpart to the word *deuteron* ("second," "the second time around") in the following clause (contra Green 2008, 73; and Davids 2006, 47, for whom this parallelism provides internal evidence in favor of this reading). If the adverb is to be taken in its stronger sense of "once for all" (hence, "decisively"), however, then this argument becomes weaker. Codex Sinaiticus would then attest to a reading in which the important contrast is between a decisive act of deliverance and the disastrous follow-up on account of the disobedience of the Hebrews (cf. NRSV).

Another challenge in reading this passage comes from Jude's use of extra-biblical sources. In particular, Jude refers to an episode following the death of Moses unknown from any scriptural source (for a detailed discussion of the sources for this legend, see Bauckham 1983, 65–76; 1990, 235–80). After being shown the promised land by God, Moses died and was buried, though no one knew his burial place (Deut. 34:5–6). Who buried Moses, such that no one knew where the grave was? A legend developed that the archangel Michael was sent to bury Moses's body. Satan, however, appeared on the scene to protest giving Moses an honorable burial, since Moses was guilty of murdering an Egyptian taskmaster out of anger (see Exod. 2:11–12). Michael did not dismiss the charge on his own authority but instead referred the matter to God.

The actual words quoted by Jude (v. 9) as Michael's response to Satan—"May the Lord rebuke you"—come from Zech. 3:2, in the context of another slanderous accusation brought by Satan against one whom the Lord had chosen (the high priest Joshua). The scene in Zech. 3:1–6, in which the Lord (or the angel of the Lord) rebukes Satan for bringing accusations against Joshua, may have provided the scriptural template for the apocryphal Moses story (with the words of the angel recontextualized in the new scene), as for several other traditions featuring some demonic figure (Satan, Mastema, or Melchiresha) contending with an angel (Michael, or "the angel of the Lord") over a particular individual, dramatizing the question of whether a person's sin puts him or her in the power of Satan or whether God's election overrules this. Jude's source is consonant with a well-attested motif (Bauckham 1983, 65–66).

It is reasonable to suppose that either *Testament of Moses* (see deSilva 1999) or *Assumption of Moses* originally ended with some version of this legend, but neither the ending of the former nor the whole of the latter survives from antiquity. We have no access to Jude's actual source, and so we simply cannot know whether Jude knew the legend from *Testament of Moses* as opposed to some other extracanonical text or even oral lore.

Knowledge of this apocryphal story was rare in the early church. When Bede sought Jude's source for this story, he caught only its correspondence with Zech. 3:1–6. Not knowing the Moses legend, he entertained the possibility that the "body of Moses" was a figurative expression for the people of Israel (Bede, *On Jude*, in Bray 2000, 252–53). Another, unnamed exegete reading this text linked this story with Christ's transfiguration and with Satan accusing God of lying, since during the transfiguration God brings Moses's spirit into the land he had earlier sworn that Moses would never enter (Bauckham 1983, 72). Already the author of 2 Peter had found it prudent to omit this material as he reworked Jude in his own polemic against new opponents in a more thoroughly gentile Christian context.

An important marker running throughout Jude is the repetition of the word *houtoi* ("these people," vv. 8, 10, 12, 16, 19) alternating with references to episodes from the Hebrew Scriptures (or their developments), drawing connections relentlessly between those prototypes and the intruders:

Reminders about the exodus generation, the Watchers, and Sodom (vv. 5–7)
Statement about "these people" (v. 8)
The example of Michael the archangel (v. 9)
Statement about "these people" (v. 10)

Scholars tend to see a parallel here with a type of exegesis exhibited at Qumran, asserting that Jude interprets the biblical (and extrabiblical) texts to which he refers as veiled predictions of the intruders' infiltration of the church (see Ellis 1978, 225).

While Jude, like the Qumran community and most sectors of the early church, believed that the Hebrew Scriptures spoke about the last days, which have now come, Jude does not fall precisely into their mode of pesher interpretation. In pesher, a brief passage of Scripture is recited, and then its interpretation is given (whence the name *pesher*, from the Hebrew word *pišrô*, "its interpretation is . . ."). The biblical text is read like a road map of the history of the Qumran sect in the emergence of the Teacher of Righteousness, the opposition of the Wicked Priest (probably Jonathan, one of the younger brothers of Judas Maccabeus) and his allies, the encroachment of the Roman Empire, the plight of the faithful community at Qumran, and the future resolution at God's judgment.

Unlike the Qumran pesharim, which read the struggles of their community and leaders in the ancient texts themselves, Jude does not claim that particular

Qumran Pesharim

"Because of the blood of men and the violence done to the land, to the city, and to all its inhabitants [Hab. 2:8].

"Interpreted, this concerns the Wicked Priest whom God delivered into the hands of his enemies because of the iniquity committed against the Teacher of Righteousness and the men of his Council. . . .

"Woe to him who causes his neighbors to drink; who pours out his venom to make them drunk that he may gaze on their feasts [Hab. 2:15].

"Interpreted, this concerns the Wicked Priest who pursued the Teacher of Righteousness to the house of his exile. . . . And at the time appointed for rest, for the Day of Atonement, he appeared before them to confuse them, and to cause them to stumble on the Day of Fasting." (1QpHab 9.8–10; 11.2–8, in Vermès 1995, 345–46)

Jude 5–10 in the Rhetorical Flow

Letter opening (1–4)

▶ **Intruders' behavior illumined from history (5–10)**

Three historical examples and their relevance (5–8)

A fourth example and its relevance (9–10)

OT texts foretell the arrival of the intruders per se (though the intruders' presence does fulfill the prophetic warnings of the apostles; vv. 17–18). Rather, the Scriptures provide a repository of historical examples that illumine the intruders' character and their standing in God's sight by comparison.

Historical examples were an important form of proof in both judicial and deliberative rhetoric. Orators urging a particular course of action in the present could compare their current situation with similar situations and choices in the past to support the outcome and consequences that they allege for the future (see Aristotle, *Rhet.* 1.9.40; 2.20.8). In judicial speeches, past examples help render an audience "more ready to believe your statements when they realize that another action resembling the one you allege has been committed in the way in which you say that it occurred" (Anaximenes, *Rhet. Alex.* 1429a.25–28). In this and the following section, Jude recalls numerous examples from the sacred past to cast interpretive light on the intruders' attitudes and practices. If the kinds of behaviors that they currently exhibit have led to God's judgment on those exhibiting such behaviors in the past, then God's judgment will surely come upon these intruders as well. This in turn serves to distance Jude's audience from them and their influence.

Tracing the Train of Thought

Three Historical Examples and Their Relevance (5–8)

5. Jude shows his esteem for his hearers' grounding in the faith, claiming to write **to remind** people whom he affirms to **have come to know all things once for all** (v. 5a). As another expression of goodwill, this enhances their receptivity to his message (Watson 1988, 50). In verses 5–7, Jude presents three historical examples to support his claim that God surely judges those who live contrary to God's order. These stories become a mental frame that sets the audience's present situation in a particular interpretive light.

Jude's first example (v. 5) recalls the fate of the exodus generation. Despite having dramatically experienced God's powerful deliverance at the Red Sea, the Hebrews faltered in trust when it came time to take possession of the promised land (see Num. 13–14; Heb. 3:7–4:11). Awed by the strength of the Canaanites, the Hebrews questioned the reliability of God's promise and disobeyed God's command to invade the land, deciding instead to return to Egypt under new leadership. As punishment, God **destroyed those who did**

not exhibit trust (v. 5b) by sentencing them to wander until the whole adult generation, except Joshua and Caleb, died in the desert (Num. 14:20–24, 30).

6. The second example moves back in time to the story of the **angels who did not keep to their realm but abandoned their proper dwelling** (v. 6a) to mate with human women (see Gen. 6:1–4). This obscure story became the focus of significant attention and expansion in the second century BCE (see *Jub.* 5.1–14; *1 En.* 6–22). Jewish writers frequently use it to warn against transgressing God's boundaries or rebelling against God (see CD 2.17–19; Sir. 16:7; *T. Reu.* 5.6–7; *2 Bar.* 56.10–16). Whereas Christians would look more to the story of Adam and Eve to explain the source of evil in the world, Jewish authors looked to these angels' corruption of humankind with their teaching of forbidden arts (such as war, sorcery, and astrology) and to the violence caused by their offspring, the giants, both before and after their deaths. The fate of these angels, to be **kept in eternal chains under the gloom of the netherworld for the judgment of the Great Day** (v. 6b), is a prominent detail in the story as told in *1 Enoch* (10.4–6, 12–14; 18.14–16; 21.3, 10), with which Jude was familiar. The story of these angels (the Watchers) may represent a reconfiguration of the Greek myth of the Titans, who revolted against the gods, brought forbidden knowledge to humans, were defeated, and eventually were chained in prisons deep in the underworld (see Hesiod, *Theog.* 718–32).

7. The third example recalls the punishment of the cities of **Sodom and Gomorrah** (v. 7a; cf. Gen. 18:16–19:29) together with two other, lesser-known "cities of the plain" (see Deut. 29:23; these cities and their kings are listed in Gen. 14:2). The distinctive fate of these cities—to suffer **punishment of eternal fire** (v. 7b)—made them prominent moral examples (see Wis. 10:6–7; 3 Macc. 2:5; Matt. 10:15; 11:24; Rev. 11:8). Natural features of the plain associated with the location of these cities were seen as evidence of God's punishment: "Evidence of their wickedness still remains: a continually smoking wasteland, plants bearing fruit that does not ripen, and a pillar of salt standing as a monument to an unbelieving soul" (Wis. 10:7 NRSV; see also Josephus, *J.W.* 4.8.4 §§483–85).

Jude claims that such punishment befell these cities because they **indulged in fornication and went after different flesh** (v. 7b). When the angelic messengers of God visited Sodom and accepted refuge in the home of Lot, the residents of the city demanded that Lot produce them so that they could violate them (Gen. 19:4–6). But Jude does not suggest that their motivation was connected with homosexual desire. He accuses the people of Sodom of seeking intercourse with "different flesh," which probably means the "flesh of a different order of being" (cf. 1 Cor. 15:39–40), sinning **in the same manner** (v. 7b) as the angels who had done the same (v. 6). The sin of Sodom, seeking intercourse with angels, serves as a counterpart to the sin of the Watchers.

Jude's litany of examples closely resembles the sequence in Sir. 16:7–10, where Ben Sira also uses the examples of the giants, Sodom, and the exodus generation to demonstrate that God's commitment to punish the rebellious is as great as God's compassion and mercy; and in 3 Macc. 2:4–7, where Simon the high priest recalls the examples of God's condemnation of the giants, Sodom, and Pharaoh for their arrogance and violence. Jude, however, departs from the canonical order of stories, preferring to build toward a climax in regard to the punishments that fall upon each group (Watson 1988, 53–54). These three precedents establish God's commitment to hold accountable and to punish those who do not honor the boundaries that God has ordained (in terms both of cosmic hierarchy and sexual activity) and who do not persevere in faith and obedience to God's commands. Whether the disobedient have known God's saving power (like the exodus generation or the angels) or not (like the residents of Sodom), their end will be the same.

8. Despite this historical evidence available to all, the intruders **in like manner, . . . while they go about dreaming, also defile flesh, reject lordship, and defame glorious beings.** Jude remains elusive in regard to the intruders' specific behaviors. Instead, he uses language that connects their behavior more explicitly with the behavior of Sodom (whose residents defiled flesh and defamed angels), the Watchers (who similarly defiled flesh and rejected God's authority), and the exodus generation (which rejected God's authority; Watson 1988, 54) so that the audience may draw the implications of the comparison more clearly: these intruders are out of line, and they will come to a bad end.

One phrase stands out in this description because it does not relate to any of the historical examples: "they go about dreaming" (*houtoi enypniazomenoi*). Early Christians believed that the Holy Spirit was once again speaking God's word to people, and congregations were open to what might be communicated in a trance or some other state of ecstasy. The intruders base their authority on their paranormal experiences, and they place greater stock in what is revealed to them during ecstatic experiences than in more traditional sources for theology and ethics. Jude, however, describes their activity using terminology found in Deuteronomy (13:1, 3, 5 [13:2, 4, 6 LXX]), where it describes the false prophet who leads the people astray to rebel against God: *prophētēs ē enypniazomenos enypnion* ("a prophet or anyone dreaming a dream"). To anyone familiar with Deuteronomy—and given that it is one of the three books of the Hebrew Scriptures most often quoted in the NT, one might assume that many Christians would have had some familiarity with it—the very choice of words suggests that the intruders' charismatically induced utterances are unreliable (Bauckham 1983, 55).

Jude's elusive language prevents certainty about the particulars of the intruders' position. The combination of the charges of "rejecting authority/lordship" and "defaming glorious beings" (a term denoting an order of angels in 1QH 18.8) suggests that the intruders particularly reject the moral constraints of the law of Moses, thought to have been delivered through angelic intermediaries (see *Jub.* 1.27–2.1; Acts 7:38, 53; Gal. 3:19; Heb. 2:2), and refuse to honor the created and moral order of which angels were commonly thought to be guardians (see 1 Cor. 11:10; Bauckham 1983, 57–59). Angels were also expected to play an important role in the final judgment, gathering the righteous and enacting punishment on the ungodly (see, e.g., *T. Levi* 3.3; Matt. 13:37–43, 47–50; 25:31–33; Rev. 14:14–20; Neyrey 1993, 66–67), and expressions of contempt for angels, or power over them, might suggest that the intruders considered themselves to be exempt from the rigorous scrutiny of the last judgment. The intruders thus disregard the moral constraints laid upon human beings by God and exercise their "freedom" in a way that indulges their sexual desires. On the basis of their alleged direct access to God's revelations, they claim to be their own moral authority, and they seek to become the moral authority for the Christian communities they visit.

A Fourth Example and Its Relevance (9–10)

9. Jude then alludes to the story of **Michael the archangel, when disputing with the devil and debating concerning Moses's body** (v. 9a), in order to advance a greater-to-lesser argument. If Michael, himself an archangel (a higher order of being than the teachers), **did not dare to pronounce judgment upon [Satan] for defamation** (against Moses's character) or dismiss Satan's charges on his own authority (v. 9b), how much less should the intruders, being mere humans, presume to acquit themselves of the charges that the holy angelic ministers of the law would bring against their self-indulgent and insubordinate practices? The contrast between Michael's and the intruders' behavior likely would have aroused indignation against the latter, showing up the arrogance inherent in their practice.

10. Rather than show appropriate respect for the guardians of God's order and boundaries, **these people defame whatever they do not understand—but then again, those things that they do know by instinct like unreasoning animals, by these things they are being destroyed.** Jude has constructed an artfully balanced reproach against the intruders. On the one hand, their arrogant attitude toward angelic beings and the divine order that they represent (and the restrictions that such order would impose on their behavior) arises out of their lack of genuine knowledge about divine matters. On the other hand, their practice does arise from a certain kind of knowledge—the knowledge that the intruders share in common with animals and all who live out of their baser cravings and impulses. Their practice, however, is ultimately self-destructive: their own lives reflect the moral disorder—cravings and impulses being in the "driver's seat" instead of piety and higher reason—that results from their rejection of God's order.

Theological Issues

Jude is deeply interested in God-ordained boundaries. The angelic Watchers failed to observe such boundaries. Following their desire led them away from their proper sphere into improper interactions in the human sphere. The inhabitants of Sodom and its neighboring cities similarly followed their cravings across the lines drawn by God between humans and angels and in other arenas as well. (In another sense, Jude is also aware that certain boundaries *are* to be crossed. The wilderness generation is blamed for its lack of courage and obedience in regard to crossing a boundary and facing the challenges to forming a holy nation.) The intruders are, in Jude's portrayal, just another example of beings who disregard divinely imposed boundaries on the behavior of God's creatures. Ethically, this manifests itself in a self-centered concern that pervades the intruders' behavior, their underlying motive being to satisfy their own desires for material gain, food, drink, and sexual gratification (a particularly powerful creaturely drive). Their practice is grounded in their conviction that traditional Jewish and Jewish Christian codes of morality are merely antique remnants of a less enlightened time, an earlier and inferior stage in human knowledge of God beyond which they have evolved.

Jude expresses the contrary conviction that when these boundaries are crossed, people become less than God intended for them to be. Following their own cravings, the intruders debase themselves to the level of "unreasoning animals," a downward spiral that leads to the ruin of their lives rather than their liberation (v. 10). The intruders' practice and Jude's critique represent two positions taken in response to two very basic questions: What does it mean to live an authentically human life? And on what basis do we know what an authentically human life looks life? The posture of the intruders suggests that we are principally animals with the power to speak (and to rationalize our animalistic behavior), and that following and fulfilling our cravings results in fullness of life. Jude suggests that we are in-spirited beings with the power to bring our cravings and impulses into line with God's ordering of the same (cf. 4 Macc. 2:21–23). He asserts that we lose something of our humanness and are diminished, rather than fulfilled, when we give our cravings and impulses too much slack.

Furthermore, we lose something of the God-given cure for our condition when we disregard the authority set over us by God to keep us out of the territory where cravings, desires, and emotions gain the upper hand. For Jude, an authentic human life is reflected in the practices commended by "the faith once for all handed on to the saints," the apostolic teaching, in continuity with the tradition of the OT and its ongoing interpretation. Without these authorities speaking to us from outside our own experience, we too easily fall prey to the distorted vision for "authentic" human life impressed upon our sense perceptions by our own passions and impulses. The intruders' reliance on their personal revelations as a reliable counterauthority for discerning God's "real" boundaries, Jude cautions, is ultimately misguided. Their "dreaming" is nothing more than a sublimated fantasy generated by the impulses and yearnings of their own lower natures, a means by which they can deceive themselves into pursuing the downward spiral as if it were, in fact, the way to authenticity. Jude's conservatism, seen in his regard for the authority of scriptural tradition and for ethics, is rooted in the conviction that nothing is more deceptive than the human heart, with the result that we need to subject its desires to the external norms of the Jewish Christian tradition, rather than the reverse, if we are to rise above our own animal natures.

Jude 11–15

Intruders' Behavior Illumined from History, Nature, and Prophecy

Introductory Matters

Jude's description of the intruders resembles other near-contemporary denunciations of rival teachers and philosophers. Dio Chrysostom of Prusa, a statesman turned philosopher, lambastes sophists as, among other things, "ungodly" (*Trojana* [*Or.* 11.14]) and boastful people (*De Homero et Socrate* [*Or.* 55.7]), flatterers (*De quod felix sit sapiens* [*Or.* 23.11]), speakers who bring no profit to their hearers (*Tarsica prior* [*Or.* 33.4–5]), peddling their philosophy for the sake of acquiring money and enjoying prestige (*Ad Alexandrinos* [*Or.* 32.30]; Johnson 1989, 430). The sophist Aelius Aristides, in turn, accuses philosophers of many of the same things, especially that they were flatterers out for their own pleasure and looking to turn a profit (*Second Platonic Discourse* 46.308.5, 10; Johnson 1989, 430). It was common to say of rival speakers-for-hire or promoters of some philosophy that they were only out for pleasure, profit, and prestige (Johnson 1989, 432, citing ample evidence from Dio Chrysostom, Epictetus, Philostratus, and Lucian).

Jude's polemic against the intruders includes several of these topics. They are "ungodly" (vv. 4, 14–15), pleasure-seeking (vv. 4, 8, 10, 12, 16, 18), arrogant and bombastic in their speech (vv. 8, 10, 16), self-serving (note the phrase "for profit" in v. 11; see also v. 12), flatterers (v. 16), of no profit to anyone ("waterless clouds" and "fruitless trees," v. 12). The conventional nature of these charges should give us some pause before assuming that they are fully accurate reflections of the intruders' behavior and motives and not merely signs that

208

they were opponents (Johnson 1989, 432–33). However, many of these charges have such a situation-specific content as to suggest that they are not merely conventional (Green 2008, 22). The boastfulness of the intruders is specifically enacted in regard to spirit beings, suggesting some specific, observable practice. Their empty message springs from attempts to follow divine revelation (their "dreaming," certainly not part of conventional polemic) apart from being grounded in the tradition. The Christian love feast provided the specific occasion for self-indulgence (v. 12). The pervasiveness of Jude's emphasis on the intruders' pursuing undue indulgence of their cravings and impulses suggests that if the audience could not confirm this through their own observation, Jude would be seen as engaging in slander beyond the pale of convention.

Jude previously alluded to a story known from *1 Enoch*. Now, in verses 11–15, he recites it as an authoritative text, making further allusions to details of the fate of the Watchers. The book of *1 Enoch* is an apocalypse that grew in stages to its present shape between the early second century BCE and the first century CE. Enoch's strange disappearance from the scriptural story made him the focal point for speculation. What did Enoch see when he was "taken up" by God, apparently still living (Gen. 5:24)? What purpose did God have for him? What did he learn from entering the realm beyond?

The earliest core of this apocalypse was written before the success of the Maccabean Revolt (i.e., before 164 BCE) and included the "Apocalypse of Weeks" (*1 En.* 91.12–17; 93.1–10) and the "Book of the Watchers" (*1 En.* 6–36). The Book of the Watchers is a highly creative expansion of Gen. 6:1–4, which tells of angels ("sons of God") leaving their natural abode in order to mate with human females ("the daughters of human beings"), thereby begetting the race of the giants. According to *1 Enoch*, the fallen angels taught human beings how to make weapons and wage war; how to incite lust through jewelry and cosmetics; how to mine precious metals (thus introducing the opportunity for greed and competition for rare goods); and how to produce magical spells, astrology, and other snares. Their offspring, meanwhile, wrought havoc on the earth. God punished the angels, chaining them in a deep, dark pit, and tells Enoch to go to them to proclaim God's sentence: they will remain chained in dark prisons until the final judgment, while God exterminates the giants (whose ghosts become the demons that plague humankind). Before returning to earth, an angel shows Enoch the places of postmortem reward and punishment and other mysteries. This expanded legend is important background for Jude, 1 Peter, 2 Peter, and Revelation.

Major additions to *1 Enoch* include the "Book of Heavenly Luminaries" (*1 En.* 72–82), the "Book of Dream Visions" (*1 En.* 83–90), the "Letter of Enoch" (*1 En.* 91–107, incorporating the earlier "Apocalypse of Weeks"), and the "Parables of Enoch" (*1 En.* 37–31). The "Book of Heavenly Luminaries" prescribes a solar year (364 days) for the calculation of Sabbaths and religious festivals rather than a lunar year (354 days, requiring the addition of an extra month every third year). The Jerusalem authorities followed the lunar calendar, but the Qumran community used the solar calendar, citing 1 Enoch as authoritative support. The Qumran community bitterly critiqued their fellow Jews for following the "lesser light" (the moon) rather than the "greater light" (the sun), with the result that they celebrated the major festivals on the wrong days. The difference in calendar allowed the Jerusalem priests to attack the Qumran community on, for example, the latter's Day of Atonement (calculated according to the solar year) without violating that holy day themselves (calculated according to the lunar year).

The "Parables of Enoch" feature the figure of the "Son of Man" and his role in the last judgment of the wicked and deliverance of God's people. No copies of this section of 1 Enoch were found among the Dead Sea Scrolls, making it difficult to be sure of the date. They may predate the Gospels and thus perhaps inform the use of the title "Son of Man" by Jesus and his disciples. But they could just as well have been written simultaneously or slightly later, bearing witness to an independent development of a "Son of Man" figure or, to some extent, a backlash against Jewish Christian claims.

Jude comes from a milieu in which 1 Enoch was regarded quite highly. It clearly was popular among apocalyptic Jewish groups, judging from the fingerprints that it has left on books such as Daniel and Revelation and on the Dead Sea Scrolls, and it likely was available to Jude in some written form.

In this section, Jude continues to draw from a wide variety of scriptural and parascriptural sources, bringing the weight of the tradition to bear upon the intruders' character, activity, and destiny. Each allusion and recitation functions rhetorically to widen the gap between the audience and their new teachers.

Tracing the Train of Thought

Three Brief, Applied Historical Examples (11)

11. Jude concisely invokes three more historical examples, asserting a connection between the historic paradigms and the intruders' activity and

---

Jude 11–15 in the Rhetorical Flow

Letter opening (1–4)

Intruders' behavior illumined from history (5–10)

▶ Intruders' behavior illumined from history, nature, and prophecy (11–15)

  Three brief, applied historical examples (11)

  Amplification of intruders' viciousness (12–13)

  Indictment from 1 Enoch (14–15)

Wikimedia Commons

Figure 8. *Cain Killing Abel* (attributed to Gaetano Gandolfi, 1734–1802). Jude accuses his opponents of walking in the "way of Cain," who failed to control his angry passions and selfishly disregarded the well-being of others.

motivations: **Woe on them, because they walked in the way of Cain and abandoned themselves to the error of Balaam for profit and perished in the rebellion of Korah!** The triple form of this verse potentially recalls—in an ironic, since antithetical, manner—the opening of the Psalter, which describes the ideal toward which all worshipers of God are to strive: "Blessed is the person who does not walk in the advice of the ungodly, nor stand in the road of sinners, nor sit in the seat of scoffers" (Ps. 1:1). Anyone hearing this correspondence of cadences will immediately grasp that Jude presents the intruders as the "anti-ideal," a paradigm for nonimitation. "Woe to them" is an idiom very much at home in the speech of Jesus (twenty-nine of forty-five NT occurrences are from the Synoptic Gospels; all but two of the remainder are in Revelation; see Brosend 2004, 176), roughly the equivalent of our modern "Shame on them!" The correspondences that Jude asserts between the intruders and their scriptural predecessors provide the rationale for his claim that they deserve to come to disgrace. As in verses 5–7, Jude sacrifices chronological order for the sake of creating a climactic movement

211

from walking to abandoning oneself to perishing, thus "ending on a strong note of judgment" (Watson 1988, 60).

God's acceptance of Abel's sacrifice and rejection of Cain's was something of a mystery. Genesis 4:6–7 provides the only internal clue: Cain and his offerings would be accepted only if he learned to master his passions and impulses, of which his anger was but one example, rather than yield to them. The sequel—Cain's murder of Abel—shows Cain still walking in his debased path. Retelling this story, Josephus claimed that Cain promoted immorality among other people (*Ant.* 1.2.2 §§52–66). Philo, the Jewish philosopher, regarded Cain as the model of the person who believes, with Protagoras, that "the human being is the measure of all things" rather than God and God's law (*Post.* 11 §§38–39), so that those who follow Cain as their teacher seek what seems good to them, not what God's instruction defines as good. Such developments of the figure of Cain would resonate well with Jude's portrait of the intruders (see Byron 2011 for a fascinating history of interpretation and development of the Cain and Abel story).

Balak, king of Moab, had summoned Balaam to curse the Hebrews (Num. 22–24). Balaam is a prophet for hire (Num 22:7; cf. Neh. 13:2), but he claims to be able to speak only what God permits, no matter how much money Balak offers (Num. 22:18). Balaam does in fact consult with God (22:19–20), who constrains him to bless rather than curse Israel. Although acting blamelessly in this episode, Balaam later taught Balak how to alienate the Hebrews from their God, using the Midianite women to seduce them first into sexual immorality and then into idolatry (25:1–3; 31:16; cf. Rev. 2:14–15), resulting in God's sending a plague to punish the people (Num. 25:3–4, 8b–9). Both Josephus and Philo suggest that Balaam offered this plan to Balak when faced with dismissal without any money or gifts, seeking to find some way to earn his pay (Philo, *Mos.* 1.53 §§293–94; Josephus, *Ant.* 4.6.6 §§126–30). The expectation that Christian teachers would receive material support (1 Cor. 9:3–7) could subvert the motives of otherwise orthodox teachers or could even attract people who ought not to be teaching in the church at all (see 1 Tim. 6:3–10; Titus 1:11, which are concerned primarily with Christian *teachers*). Jude asserts that, like Balaam, the intruders are seeking to profit themselves by promoting immorality and thus disloyalty to the covenant God. The congregation will come to grief if they allow the intruders' influence to continue.

Korah (together with Dathan, Abiram, and 250 supporters) challenged the right of Moses and Aaron to lead and legislate, claiming that all the Hebrews were holy to the Lord and chosen by God (Num. 16:1–35). Korah's faction used an egalitarian premise to undermine Moses and Aaron's authority, while also seeking to gain power for themselves. Jude sees further reflections here of the intruders, insofar as they reject the moral authority of the law and of the apostolic teaching on the basis of their own access to God—that is, on the basis of the Christian "democratic" idea that all could possess the Spirit and receive equally valid spiritual revelations—while using this premise to increase their own prestige and make a living. God adjudicated the debate by opening up the ground beneath the tents of Korah's clan and consuming his 250 partisans with fire (Num. 16:31–35), while the remainder of the congregation hastened to withdraw from proximity to the rebels (16:34). Jude hopes that his own hearers will imitate the congregation of the Hebrews, not waiting to see judgment (which is surely looming over the intruders' heads!) actually fall upon them.

Amplification of Intruders' Viciousness (12–13)

12a. Jude follows these compressed historical examples with a series of five rich images drawn from nature, each of which continues to characterize these intruders as unworthy of a hearing and of support and indeed also as a danger to the community's health. Jude poignantly captures this danger by describing them as **hidden reefs in your love feasts, as they carouse together irreverently, shepherds looking out for themselves.** The image of "hidden reefs" (*spilades*) is obscured in some English translations, though ESV, NASB, and NLT have it right. Following the lead of 2 Pet. 2:13, some versions (e.g., NIV, RSV, NRSV) substitute "blemishes, stains" because 2 Peter uses the image of "blemishes" (*spiloi*) at the point where it is otherwise drawing on Jude 12. Some early commentators on Jude also read the image from 2 Peter back into Jude, perhaps because it seemed less arcane. No textual variants in the manuscript tradition, however, suggest that Jude intended anything other than "hidden reefs." Jude drew this image from the danger faced by ships following or approaching a coastline—a very common danger, to judge from Paul's example ("shipwrecked three times" [2 Cor. 11:25] already before the shipwreck on Malta [Acts 27:39–41]). This image highlights the intruders' deceptive appearances and hidden agendas, asserting again that the intruders pose grave danger "below the surface."

It is not at all difficult to see how the metaphor applies to the communal gatherings of the "love feast" (contra Neyrey 1993, 75), where the intimate setting of sharing a sacred meal among "insiders," where the defenses are lowered, gives the intruders access to the minds and indeed the bodies of the gathered Christians. At these feasts, the intruders indulge their cravings without regard for the presence of the Holy (hence, "irreverently," "without due reverence"), acting as "shepherds looking out for themselves" (literally, "shepherding themselves," v. 12a). Ezekiel called the rulers of Judea "shepherds" who "fed themselves" at the expense of the flock that God entrusted to their care (Ezek. 34:1–10). In the Fourth Gospel, Jesus uses this familiar metaphor to contrast himself, the "good shepherd," with other leaders of God's people who, in the end, look out only for themselves (John 10:1–18). Jude succinctly reminds the hearers both of the intruders' self-interest and of their lack of self-mastery.

12b–13. Some scholars have suggested that the images describing the intruders as **waterless clouds being driven on by winds, trees without any fruit at harvest-time, twice dead, torn up by the roots, wild waves of the sea, dredging up their degradation like sea foam, wandering stars for whom the dark gloom of the netherworld has been kept forever** derive from *1 En.* 2.1–5; 5.1–4, where the author speaks of God's proper order (Watson 1988, 62). There, among many other observations of natural phenomena, the lights in heaven do not alter their courses, clouds with rain and trees with fruit come along in their proper seasons, and seas and rivers flow where they ought. Another suggested source is *1 En.* 80.2–8, where the author speaks of rain being withheld, fruits appearing late in the season, and stars changing their courses (Bauckham 1983, 90–91; Osburn 1985).

Granted that Jude was familiar with *1 Enoch*, he shares no more with that author here than the tendency to look to nature for images to illustrate order or disorder in the human sphere. The precise imagery and wording in Jude has much more in common with scriptural texts. The image of "waterless clouds" (recalling Prov. 25:14 NRSV: "clouds and wind without rain") asserts that the intruders blow a lot of wind but bring forth nothing profitable or refreshing. The next image reinforces this. As "trees without any fruit at harvesttime, twice dead, torn up by the roots," the intruders are the antithesis of the godly person, who stands "like a tree rooted by streams of water, yielding its fruit in its season, and its leaf does not wither" (Ps. 1:3). Again, the intruders have no life and no fruit to offer the congregation. Jude's image of "wild waves of the sea, dredging up their degradation like sea foam" closely resembles "the tossing sea" whose "waters toss up mire and mud" in Isa. 57:20 (NRSV). The raging sea corresponds to the intruders' passions and impulses, which they do not keep in check, with the result that they exhibit self-indulgence rather than virtuous self-mastery (cf. 4 Macc. 7:1–3, 5; 15:31–32).

The final image speaks of the intruders as "wandering stars." They are like the planets (*planētai*, "wanderers") and other astral bodies that do not keep their proper place, as it were, and thus, unlike the "fixed stars," cannot be used reliably for navigation. Following the intruders' example and teaching will similarly lead the congregation astray. But this image now also connects with the story of the rebellious angels, who are spoken of as fallen stars (*1 En.* 18.14; 21.3, 6) and are shut up in the "dark gloom of the netherworld" (*1 En.* 10.4–5; 88.1–3) to suffer fiery torments (*1 En.* 18.3–6; 21.3–6). The place of torment as a place of darkness is well established in this period (see Ps. 88:12; Tob. 4:10; 14:10; *1 En.* 63.6; *Pss. Sol.* 14.9; 15.10; Matt. 8:12; 25:30), held alongside the images of punishment by burning—"yet from those flames no light, but rather darkness visible" (John Milton, *Paradise Lost* 1.63). Recalling the Watchers' story, Jude subtly reasserts that these intruders have "crossed the line" by coming into the congregation, that their instruction leads to being overpowered by human passions and other evils (recall the teaching of the Watchers), and that (social) intercourse with them will only breed evil.

Common to these major biblical allusions is the end that befalls each subject. God judges Cain, Balaam (who dies with the Midianites during the Israelite conquest), Korah, the shepherds who fatten themselves and fleece the flock of God, and the wandering stars. To the extent that the intruders do in fact mirror these precedents, they will also mirror their fate. Joining in their practices and teaching will by no means, therefore, be advantageous.

Indictment from 1 Enoch (14–15)

14–15. This allusion to *1 Enoch* prepares the way for Jude's recitation of *1 En.* 1.9–10: **Enoch, the seventh from Adam, prophesied even about these, saying: "Look! The Lord came with tens of thousands of his holy ones to execute judgment against all and to convict every soul concerning all their ungodly deeds through which they lived in an ungodly manner, and concerning all the harsh things which ungodly sinners spoke against him."** The text supplies an authoritative prediction of God's certain judgment on ungodliness and disrespectful speech directed against God (and God's agents), two areas in which, Jude asserts, the intruders have distinguished themselves.

Starting a prophecy with the declaration that "the Lord came [*ēlthen*]" seems strange. The past tense may simply reflect Jude's literal translation into Greek of a Hebrew or Aramaic perfect tense verb (VanderKam 1973, 148; Osburn 1976–77, 337). The existing Greek and Ethiopic versions of *1 Enoch* render this more idiomatically with a verb in the present tense: "He is coming [*erchetai*]." But could Jude have regarded this divine act of judgment as something already accomplished? The author of *1 Enoch* had, in fact, prophesied about the judgment upon the "wandering stars" (the angelic Watchers) and had even proclaimed to them God's judgment. Enoch's predictions focused primarily on the fate of the Watchers, the flood, and the fate of all who were caught up in ungodliness in that period (see *1 En.* 10.1–3). Jude may be presenting Enoch's prophecy as a fait accompli, a historical precedent displaying God's response to ungodliness in speech and deed (as it certainly is for the author of 2 Pet. 3:5–7), and thus an admonitory precedent to the congregation and the intruders.

On the other hand, Jude's description of the intruders themselves as "wandering stars" facilitates applying Enoch's declaration of God's judgment more directly to them. It is not immediately clear whether Jude envisions Enoch as prophesying *about* the intruders (as successors to the wandering stars) or *to* the intruders, warning them of the certitude of God's judgment against all ungodliness. The dative case of *toutois* ("about/to these," v. 14) more often bears the latter sense. If taken in this way, Jude asserts that the intruders have heard the divine warnings against behavior such as theirs but have foolishly persevered in a self-destructive path. Most scholars (e.g., Bauckham 1983, 93; Watson 1988, 64; Green 2008, 103), however, prefer to read the dative here as "about these," reading Jude's citation of *1 En.* 1.9 as the textual warrant for

Jude's claim in verse 4 that the intruders are in fact "*the* ungodly people long ago marked out for this condemnation." The text's emphasis on God's holding people accountable for impious speech makes it especially amenable to Jude's portrait of the intruders (cf. Jude 8, 10), as does its repetition of forms of the word "ungodly," which Jude had used to characterize the intruders at the outset (v. 4).

The scope of *1 En.* 1.9, however, encompasses more than the intruders, and Jude has not so dramatically reshaped the quotation as to bring it to bear only on the intruders and not leave the congregation (and all future readers) exposed as well. "All" remain the objects of judgment explicitly at the beginning of the citation: God comes "to execute judgment against all and to convict every soul concerning all their ungodly deeds." Even if Jude uses this text specifically to implicate the intruders as standing among the "ungodly" whom God will come to judge, it does so within the context of a broader vision of God's commitment to hold all people accountable for all their deeds and speech. (The teachings of Jesus and the book of Revelation also prominently foreground the angels' involvement in judgment; see, e.g., Matt. 13:36–42, 47–50; 16:27; 24:29–31; 25:31; Rev. 14:14–20.) All who have affronted God's honor through their lack of regard for God's appointed order of individual and social life will encounter the Lord's "riposte" to their ill-advised challenges (Neyrey 1993, 78).

Theological Issues

Jude's portrayal of the intruders continues to confront religious leaders with a stark picture of the "antihero." It is a mirror into which Christian leaders in any capacity can look only with trepidation, but they must look nonetheless because such self-examination now may spare judgment later. Jude's portrait shows us Christian teachers perverting the gospel to accommodate and legitimate, rather than to tame and transform, our animal nature, our "old self." These teachers deceive themselves into thinking, on the basis of whatever authority they have chosen to follow (their own spiritual experience, what the spirit of the age deems to be in keeping with "reasonable" religion, and so forth), that they stand in a superior position to the tradition they have inherited and see more clearly than those who have stood closer to the realities of which that tradition speaks. But in so doing, they have deprived themselves of all spiritual power and have emptied themselves of whatever profit they might have brought to those who listen to them. In place of seeking God's transformation of themselves and their hearers, they have dropped their sights to the level of seeking to make a living, to enjoy a span of prestige, perhaps even to steal a few pleasurable moments with those who are too easily enamored with their show of spirituality. In the end, they lead themselves and their followers into deeper slavery to their cravings and impulses and thus into the bondage that death holds over all for whom this present life is the primary concern. Those who might have led others to the divine rock that delivers in a storm have instead become the hidden rocks that cause shipwreck. Jude calls Christian leaders to look long and hard at themselves in front of this portrait, to see if any part of themselves is reflected therein, and to disentangle themselves immediately from the way of Cain and error of Balaam before they too share in the fate of Korah or the Watchers.

The portrait of God throughout Jude, but especially here in the recitation from *1 Enoch*, raises theological problems for many. Jude proclaims the God who holds all creatures accountable in judgment, punishing those who have rebelled against God's order and boundaries, exacting satisfaction for affronts to God's honor. This is the God who sentenced an entire generation of Hebrews to die in the desert, who buried the cities of the plain under fire and sulfur, who punished with an epidemic the Hebrews who succumbed to Balaam's wiles, who caused the ground to swallow up Korah's partisans and their families, who wiped away the ungodly in a great deluge. But this is simply to say that Jude speaks about God in ways that are prominently featured in the tradition that he has received.

The Hebrew Scriptures speak with exuberance about God's reign, particularly God's commitment to bring justice to this world, vindicating the pious and bringing down their oppressors. The Psalter, for example, bears frequent witness to this as the hope of Israel and the consequence of God's lordship (e.g., Pss. 96:10, 13; 97:2; 98:9; 99:1, 4). Jesus himself sustains the expectation that God will hold rebellious humanity accountable for refusing God's rightful claim to obedience (Matt. 13:41–43; 25:41–45), using the same images of fire and darkness to speak of the fate that awaits the impious. Jude is not more exclusive or vindictive than Jesus (at least as the latter is represented in the traditions attributed to him).

At the same time, it is important not to lose sight of Jude's proclamation of the love of God throughout his brief letter. Those who follow the apostles' teaching and use God's grace to pursue holiness rather than self-indulgence are "beloved" (vv. 1, 3, 5, 17, 20), urged to keep themselves in God's love (v. 21), and assured of God's commitment to keep them so that they will encounter God without fear or cause for rejection (v. 24). Jude, like John the Seer and like Jesus himself, will not allow us to lose sight of God's holiness and honor alongside God's love. In this, he bears witness to the fuller character of God known from the larger tradition, rather than the more popular but distorted (since partial) focus only on the forgiving, loving, forbearing God.

Jude 16–25

Exhortations and Conclusion

Introductory Matters

This commentary has used classical rhetorical theory as an aid to understanding the strategy and effect of many features of Jude, but it has not attempted to use the typical outline of a Greco-Roman speech as a framework for understanding Jude's structure. It is precisely here that rhetorical critics are most often justly taken to task for imposing a foreign grid onto the text or stretching the text to fit an unnatural frame. Duane Watson (1988), a deservedly leading figure in rhetorical criticism of the NT, makes an uncharacteristic misstep with Jude's conclusion along these very lines.

The typical judicial oration fell into four parts: (1) an exordium, which sounded the keynote of the speech, established credibility, and removed prejudice; (2) a narration, which briefly gave the facts of the case up to the point to be disputed; (3) proofs, which established the orator's interpretation of the case; (4) a conclusion, which generally contained a closing summary (the *repetitio*) and closing appeal to emotions (the *adfectus*, further divided into the *indignatio*, which sought to arouse indignation against opponents or the defendant, and the *conquestio*, which sought to arouse pity for the defendant, or other emotions favorable to one's case; so *Rhet. Her.* 2.30.47–2.31.50). Aristotle (*Rhet.* 3.10.1–4) understands the function of the conclusion to be "to dispose the hearer favorably toward oneself and unfavorably toward the adversary; to amplify and depreciate; to excite the emotions of the hearer; to recapitulate [by means of a summary statement of the proofs]." For Jude, Watson categorizes verses 17–19 as the *repetitio* (closing summary) and verses

20–23 as the *adfectus* (closing emotional appeal; Watson 1988, 67–68, 71–73; see also Neyrey 1993, 26; Witherington 2007, 625).

Identifying verses 17–19 as a closing summation is problematic. Ben Witherington (2007, 627) supports this identification, claiming that a "trump card" such as verses 17–19 is suitable for a peroration (citing Cicero, *De or.* 2.77.314). However, a "trump card" is equally if not more suitable either at the outset or at the close of the proof section (*Rhet. Her.* 3.10.18), while the closing summation generally "recalls the points we have made" rather than introducing new material (*Rhet. Her.* 2.30.47). It seems more prudent to regard these verses as a fifth argument (with Green 2008, 42), calling forward another "witness," as it were, against the intruders, following upon Jude's earlier "witness" (the recitation of *1 En.* 1.9) and his arguments based on historical examples (Jude's presentation of the apostolic witness harks back explicitly to the recitation from *1 Enoch* by means of the catchword "ungodly" in vv. 15, 18). Moreover, directly addressing the audience and using verbs of reminding/remembering link verse 5 and verse 17 together in a kind of inclusio, unifying the section that examines the intruders in light of the shared, received tradition.

Verses 17–23 also do not arouse the emotions expected in the (forensic) *adfectus*. While verses 17–19 do arouse indignation, they do not do so to any degree or in any manner different from verses 4–16. Verses 20–23 contain a series of closing exhortations to particular behaviors. While these may incidentally arouse emotions (e.g., feelings of friendship as people contemplate some of these actions, or fear in connection with reclaiming the wayward), the section is so unlike the kind of material that the rhetorical theorists envisioned for the *adfectus*—pulling out all the stops to arouse indignation against, or pity for, a defendant—that the rhetorical category obscures more than it reveals about this material.

Watson's delineation of the structure seems to be based on identifying the shift to the letter closing at verse 17 with "But as for you, beloved." But does this phrase (either here or in v. 20) indeed signal a new section? A more compelling structural marker for the letter's climax is the alternation between descriptions of the intruders and exhortations addressed to the readers:

Contrast 1 (vv. 16–18)	Contrast 2 (vv. 19–23)
These people (v. 16)	These people (v. 19)
But as for you, beloved (v. 17)	But as for you, beloved (v. 20)

Jude repeats key phrases or terms within each block to give each greater unity and coherence. In the first contrast, he describes the intruders as people "walking in line with their own cravings" (v. 16), using a phrase that anticipates (verbatim) the content of the apostles' warning to the beloved congregation (v. 18: "walking in line with their own cravings for ungodly things"). In the second contrast, Jude describes the intruders as people "not having the Spirit"

(v. 19), differentiating them from the beloved congregation, which is to pray "in the Holy Spirit" (v. 20). These paired alternations are rhetorically significant, driving verbal wedges between the intruding teachers and the congregation about which Jude passionately cares.

There are some significant textual issues in verses 22–23. Some early manuscripts identify two restorative actions that the congregation is to undertake, and others identify three. Although the earliest manuscript ($\mathfrak{P}^{72}$) supports the shorter reading (Osburn 1972; Neyrey 1993, 85–86), the longer reading is attested, with some variation, by the three major codices: Sinaiticus, Alexandrinus, and Vaticanus. These witnesses tip the scales in favor of the longer form here, outweighing the force of the text-critical rule that, all things being equal, a shorter reading is to be preferred (because scribes tended to expand the text rather than abbreviate it). The remaining variation concerns whether the first

Variant Readings of Jude 22–23

Some early manuscripts of Jude 22–23 identify two restorative actions that the congregation is to undertake, and others identify three.

Evidence in support of three restorative actions is as follows:

"Have mercy on some who doubt/dispute; save others, snatch [them] from fire; have mercy on others in fear, hating . . ." (Codex Sinaiticus [fourth century])

"Have mercy on some who doubt/dispute; save others, snatching [them] from fire; have mercy on others in fear, hating . . ." (correction to Codex Sinaiticus [twelfth century])

"Have mercy on some who doubt/dispute; save, snatching [them] from fire; have mercy on others in fear, hating . . ." (Codex Vaticanus [fourth century])

"Convict some who doubt/dispute; save others, snatching [them] from fire; have mercy on others in fear, hating . . ." (Codex Alexandrinus [fifth century])

Evidence in support of two restorative actions is as follows:

"Snatch some from fire; have mercy in fear on those who doubt/dispute, hating . . ." ($\mathfrak{P}^{72}$ [third/fourth century])

"Convict some who doubt/dispute; save others, snatching [them] from fire in fear, hating . . ." (Codex Ephraem Rescripti [fifth century])

"Have mercy on some who doubt/dispute; save others, snatching [them] from fire in fear, hating . . ." (correction to Codex Ephraem Rescripti [sixth century])

"Have mercy on some while disputing [with them]; save others in fear, seizing [them] from fire, hating . . ." (three ninth-century MSS)

Jude 16–25 in the Rhetorical Flow

Letter opening (1–4)
Intruders' behavior illumined from history (5–10)
Intruders' behavior illumined from history, nature, and prophecy (11–15)
▶ **Exhortations and conclusion (16–25)**
    First contrast and exhortation (16–18)
    Second contrast and exhortation (19–23)
    Liturgical conclusion (24–25)

action is to "have mercy upon" or "correct" those who doubt or dispute. The first reading has by far the stronger manuscript attestation. Moreover, the reading "correct" in Codex Alexandrinus can be explained as an attempt to eliminate the repetition of "have mercy" in verses 22–23, replacing it with another suitable verb in regard to the first group (Metzger 1994, 659–60).

Tracing the Train of Thought

First Contrast and Exhortation (16–18)

16. Jude has undermined the intruders' credibility by associating them with the most infamous false teachers in the story of God's people and also by showing their behaviors to stand condemned according to the standards revealed in God's previous judgments. Jude piles together several topics that denounce these intruders as insincere sophists who serve their own appetites and approach the believers as admiring friends only to get what they want out of them: **These people are grumblers, complaining about their lot while walking according to their own cravings, and their mouth speaks arrogant things, while admiring appearances for the sake of [their own] advantage.** Jude makes a further connection between the intruders and the rebellious exodus generation, whose members were frequently described as "grumblers" (*gongystai*), especially in regard to the incident at Kadesh-barnea (Num. 14:2, 27, 29, 36) and Korah's rebellion (Num. 16:11; see also Exod. 16:1–12; Num. 16:41–50), the two incidents to which Jude alluded in verses 5, 11 (Watson 1988, 66). He suggests that they are the sort of people who blame fate for their sorrows, when instead they should blame their own self-gratifying agendas and practices. Jude adds something new here by accusing them of "showing partiality in order to get on the good side of their potential patrons" (Witherington 2007, 625; see also Neyrey 1993, 82), though here his polemics may reflect convention more than the intruders' actual practice and motives (for an accusation of partiality against church members, see James 2:1).

17–18. This accumulation of charges against the intruders heightens the contrast when he turns to his hearers: they are truly bad news, **But as for you, beloved** (v. 17a), you are in a different class altogether. Jude calls the congregation's attention to their shared tradition once again: **Remember the words spoken in advance by the apostles of our Lord Jesus Christ, that they used to say to you: "In the last period of the time there will be scoffers walking in line with their own cravings for ungodly activities"** (vv. 17b–18). Jude has already recontextualized a portion of this recitation of tradition in verse 16 ("walking in line with their own cravings"), facilitating the cementing of a connection between the intruders and the apostolic warning.

Jude does not quote any known apostolic text. He may be giving a verbatim quotation of some current apostolic formulation, but more probably he is simply capturing the essence of the many warnings against false teachers given by Jesus (as in Matt. 7:15; 24:11–12) and the apostles. Luke portrays Paul as putting his churches on alert against the "savage wolves" that would come to prey upon the flock, seeking power and profit at the expense of the church and the faith (Acts 20:29–31). Indeed, Luke calls this a common theme in Paul's preaching. Both Pauline and Johannine traditions connect the emergence of false teachers with the "last times" (1 Tim. 4:1–5; 1 John 2:18), as here in verse 18.

The apostles who evangelized Jude's audience had also prepared them to recognize the false teachers who would inevitably come. Indeed, this apostolic warning highlights a scornful attitude toward the authority of the received tradition and an orientation toward self-gratification as marks of those false teachers, aligning well with Jude's consistent portrayal of the intruders. The congregation should now heed the earlier warning, reject these intruders' influence as a mockery of God's moral norms, and continue to pursue blamelessness before God without further distraction.

Second Contrast and Exhortation (19–23)

19. In the second pair of contrasts, Jude denounces the teachers as **the ones making divisions, worldly-minded, not having the Spirit.** The intruders break down the unity of congregations by not walking in line with "the faith that had been handed down once for all to the saints" (v. 3), eroding the commitment of some to continue to pull in the direction of the whole (v. 20). "Worldly-minded" translates the Greek *psychikoi*, a word used to describe whatever pertains to the natural person and natural life. It is qualitatively different from, and inferior to, the Spirit-led, Spirit-infused life (cf. 1 Cor. 2:14; 15:46; James 3:15). Jude asserts that the intruders operate only with the wisdom and knowledge that come through the natural mind and reasoning faculties. Their "dreaming" (v. 8)—whatever they claim to learn through ecstatic experience—must therefore be deceptive. The characterization of the intruders throughout, but especially in verses 16, 18, as people who "walk in line with their own desires" lends implicit proof to Jude's claim that they do not possess the Spirit. Paul also, and more explicitly, emphasized the incompatibility of following one's self-centered cravings and impulses and following the guidance of the Spirit (Gal. 5:16–25). James contrasts the wisdom from above, which manifests itself in virtue, with the wisdom of the natural person, which is earthbound, death-bound, and manifests itself in cravings driving the individual (James 3:13–4:1). This larger ethical conversation might explain the logical flow of verses 18–19.

The intruders cannot, therefore, be reliable teachers of Christians, who, unlike the intruders, both possess the Spirit (in which they pray, v. 20) and require teachers who are themselves "spiritual," guided and transformed by the wisdom the Spirit bestows.

20–21. When Jude turns again to address his audience, he provides a picture of what "contending for the faith" (v. 3) looks like in day-to-day practice (Cantinat 1973, 267, 279): **But as for you, beloved, as you build yourselves up in your most holy faith, praying in the Holy Spirit, keep yourselves in the love of God, waiting for the mercy of our Lord Jesus Christ unto eternal life.** Jude returns to the theme of the faith shared by all who stand in the tradition of the apostles' teaching. As he himself was engaged in encouraging them in their shared faith before having to address the immediate threat posed by the intruders (vv. 3–4), so he urges the members of the congregation to engage in mutual encouragement, supporting one another on the path toward spiritual maturity and toward the full transformation that God's grace seeks to work within and among them. Jude shares the broader Christian conviction that disciples must be involved in, and supportive of, one another's growth if each is to make progress in the life of faith (see Col. 3:16; 1 Thess. 4:18; 5:11, 14; Heb. 3:12–13; 10:24–25; 12:15–16). Alongside this, the congregation enjoys the spiritual strength and guidance supplied by the Spirit (v. 20).

Both social and supernatural support, therefore, help the disciples keep themselves connected with God's love and directed in their love toward God (it is not clear whether "the love of God" should be taken in a subjective or objective sense, or even whether a choice should be made between the two). Jude again harks back to themes from the letter's opening ("beloved in Father God and kept for Jesus Christ," v. 1), calling here for "faithful human response" to God's act of keeping them (Bauckham 1983, 27). Where the intruders focus their attention on the fulfillment of their cravings, leading eventually to their condemnation (vv. 14–15), the disciples are to focus their attention on growing in the love of God and to focus their yearnings toward the experience of mercy on the day of judgment and the enjoyment of the life that lies beyond (v. 21). As long as the orientation of their hearts is thus directed, the disciples can be confident of this good outcome (v. 24).

22–23. "Contending for the faith" also involves struggling to reclaim those whose foothold on the path of faith has faltered: **And have mercy on some who persist in disputing; save others, snatching them from the fire; have mercy on others in fear, hating even the tunic soiled from contact with the flesh.** Jude joins a chorus of other canonical witnesses to the necessity of community discipline (cf. Matt. 18:15–18; Gal. 6:1–2; Heb. 3:12–13; James 5:19–20). A disciple who begins to walk out of alignment with the faith is not simply to be expelled from the community nor allowed to continue in the way of error, straying farther from the path to life. Responsibility is laid on the Christian family to make every effort to rally around the wayward to restore them, while also taking care not to let themselves become ensnared in sin.

Jude colors his language with images drawn from Zech. 3:1–5. This text had already contributed the words "The Lord rebuke you" in verse 9 (cf. Zech. 3:2), by way of a tradition about the burial of Moses's body (for which Zech. 3:1–5 had served as a kind of template or prototype). Zechariah depicts the high priest Joshua (active during the rebuilding of the temple after the Babylonian exile) clad in soiled clothing (Zech. 3:3). The angel of the Lord removes these and provides clean, festive robes (Zech. 3:4–5), calling him "a brand snatched from the fire" (Zech. 3:2). Jude may have this passage in mind as he exhorts his hearers to "snatch others from the fire," while "hating even the tunic soiled by the flesh" (v. 23). The image of fire, commonly associated with judgment and postmortem retribution, underscores the peril of those who succumb to the intruders' influence. But Jude also seeks to safeguard the disciples who attempt to reclaim the wayward, warning them to remain conscious of the vileness of the pollution of sinful behavior so that they themselves, while trying to restore the sinner, will not be enticed.

Is Jude interested not only in preserving the spiritual health of his congregation but also in reclaiming the intruders from their error, as many interpreters suggest (e.g., Didymus the Blind, *Commentary on Jude*, in Bray 2000, 249; Marshall 1969, 167–68; Bauckham 1983, 116–17; 1990, 158; Witherington 2007, 637; Reese 2007, 83)? Does not Jude's claim that the intruders are "the ungodly ones long ago marked down for this condemnation" (v. 4) indicate, on the contrary, that their fate is sealed (Neyrey 1993, 91–92)? The content of a prophetic denunciation may not be the same as its intended effect. Jonah declared, "Forty days more, and Nineveh shall be overthrown" (Jon. 3:4 NRSV). He did not call for repentance, nor did he suggest that this fate could be avoided. Nevertheless, the Ninevites did repent and were spared by the God who is concerned with all persons, a fact that greatly upset Jonah (Jon. 4:1–2). Jude's words might have a similar effect on at least some of the intruders, with the result that they look at their own path differently and begin to move away from it toward a different use of God's grace. Jude nowhere calls for the expulsion of the intruders in this epistle (Reese 2007, 85); if they remain in the midst of the congregation, the disciples might well identify them as people to be restored—with all due caution!

Liturgical Conclusion (24–25)

24–25. Jude closes his letter with a rich doxology appropriate to the liturgical setting of the gathered congregation: **And to the One who is able to guard you so that you do not stumble and to make you stand blameless and exceedingly joyful in the presence of his glory, to our only God, our Savior, through Jesus Christ our Lord, [belong] glory, majesty, power, and authority from before this whole age and now and unto all ages. Amen!** Jude's final words speak of the confidence that the disciples can have as they contend for the faith. God is able to guard them, in the first instance, from defilement as they engage the wayward and seek to bring them back to the way of the faith but also, secondarily, from making missteps themselves that would render them unfit to stand in the presence of the Holy God. The perfection, completeness, and otherness of God requires that all who approach God, and all sacrifices that are offered to God, be "blameless" or "without blemish" (Neyrey 1993, 99). While the Levitical codes tended to focus on the absence of physical blemishes, this soon expanded to include the absence of moral blemishes as well.

Jude has woven the language of holiness and defilement throughout his letter as part of his strategy for distancing the congregation from the intruders. As a body of "holy ones" ("saints," v. 3), the Christian community has the privilege of standing in a special relationship to the Holy God. The congregation's call is to continue to build itself up in its "holy faith" in conversation with the "Holy Spirit" (v. 20), the power of God working in them to present them "blameless" (v. 24) before God at the judgment. The intruders, on the other hand, bring defilement into the community (vv. 8, 23), threatening the believers' fitness to stand before the Holy God. Refusing to be influenced by the intruders, the disciples have the opportunity to reverse that influence, reclaiming even the self-serving teachers from the polluting grip of their own impulses and cravings. For all glory, majesty, power, and authority belong to the One whose desire is to establish them blameless before God and to give them a joy that the natural cravings cannot attain.

Theological Issues

From beginning to end, Jude raises the critical question of the location of authority, the bottom-line norm that guides the congregation in the discernment of what is good and edifying and what is base and damaging. The charismatic intruders locate authority in their own spiritual insights and experience, legitimating their innovations with claims to new divine revelation. When final authority is located in a teacher's professed access to the divine, it is exceedingly difficult to bring any external criteria to bear on evaluating the teacher's claims or instructions—as anyone who lost family and friends to the cults in

Guyana (People's Temple), Waco (Branch Davidians), and Rancho Santa Fe (Heaven's Gate) can attest.

Jude locates final authority in the divine revelations handed down by the people of God through the ages: the Jewish Scriptures, other texts that are consonant with those Scriptures, the teachings of Jesus, and the apostolic teaching. The apostolic teaching is inspired by the Spirit and thus is "new" revelation, but it too is thoroughly grounded in the Jewish Scriptures (hence the vast amount of Jewish scriptural intertexture throughout the Christian texts that come to be recognized as authoritative Scriptures by the early church).

Jude is not at all opposed to the fresh winds of the Spirit. On the contrary, he depends on it and urges his audience to seek it out. However, he asserts that the Spirit's voice and prompting will be recognized by consonance with what the Spirit has spoken before to the people of God. Thus those who remain grounded in the scriptural and apostolic tradition have the Spirit (v. 20), but those who locate authority in their own "dreaming" do not (v. 19).

The dynamics of Jude's situation and response suggest that new teachers will either be evaluated on the basis of the words of the apostles and prophets or be allowed potentially to divert the congregation from the trajectory set by the apostles and prophets (vv. 17–18). In current church settings, it is often too easy and attractive to apply dismissive labels to those with whom we disagree and, in doing so, to become mere sophists defending our turf rather than disciples contending for the faith. Nonetheless, Jude would have us be watchful for instances when we need to call teachers to account on the pavement of the apostolic foundation. Does a preacher proclaim a "gospel" that gives quarter to the passions of the flesh that wage war against the soul? Does a teacher or writer dismiss the witness of the apostolic teaching as "outdated" or "uninformed," nurturing new disruptions of the unity of the church? For Jude, a teacher's authority comes from teaching in harmony with the tradition, which can include development and reconfiguration but never a change in trajectory, and a message that lacks such consonance lacks authority and Spirit. Jude's example and instructions counsel careful discernment through prayer and study done in a spirit of humility before the God who alone knows the complete truth but gives wisdom to those who ask.

The closing instructions of Jude, in concert with numerous other NT texts, raise the difficult issue of intragroup "discipline" (vv. 20–23). These texts are abused equally through loveless, rigid, debilitating enforcement and through neglect. Churches too often fall into the one extreme of excluding sinners from receiving forgiveness and restoration or the other extreme of embracing behavioral practices incompatible with the Christian tradition in an effort to show love to all people. Jude encourages the exercise of discernment regarding when a disciple has failed to take hold of God's grace for God's purposes unto God's good ends. He encourages the congregation (and not only its leaders) to respond in a redemptive, restorative fashion. Discernment is for the purpose of mercy and rescue, not condemnation and exclusion. For Jude, one manifestation of Christian love involves the investment of time that dialogue requires and the boldness that allows disciples to move into uncomfortable areas with their wayward sisters and brothers—all with the combination of caution and humility that keeps a vigilant watch over one's own passions and weaknesses in the process.

Bibliography

Adamson, James B. 1989. *James: The Man and His Message*. Grand Rapids: Eerdmans.

Aland, Barbara, and Kurt Aland, et al. 1997. *James*. Installment 1 of *Novum Testamentum Graecum: Editio Critica Maior*. Vol. 4, *Catholic Letters*, part 2. Edited by the Institute for Textual Research. Stuttgart: Deutsche Bibelgesellschaft.

Aymer, Margaret P. 2007. *First Pure, Then Peaceable: Frederick Douglass Reads James*. Library of New Testament Studies 379. London: T&T Clark International.

Barclay, S. M. 1885. *The Self-Revealing Jehovah of the Old Testament the Christ of the New Testament*. London: Nisbet.

Barrett, C. K. 1974. "Pauline Controversies in the Post-Pauline Period." *New Testament Studies* 20:229–45.

———. 1986. "Boasting (καυχᾶσθαι κτλ.) in the Pauline Epistles." In *L'apôtre Paul: Personnalité, style et conception du ministère*, by Albert Vanhoye et al., 363–68. Bibliotheca ephemeridum theologicarum lovaniensium 73. Louvain: Louvain University Press.

Bauckham, Richard J. 1983. *Jude, 2 Peter*. Word Biblical Commentary 50. Waco: Word.

———. 1990. *Jude and the Relatives of Jesus in the Early Church*. Edinburgh: T&T Clark.

———. 1995. "James and the Jerusalem Church." In *The Book of Acts in Its Palestinian Setting*, edited by Richard Bauckham, 415–80. Grand Rapids: Eerdmans

———. 1999. *James: Wisdom of James, Disciple of Jesus the Sage*. London: Routledge.

———. 2003. "James." In *Eerdmans Commentary on the Bible*, edited by James D. G. Dunn and John W. Rogerson, 1483–92. Grand Rapids: Eerdmans.

Brandon, S. G. F. 1957. *The Fall of Jerusalem and the Christian Church: A Study of the Effects of the Jewish Overthrow of A.D. 70 on Christianity*. London: SPCK.

Bray, Gerald, ed. 2000. *James, 1–2 Peter, 1–3 John, Jude*. Ancient Christian Commentary on Scripture: New Testament 11. Downers Grove, IL: InterVarsity.

Brooke, A. E., trans. and ed. 1896. *The Commentary of Origen on St. John's Gospel*. 2 vols. Cambridge: Cambridge University Press.

Brosend, William. 2004. *James and Jude*. New Cambridge Bible Commentary. Cambridge: Cambridge University Press.

Brown, Raymond E., and John P. Meier. 1983. *Antioch and Rome: New Testament Cradles of Catholic Christianity*. New York: Paulist Press.

Bultmann, Rudolf. 1958. *Jesus Christ and Mythology*. London: SCM.

———. 1965. "Καυχᾶσθαι κτλ." In *Theological Dictionary of the New Testament*, edited by Gerhard Kittel and Gerhard Friedrich, translated by Geoffrey W. Bromiley, 3:645–54. Grand Rapids: Eerdmans.

Byron, John. 2011. *Cain and Abel in Text and Tradition: Jewish and Christian Interpretations of the First Sibling Rivalry*. Leiden: Brill.

Cantinat, Jean. 1973. *Les épîtres de Saint Jacques et de Saint Jude*. Sources bibliques. Paris: Gabalda.

Charles, J. Daryl. 1990. "'Those' and 'These': The Use of the Old Testament in the Epistle of Jude." *Journal for the Study of the New Testament* 38:109–24.

———. 1991a. "Jude's Use of Pseudepigraphical Source Material as Part of a Literary Strategy." *New Testament Studies* 37:130–45.

———. 1991b. "Literary Artifice in the Epistle of Jude." *Zeitschrift für die neutestamentliche Wissenschaft* 82:106–24.

———. 1993. *Literary Strategy in the Epistle of Jude*. Scranton: University of Scranton Press; London: Associated University Press, 1993.

Cheung, Luke L. 2003. *The Genre, Composition and Hermeneutics of the Epistle of James*. Paternoster Biblical and Theological Monographs. London: Paternoster.

Chilton, Bruce, and Craig Evans, eds. 1999. *James the Just and Christian Origins*. Supplements to Novum Testamentum 98. Leiden: Brill.

———, eds. 2005. *The Missions of James, Peter, and Paul: Tensions in Early Christianity*. Supplements to Novum Testamentum 115. Leiden: Brill.

Chilton, Bruce, and Jacob Neusner, eds. 2001. *The Brother of Jesus: James the Just and His Mission*. Louisville: Westminster John Knox.

Daube, David. 1949. "Rabbinic Methods of Interpretation and Hellenistic Rhetoric." *Hebrew Union College Annual* 22:239–62.

Davids, Peter H. 1982. *The Epistle of James: A Commentary on the Greek Text*. New International Greek Testament Commentary. Grand Rapids: Eerdmans.

———. 2005a. "James and Peter: The Literary Evidence." In *The Missions of James, Peter, and Paul: Tensions in Early Christianity*, edited by Bruce Chilton and Craig Evans, 29–52. Supplements to Novum Testamentum 115. Leiden: Brill.

———. 2005b. "The Test of Wealth in James and Paul." In *The Missions of James, Peter, and Paul: Tensions in Early Christianity*, edited by Bruce Chilton and Craig Evans, 355–84. Supplements to Novum Testamentum 115. Leiden: Brill.

———. 2005c. "Why Do We Suffer? Suffering in James and Paul." In *The Missions of James, Peter, and Paul: Tensions in Early Christianity*, edited by Bruce Chilton and Craig Evans, 435–66. Supplements to Novum Testamentum 115. Leiden: Brill.

———. 2006. *The Letters of 2 Peter and Jude*. Pillar New Testament Commentary. Grand Rapids: Eerdmans.

Davies, W. D. 1955. *Paul and Rabbinic Judaism*. 2nd ed. London: SPCK.

———. 1964. *The Setting of the Sermon on the Mount*. Cambridge: Cambridge University Press.

Deissmann, Adolf. 1910. *Light from the Ancient East: The New Testament Illustrated by Recently Discovered Texts of the Graeco-Roman World*. Translated by Lionel R. M. Strachan. Rev. ed. Reprint, Grand Rapids: Baker, 1978.

deSilva, David A. 1999. "Testament of Moses." In *Dictionary of New Testament Background*, edited by Craig A. Evans and Stanley E. Porter, 1192–99. Downers Grove, IL: InterVarsity.

———. 2000. *Honor, Patronage, Kinship and Purity: Unlocking New Testament Culture*. Downers Grove, IL: InterVarsity.

———. 2002. *Introducing the Apocrypha: Message, Context, and Significance*. Grand Rapids: Baker Academic.

———. 2004. *An Introduction to the New Testament: Contexts, Methods and Ministry Formation*. Downers Grove, IL: InterVarsity.

———. 2012. *The Jewish Teachers of Jesus, James, and Jude: What Earliest Christianity Learned from the Apocrypha and Pseudepigrapha*. New York: Oxford University Press.

Desjardins, Michel. 1987. "The Portrayal of the Dissidents in 2 Peter and Jude." *Journal for the Study of the New Testament* 30:89–102.

Dibelius, Martin. 1976. *James: A Commentary on the Epistle of James*. Revised by Heinrich Greeven. Translated by Michael A. Williams. Edited by Helmut Koester. Hermeneia. Philadelphia: Fortress.

Dodd, C. H. 1946. *The Johannine Epistles*. Moffatt New Testament Commentary. London: Hodder & Stoughton.

———. 1953a. *The Interpretation of the Fourth Gospel*. Cambridge: Cambridge University Press.

———. 1953b. "The Mind of Paul I." In *New Testament Studies*, 67–82. Manchester: Manchester University Press.

Dunnett, W. M. 1988. "The Hermeneutics of Jude and 2 Peter: The Use of Ancient Jewish Traditions." *Journal of the Evangelical Theological Society* 31:287–92.

Easton, B. S. 1957. "The Epistle of James." In *The Interpreter's Bible*, edited by George A. Buttrick, 12:3–74. Nashville: Abingdon.

Elliott, J. K., ed. 1993. *The Apocryphal New Testament: A Collection of Apocryphal Christian Literature in an English Translation Based on M. R. James*. Oxford: Clarendon.

Elliott-Binns, L. E. 1957. *Galilean Christianity*. Studies in Biblical Theology 16. London: SCM.

Ellis, E. Earle. 1978. *Prophecy and Hermeneutic in Early Christianity: New Testament Essays*. Wissenschaftliche Untersuchungen zum Neuen Testament 18. Tübingen: Mohr Siebeck.

Eusebius. 1926–32. *The Ecclesiastical History*. Translated by Kirsopp Lake, J. E. L. Oulton, and Hugh Jackson Lawlor. 2 vols. Loeb Classical Library. Cambridge, MA: Harvard University Press.

————. 1927–28. *The Ecclesiatical History and the Martyrs of Palestine.* Translated with introduction and notes by Hugh Jackson Lawlor and J. E. L. Oulton. 2 vols. London: Macmillan.

————. 1965. *The History of the Church.* Translated and edited by G. A. Williamson. Hammondsworth: Penguin.

————. 1979. *The Church History of Eusebius.* In *The Nicene and Post-Nicene Fathers,* 2nd series, edited by Philip Schaff and Henry Wace, 1:3–1039. Reprint, Grand Rapids: Eerdmans.

Eybers, I. E. 1975. "Aspects of the Background of the Letter of Jude." *Neotestamentica* 9:113–23.

Freyne, Séan. 1980. *Galilee, from Alexander the Great to Hadrian, 323 B.C.E. to 135 C.E.: A Study of Second Temple Judaism.* Wilmington, DE: Michael Glazier.

————. 2004. *Jesus, a Jewish Galilean: A New Reading of the Jesus-Story.* London: T&T Clark.

Fuchs, Eric, and Pierre Raymond. 1980. *La deuxième épître de saint Pierre; L'épître de saint Jude.* Commentaire du Nouveau Testament 13B. Neuchâtel: Delachaux & Niestlé.

Gertner, M. 1962. "Midrashim in the New Testament." *Journal of Semitic Studies* 7:283–91.

Goodblatt, David M. 1994. *The Monarchic Principle: Studies in Jewish Self-Government in Antiquity.* Texte und Studien zum antiken Judentum 38. Tübingen: Mohr Siebeck.

Green, Gene L. 2008. *Jude and 2 Peter.* Baker Exegetical Commentary on the New Testament. Grand Rapids: Baker Academic.

Grundmann, Walter. 1974. *Der Brief des Judas und der zweite Brief des Petrus.* Theologischer Handkommentar zum Neuen Testament 15. Berlin: Evangelische Verlagsanstalt.

Hartin, Patrick J. 1991. *James and the "Q" Sayings of Jesus.* Journal for the Study of the New Testament: Supplement Series 47. Sheffield: JSOT Press.

————. 1996. "Call to Be Perfect through Suffering (James 1,2–4): The Concept of Perfection in the Epistle of James and the Sermon on the Mount." *Biblica* 77:477–92.

————. 1999. *A Spirituality of Perfection: Faith in Action in the Letter of James.* Collegeville, MN: Liturgical Press.

————. 2003. *James.* Sacra pagina 14. Collegeville, MN: Liturgical Press.

Hartmann, Gerhard. 1942. "Der Afbau des Jacobusbriefes." *Zeitschrift für Theologie und Kirche* 66:63–70.

Havener, Ivan. 1987. *Q: The Sayings of Jesus, with a Reconstruction of Q by Athanasius Polag.* Good News Studies 19. Wilmington, DE: Michael Glazier.

Heidegger, Martin. 1976. "Brief über den 'Humanismus.'" In *Gesamtausgabe,* vol. 9, edited by F.-W. von Hermann, 312–64. Frankfurt: Klostermann, 1976. The original "Letter on Humanism" appeared in 1947.

————. 1979. "Der Anfang des abendländischen Denkens (Heraklit)." In *Gesamtausgabe,* vol. 55, edited by Manfred S. Frings, 1–184. Frankfurt: Klostermann, 1979. The original "Lecture on Heraclitus" appeared in 1943.

Hengel, Martin. 1974. *Judaism and Hellenism*. Translated by John Bowden. 2 vols. London: SCM.

———. 1989. *The "Hellenization" of Judaea in the First Century after Christ*. Translated by John Bowden. Philadelphia: Trinity Press International.

Hippolytus. 1989–90. "On the Seventy Apostles." In *The Ante-Nicene Fathers: Translations of the Writings of the Fathers Down to A.D. 325*, edited by Alexander Roberts and James Donaldson, 5:255–56. Reprint, Grand Rapids: Eerdmans.

Horsley, Richard. 1996. *Archaeology, History, and Society in Galilee: The Social Context of Jesus and the Rabbis*. Valley Forge, PA: Trinity Press International.

Howard, George, 1992. "Tetragrammaton in the New Testament." In *Anchor Bible Dictionary*, edited by David Noel Freedman, 6:392–93. New York: Doubleday.

Ilan, Tal. 1989. "Notes on the Distribution of Jewish Women's Names in Palestine in the Second Temple and Mishnaic Periods." *Journal of Jewish Studies* 40:186–200.

———. 2002. *Lexicon of Jewish Names in Late Antiquity*. Part 1, *Palestine 330 BCE–200 CE*. Texte und Studien zum antiken Judentum 91. Tübingen: Mohr Siebeck.

Irenaeus. *Works*. 1872. Translated by John Keble. Oxford: James Parker.

———. 1989–90. *Against Heresies*. In *The Ante-Nicene Fathers: Translations of the Writings of the Fathers Down to A.D. 325*, edited by Alexander Roberts and James Donaldson, 1:309–567. Reprint, Grand Rapids: Eerdmans.

Jackson-McCabe, Matt A. 2001. *Logos and Law in the Letter of James: The Law of Nature, the Law of Moses, and the Law of Freedom*. Supplements to Novum Testamentum 100. Leiden: Brill.

Jeremias, Joachim. 1964. "Γέεννα." In *Theological Dictionary of the New Testament*, edited by Gerhard Kittel and Gerhard Friedrich, translated by Geoffrey W. Bromiley, 1:657–58. Grand Rapids: Eerdmans.

Jerome. 1896. *De viris illustribus*. Edited by E. C. Richardson. Texte und Untersuchungen 14/2. Berlin: Akademie.

———. 1956a. *Lives of Illustrious Men*. In *The Nicene and Post-Nicene Fathers*, 2nd series, edited by Philip Schaff and Henry Wace, 3:359–84. Grand Rapids: Eerdmans.

———. 1956b. "The Perpetual Virginity of Blessed Mary: Against Helvidius." In *The Nicene and Post-Nicene Fathers*, 2nd series, edited by Philip Schaff and Henry Wace, 6:334–46. Grand Rapids: Eerdmans.

Johnson, Luke Timothy. 1989. "The New Testament's Anti-Jewish Slander and the Conventions of Ancient Polemic." *Journal of Biblical Literature* 108:419–41.

———. 1995. *The Letter of James: A New Translation with Introduction and Commentary*. Anchor Bible 37A. New York: Doubleday.

———. 1998. "The Letter of James: Introduction, Commentary, and Reflections." In *The New Interpreter's Bible*, edited by Leander E. Keck, 12:175–225. Nashville: Abingdon.

———. 2004. *Brother of Jesus, Friend of God: Studies in the Letter of James*. Grand Rapids: Eerdmans.

Jones, Peter Russell. 2001. *The Epistle of Jude as Expounded by the Fathers—Clement of Alexandria, Didymus of Alexandria, the Scholia of Cramer's Catena, Pseudo-Oecumenius, and Bede*. Lewiston, NY: Edwin Mellen.

Joubert, Stefan J. 1990. "Language, Ideology, and the Social Context of the Letter of Jude." *Neotestamentica* 24:335–49.

———. 1995. "Persuasion in the Letter of Jude." *Journal for the Study of the New Testament* 58:75–87.

Jüngel, Eberhard. 1983. *God as the Mystery of the World: On the Foundation of the Theology of the Crucified One in the Dispute between Theism and Atheism.* Translated from the 3rd German edition (1977) by Darrell L. Guder. Grand Rapids: Eerdmans.

Kelly, J. N. D. 1963. *A Commentary on the Pastoral Epistles: I Timothy, II Timothy, Titus.* Harper's New Testament Commentaries. New York: Harper & Row.

———. 1969. *The Epistles of Peter and Jude.* Black's New Testament Commentaries. London: Black.

Knight, Jonathan. 1995. *2 Peter and Jude.* New Testament Guides. Sheffield: Sheffield Academic Press.

Knox, W. L. 1945. "The Epistle of St. James." *Journal of Theological Studies* 46:10–17.

Koester, Helmut, 1982. *Introduction to the New Testament.* Vol. 2, *History and Literature of Early Christianity.* New York: de Gruyter.

Kooiman, Willem Jan. 1961. *Luther and the Bible.* Translated by John Schmidt. Philadelphia: Muhlenberg.

Kubo, Sakae. 1981. "Jude 22–23: Two-Division Form or Three?" In *New Testament Text Criticism: Its Significance for Exegesis*, edited by Eldon J. Epp and Gordon D. Fee, 239–53. Oxford: Clarendon.

Lake, Kirsopp, J. E. L. Oulton, and Hugh Jackson Lawlor, trans. and eds. 1926–32. *The Ecclesiastical History*, by Eusebius. 2 vols. Loeb Classical Library. Cambridge, MA: Harvard University Press.

Lamprecht, J. 1996. "Dangerous Boasting: Paul's Self-Communication in 2 Cor 10–13." In *The Corinthian Correspondence*, edited by R. Bieringer, 325–46. Bibliotheca ephemeridum theologicarum lovaniensium 125. Louvain: Louvain University Press.

Landon, Charles. 1996. *A Text-Critical Study of the Epistle of Jude.* Journal for the Study of the New Testament: Supplement Series 135. Sheffield: Sheffield Academic Press.

Laws, Sophie. 1980. *A Commentary on the Epistle of James.* Black's New Testament Commentaries. London: Black.

Lemaire, André. 2002. "Burial Box of James the Brother of Jesus." *Biblical Archaeology Review* 28 (6): 24–33, 70.

Levine, L. I. 1979. "The Jewish Patriarch (*Nasi*) in Third Century Palestine." In *Aufstieg und Niedergang der römischen Welt*, part 2, vol. 19, edited by Wolfgang Haase, 2:649–88. Berlin: de Gruyter.

Lightfoot, J. B. 1865. "The Brethren of the Lord." In *Saint Paul's Epistle to the Galatians: A Revised Text and Introduction, Notes, and Dissertations*, 252–91. London: Macmillan.

Lockett, Darian. 2008. *Purity and Worldview in the Epistle of James.* Library of New Testament Studies 366. New York: T&T Clark.

Lohse, Eduard. 1981. *The Formation of the New Testament*. Translated by M. Eugene Boring. Nashville: Abingdon.

Luther, Martin. 1982. *Commentary on the Epistles of Peter and Jude*. Translated by J. G. Walch. Reprint, Grand Rapids: Kregel.

Malherbe, Abraham J. 1988. *Ancient Epistolary Theorists*. Sources for Biblical Study 19. Atlanta: Scholars Press.

Marshall, I. Howard. 1969. *Kept by the Power of God: A Study of Perseverance and Falling Away*. Minneapolis: Bethany Fellowship.

———, ed. 2002. *Moulton and Geden Concordance to the Greek New Testament*. 6th ed. London: T&T Clark.

Martin, G. Currie. 1907. "The Epistle of James as a Storehouse of the Sayings of Jesus." *The Expositor*, series 7, 3: 174–84.

Martin, Ralph P. 1988. *James*. Word Biblical Commentary 48. Waco: Word.

Massebieau, Louis. 1895. "L'épître de Jacques, est-elle l'oeuvre d'un Chrétien?" *Revue de l'histoire des religions* 32:249–83.

Mayor, J. B. 1892. *The Epistle of St. James: The Greek Text with Introduction, Notes and Comments*. 2nd ed. 1897. Reprint, Grand Rapids: Zondervan, 1954.

McCartney, Dan G. 2009. *James*. Baker Exegetical Commentary on the New Testament. Grand Rapids: Baker Academic.

Metzger, Bruce M. 1968. *The Text of the New Testament: Its Transmission, Corruption, and Restoration*. 2nd ed. Oxford: Clarendon.

———. 1975. *A Textual Commentary on the Greek New Testament*. Corrected ed. New York: United Bible Societies.

———. 1987. *The Canon of the New Testament: Its Origin, Development, and Significance*. Oxford: Clarendon.

———. 1992. *The Text of the New Testament: Its Transmission, Corruption, and Restoration*. 3rd ed. New York: Oxford University Press.

———. 1994. *A Textual Commentary on the Greek New Testament*. 2nd ed. Stuttgart: Deutsche Bibelgesellschaft.

Meyer, Arnold. 1930. *Das Rätsel des Jacobusbriefes*. Beihefte zur Zeitschrift für die neutestamentliche Wissenschaft und die Kunde der älteren Kirche 10. Giessen: Topelmann.

Neusner, Jacob. 1973. *The Idea of Purity in Ancient Judaism: The 1972–1973 Haskell Lectures*. Studies in Judaism in Late Antiquity 1. Leiden: Brill.

———. 1974–77. *A History of the Mishnaic Law of Purities*. 22 vols. Studies in Judaism in Late Antiquity 6. Leiden: Brill.

———. 2002a. "Gamaliel and the Patriarchate." Paper prepared for the Institute of Advanced Theology Colloquium "Jerusalem after Jesus: 30–66 CE," at Bard College, November 2002, 3–25.

———. 2002b. "The Halakhic Agenda of the Patriarchal House Identified by Form-Analysis of the Mishnah-Pericopae." Paper prepared for the Institute of Advanced Theology Colloquium "Jerusalem after Jesus: 30–66 CE," at Bard College, November 2002, 27–40.

Neusner, Jacob, and Bruce Chilton. 2002. "Paul and Gamaliel." Paper prepared for the Institute of Advanced Theology Colloquium "Jerusalem after Jesus: 30–66 CE," at Bard College, November 2002, 41–68.

Neyrey, Jerome H. 1980. "The Form and Background of the Polemic in 2 Peter." *Journal of Biblical Literature* 99:407–31.

———. 1993. *2 Peter, Jude: A New Translation with Introduction and Commentary.* Anchor Bible 37C. New York: Doubleday.

Origen. 1896. *The Commentary of Origen on St. John's Gospel.* Translated and edited by A. E. Brooke. 2 vols. Cambridge: Cambridge University Press.

———. 1980. *Contra Celsum.* Edited by Henry Chadwick. Library of Christian Classics. Philadelphia: Westminster.

Osburn, Carroll D. 1972. "The Text of Jude 22–23." *Zeitschrift für die neutestamentliche Wissenschaft* 63:139–44.

———. 1976–77. "The Christological Use of I Enoch i.9 in Jude 14, 15." *New Testament Studies* 23:334–41.

———. 1985. "I Enoch 80.2–8 (67.5–7) and Jude 12–13." *Catholic Biblical Quarterly* 47:296–303.

Painter, John. 1997a. *Just James: The Brother of Jesus in History and Tradition.* Studies on Personalities of the New Testament. Columbia: University of South Carolina Press.

———. 1997b. *Mark's Gospel: Worlds in Conflict.* New Testament Readings. London: Routledge.

———. 2001. "Who Was James?" In *The Brother of Jesus: James the Just and His Mission*, edited by Bruce Chilton and Jacob Neusner, 10–65. Louisville: Westminster John Knox.

———. 2002a. *1, 2, and 3 John.* Sacra pagina 18. Collegeville, MN: Liturgical Press.

———. 2002b. Review of *The Voice of Jesus in the Social Rhetoric of James*, by Wesley Hiram Wachob. *Journal of Theological Studies*, n.s., 53 (1): 272–78.

———. 2004. *Just James: The Brother of Jesus in History and Tradition.* 2nd ed. Studies on Personalities of the New Testament. Columbia: University of South Carolina Press.

———. 2005a. "James and Peter: Models of Leadership and Mission." In *The Missions of James, Peter, and Paul: Tensions in Early Christianity*, edited by Bruce Chilton and Craig Evans, 143–209. Supplements to Novum Testamentum 115. Leiden: Brill.

———. 2005b. "The Power of Words: Rhetoric in James and Paul." In *The Missions of James, Peter, and Paul: Tensions in Early Christianity*, edited by Bruce Chilton and Craig Evans, 235–73. Supplements to Novum Testamentum 115. Leiden: Brill.

———. 2006. "James as the First Catholic Epistle." *Interpretation* 60:245–59.

———. 2008. "Matthew and John." In *Matthew and His Christian Contemporaries*, edited by David C. Sim and Boris Repschinski, 66–86. Library of New Testament Studies 333. London: T&T Clark.

Patrick, John, trans. 1969. "Origen's Commentary on John, Books I–X; and Commentary on Matthew, Books I–II, X–XIV." In *The Ante-Nicene Fathers: Translations of the Writings of the Fathers Down to A.D. 325*, edited by Alexander Roberts, James Donaldson, and Allan Menzies, 10:291–512. Reprint, Grand Rapids: Eerdmans.

Perkins, Pheme. 1995. *First and Second Peter, James and Jude*. Interpretation. Louisville: John Knox.

Popkes, Wiard. 2001. *Der Brief des Jakobus*. Theologischer Handkommentar zum Neuen Testament 14. Leipzig: Evangelische Verlagsanstalt.

Pratscher, Wilhelm. 1987. *Der Herrenbruder Jakobus und die Jakobustradition*. Forschung zur Religion und Literatur des Alten und Neuen Testaments 139. Göttingen: Vandenhoeck & Ruprecht.

Prideaux, Richard. 1985. "The Place of the Epistle of James in the Growth of the Primitive Church." MA thesis, La Trobe University, Melbourne.

Priest, J. 1983. "Testament of Moses." In *The Old Testament Pseudepigrapha*, edited by James H. Charlesworth, 1:919–34. Garden City, NY: Doubleday.

Rabil, Albert. 1972. *Erasmus and the New Testament: The Mind of a Christian Humanist*. San Antonio: Trinity University Press.

Reese, Ruth Ann. 2007. *2 Peter and Jude*. Two Horizons New Testament Commentary. Grand Rapids: Eerdmans.

Richards, E. Randolph. 2004. *Paul and First-Century Letter Writing: Secretaries, Composition and Collection*. Downers Grove, IL: InterVarsity.

Rollins, H. E., ed. 1958. *Letters of John Keats, 1814–1821*. 2 vols. Cambridge, MA: Harvard University Press.

Ropes, J. H. 1916. *A Critical and Exegetical Commentary on the Epistle of St. James*. International Critical Commentary. Edinburgh: T&T Clark.

Rowston, D. J. 1975. "The Most Neglected Book in the New Testament." *New Testament Studies* 21:554–63.

Schnabel, Eckhard J. 2004. *Early Christian Mission*. 2 vols. Downers Grove, IL: InterVarsity.

Schreiner, Thomas R. 2003. *1, 2 Peter, Jude*. New American Commentary. Nashville: Broadman & Holman.

Shanks, Hershel, ed. 2002. *Biblical Archaeology Review* 28 (6).

Shepherd, James M. H. 1956. "The Epistle of James and the Gospel of Matthew." *Journal of Biblical Literature* 75:40–51.

Spitta, Friedrich. 1896. *Der Brief des Jakobus*. Göttingen: Vandenhoeck & Ruprecht.

Stählin, Gustav. 1976. "Φιλία." In *Theological Dictionary of the New Testament*, edited by Gerhard Kittel and Gerhard Friedrich, translated by Geoffrey W. Bromiley, 9:146–71. Grand Rapids: Eerdmans.

Stauffer, Ethelbert. 1952. "Zum Kalifat des Jacobus." *Zeitschrift für Religions- und Geistesgeschichte* 4:193–214. English translation: "The Caliphate of James." *The Journal of Higher Criticism* 4 (1997): 120–43.

Streeter, B. H. 1929. *The Primitive Church: Studied with Special Reference to the Origins of the Christian Ministry*. London: Macmillan.

———. 1956. *The Four Gospels: A Study of Origins Treating of the Manuscript Tradition, Sources, Authorship, and Dates*. London: Macmillan. First published in 1924.

Svartvik, Jesper. 2008. "Matthew and Mark." In *Matthew and His Christian Contemporaries*, edited by David C. Sim and Boris Repschinski, 27–49. Library of New Testament Studies 333. London: T&T Clark.

Talbert, Charles H. 2007. *Ephesians and Colossians*. Paideia Commentaries on the New Testament. Grand Rapids: Baker Academic.

Taylor, Mark Edward. 2006. *A Text-Linguistic Investigation into the Discourse Structure of James*. Library of New Testament Studies 311. London: T&T Clark.

Thurén, Lauri. 1997. "Hey Jude! Asking for the Original Situation and Message of a Catholic Epistle." *New Testament Studies* 43:451–65.

Urbach, Ephraim E. 1979. *The Sages: Their Concepts and Beliefs*. Vol 1. Translated by Israel Abrahams. 2nd ed. Jerusalem: Magnes.

Van Buren, Paul M. 1980–88. *A Theology of the Jewish-Christian Reality*. 3 vols. San Francisco: Harper & Row.

VanderKam, James. 1973. "The Theophany of Enoch I 3b–7, 9." *Vetus Testamentum* 23:129–50.

Vermès, Géza. 1995. *The Dead Sea Scrolls in English*. 4th ed. London: Penguin.

Wachob, Hiram. 2000. *The Voice of Jesus in the Social Rhetoric of James*. Society for New Testament Studies Monograph Series 106. Cambridge: Cambridge University Press.

Wall, Robert W. 1997. *Community of the Wise: The Letter of James*. New Testament in Context. Valley Forge, PA: Trinity Press International.

Watson, Duane F. 1988. *Invention, Arrangement, and Style: Rhetorical Criticism of Jude and 2 Peter*. Society of Biblical Literature Dissertation Series 104. Atlanta: Scholars Press.

Webb, Robert L. 1996. "The Eschatology of the Epistle of Jude and Its Rhetorical and Social Functions." *Bulletin for Biblical Research* 6:139–51.

Webb, Robert L., and John S. Kloppenborg, eds. 2007. *Reading James with New Eyes: Methodological Reassessments of the Letter of James*. Library of New Testament Studies 342. London: T&T Clark.

White, John Lee. 1972. *The Form and Function of the Body of the Greek Letter: A Study of the Letter-Body in the Non-literary Papyri and in Paul the Apostle*. Society of Biblical Literature Dissertation Series 2. 2nd ed. Missoula, MT: Scholars Press.

———. 1986. *Light from Ancient Letters*. Philadelphia: Fortress.

Wikgren, Allen. 1967. "Some Problems in Jude 5." In *Studies in the History and Text of the New Testament in Honor of Kenneth Willis Clark*, edited by Boyd L. Daniels and M. Jack Suggs, 147–52. Salt Lake City: University of Utah Press.

Windisch, Hans. 1951. *Die katholischen Briefe*. 3rd ed. Handbuch zum Neuen Testament 15. Tübingen: Mohr Siebeck.

Witherington, Ben, III. 2007. "James the Homily." In *Letters and Homilies for Jewish Christians: A Socio-Rhetorical Commentary on Hebrews, James and Jude*, 383–555. Downers Grove, IL: IVP Academic.

Wolthius, T. R. 1987. "Jude and Jewish Traditions." *Calvin Theological Journal* 22:21–41.

Index of Subjects

Index of Modern Authors

Index of Scripture and Ancient Sources